*To my husband, Jay,
whose love, patience, and support
have made the difference*

THE RISE,

FALL, AND

STRUGGLE

FOR RECOVERY

OF GENERAL

MOTORS

Maryann Keller

WILLIAM MORROW AND COMPANY, INC.
NEW YORK

Library of Congress Cataloging-in-Publication Data

Keller, Maryann.
    Rude awakening : The rise, fall, and struggle for recovery of General Motors / by
    Maryann Keller.
       p.   cm.
    ISBN 0-688-07527-4
    1. General Motors Corporation.   2. Automobile industry and trade—
United States.   I. Title.
    HD9710.U54G4744   1989
    338.7'6292'0973—dc20   89-32050
                                           CIP

Printed in the United States of America

First Edition

1 2 3 4 5 6 7 8 9 10

BOOK DESIGN BY OKSANA KUSHNIR

ACKNOWLEDGMENTS

Many people contributed their time, talent, experiences, and support to produce this book. I could never have completed such an ambitious project without them. Specifically, I want to thank: Lisa Drew, my editor at William Morrow, for her confidence in me and the guidance she gave during the three years it took to complete the book; Jane Dystel, my literary agent, for her belief in the idea and her tireless work on my behalf; Catherine Whitney, the writer who worked with me to tell the story in just the right way, and whose insight and skill with words made the book possible; and Chris Winans, who spent long hours researching General Motors and compiling the information that would form the basis for much of the book.

During the past three years, I have spent hundreds of hours interviewing GM executives past and present, and touring various plants across the country. I am grateful to those who gave me their time and contributed their unique perspectives, and would like to mention in particular Roger Smith, Thomas A. Murphy, James McDonald, and Alex Mair. I also appreciate the time Terry Sullivan spent setting up and coordinating interviews and reviewing transcripts. Don Ephlin and the members of his staff have provided a valuable perspective.

I wish there were a way I could thank personally all the people who spoke to me, on and off the record—the managers, executives, hourly workers, and plant staffs who were so helpful to me during my visits. I would also like to thank the car dealers who were very generous with their time.

Roger Smith made my job easier by giving me access within the company, and spending long hours with me himself.

There are many GM executives, managers, and employees, past and present, who spoke to me in confidence and supplied many forms of information and documentation. I was repeatedly impressed with their love for and loyalty to General Motors, even when they expressed frustration with its policies. They are dedicated, hard-working people whose primary interest is in doing the best jobs they can. They are the true resources and talent of the company.

AUTHOR'S NOTE: Many sources requested that their identities remain confidential. For this reason, some of the remarks by General Motors workers, executives, and former employees are repeated without attribution.

CONTENTS

INTRODUCTION

As a financial analyst for the automotive industry, I find much of my professional life is consumed with looking at the numbers and making judgments based on what they tell me. But contrary to what many people might think, an analyst's job isn't abstract. It's really about talking and listening and observing. My trips from New York to Detroit are so frequent that I sometimes feel like a commuter. I spend a large percentage of my time meeting with executives and workers from the auto companies, talking with the union leadership, visiting with car dealers and suppliers, and talking to people in the automotive media and industry analysts. Our conversations usually focus on *why* the numbers say what they do. What's happening beneath the surface? Who are the key players? What mistakes have been made—and why? How can problems be resolved?

When I set out to write a book about General Motors during the 1980s, I wanted to give the average person a sense of the drama that exists within the largest industrial corporation in America. I wanted to take apart the internal dynamics in the same way one might take apart a car's engine, and spread it out to full view. This exercise was valuable, I believed, because such a large segment of the American population (and the world) is directly affected by what happens at General Motors. And everyone is affected indirectly, not just because GM plays a major role in the American economy, but because for so long it has served as a prototype for what is both right and wrong with American business.

What has occurred at General Motors during the 1980s makes for a fascinating story. It is the story of a company that recognized it needed to change, but found itself hopelessly tangled in a complex corporate culture that resisted change. The decade became an often painful learning process for the leadership of GM, as they struggled to meet the imperatives of a changing marketplace.

It is a very human story, yet you will find that there are no heroes or villians, no stupid people or self-serving leaders. Those who would place praise or blame at the feet of one person or group of people miss the point that the task of transforming a corporate culture, whether it is done well or poorly, is a far more complex dynamic than can be controlled by single individuals, no matter how powerful they are. In that respect, the "ghosts" of GM's past are central, if invisible, characters in the drama.

To be sure, individuals within the company have made decisions during the past decade that have created tremendous momentum. Some of these decisions appear to miss the point of what is needed; others seem to be revolutionary in their impact.

But the leading character in this story is General Motors itself, a corporate entity that long has been a patriarch in the American family. Many people have written about GM over the years, characterizing it in various ways—the heartless monster that tramples the little guy; the greedy dictator who doesn't care who gets hurt in its quest for power; the blind elder who doesn't recognize that times have changed; the sleeping giant who doesn't see the competition sneaking up behind it.

But these books, while they sometimes make juicy reading (Americans have a fondness for hearing the worst about powerful companies and people), rarely observe the more compelling drama that is going on within General Motors. Nor do they appreciate the extent to which GM reflects the American mentality. Like it or not, GM's struggle during the past ten years says a lot about who we are as a people, and GM's prospects for the future are a reflection of where our nation is going—in far more than simply a financial sense.

It is my hope that this examination of the inner workings of General Motors will give readers a new insight into these facts. GM is not an abstract reality for any person in America. It is everything about our country that we are proud of, and everything that we wrestle with. The story of General Motors during the 1980s is, more than anything else, a true American story.

1

The GM Corporate Culture
Full of Fuel, Running on Empty

He hunched over the wheel and gunned her; he was back in his element, everybody could see that. We were all delighted, we all realized we were leaving confusion and nonsense behind and performing our one and noble function of the time, *move*. And we moved! The white line in the middle of the highway unrolled and hugged our left front tire as if glued to our groove.

—*On the Road*, Jack Kerouac

It is behind the wheels of our automobiles that we realize our most tangible experience of freedom. We may be tied down in so many ways, locked into nine-to-five jobs, trapped in suburban communities with family responsibilities, mortgages, lawns to mow—but in those precious moments behind the wheel we possess the grand fantasy of our freedom, and the understanding that the open roads belong to us if only we choose to take them. We too could press a foot to the pedal and, like Jack Kerouac, hit the road.

Americans have had a love affair with this freedom-machine from the moment it was first invented—it easily replaced the horse in our macho adventure fantasy. "A man and his car"— what a grand symbol it has become! We romanticize the burly truckers who gather for coffee in their private neon islands at three in the morning. We idolize the mastery of skilled racers who play with the ultimate danger of speed. And we ourselves become different in our cars—insulated from the tiresome pressures of ordinary life. It is a personal space in a cluttered society, a dream machine in an often mundane existence.

Can anyone deny that the most eagerly anticipated rite of passage into American adulthood is the day we acquire a license to go on the road?

Cut to Detroit, Michigan, the motherland of the automobile industry, the place where it all began. The romantic mood begins to unravel as soon as you leave the airport, welcomed by a towering symbol of cardom . . . a monolithic black-ribbed doughnut—a tire. Traveling along Interstate 94, you pass a giant illuminated car-counter, endlessly ticking away the number of American cars being built—by minute, by hour, by day. Everywhere you look there are signs that you are at the center of the car industry. The Marlboro Man smiles down from billboards flanked by ads for metal stamping, engineered plastics, and castings. Trucks loaded with car parts lumber up and down the highway. You pass factory after factory, spewing dark gray clouds into the sky.

One might expect to find a different ambiance in the hometown of our nation's first love—one of sparkling lights and flashy displays, a little of the razzle-dazzle of an ever-evolving technology. But Detroit is not a particularly pretty city and it doesn't compensate for the lack of physical beauty by showing visitors a twenty-first-century light show. Oh, you feel the car industry here, to be sure. But the symbolism is flat and uninspired.

Those who live and work at the center of the auto industry might defend the drabness with an explanation that the car industry is not about romance. It's a nuts-and-bolts, nose-to-the-grindstone business. And Detroit isn't one of those crazy razzle-dazzle places like New York or LA. Here, the primary interest is to get the job done. Quality, performance, corporate excellence, loyalty, family values, the work ethic. This is the Midwest, and what you see is what you get.

The General Motors building rises up from the New Center area, a struggling community in the middle of the city. Once a thriving commercial area, buoyed by General Motors' early growth, it was rocked by riots during the 1960s. It is now a transitional site, in the process of undergoing corporate gentrification, sponsored by GM in an effort to improve the area.

Trees and grass have been planted in islands in the road in front of the headquarters, and in vacant lots nearby in an effort to create the suburban office complex look of Electronic Data Systems (EDS) and Hughes Aircraft, two companies GM owns. But it's hard to create a suburban flavor in the middle of Detroit, knowing that some of the city's worst slums are within easy walking distance of the GM building.

Many employees are entirely insulated from the community, entering the GM building from underground garages or covered walkways that bypass the shops. Once Saks Fifth Avenue was the anchor of a thriving retail trade; today, the typical retailer is a small outfit, selling fast food, health food, books, and low- to medium-priced clothing. Merchants complain that at 5:00 P.M. everyone gets into his/her car and retreats to the suburbs. The sidewalks roll up at night; gutted, burned-out buildings remain as a testimony to urban crisis past and present.

The GM headquarters itself is in a rather drab building, its interior decor haphazard and lacking the skill of a designer's touch. Cars are on display everywhere, as one might expect, in the main floor–showroom and in the lobbies on individual floors. But they seem carelessly parked on the frayed carpets, and are flanked by plastic flowers and trees. The building has none of the high-tech characteristics or luxurious styling touches one might expect to find at the headquarters of the nation's most prominent employer. Even the air-conditioning doesn't quite work. The old-fashioned window units groan and sputter on hot Detroit days; the corridors are like steam baths. Yet, the building is oddly impressive. It is massive, and the extensive use of marble and granite reflects an era of craftsmanship and durability that are not found in today's modern glass towers.

And then there's the Fourteenth Floor. In Detroit, you can mention to anyone that an event occurred on the Fourteenth Floor, and they will know exactly what you mean. *The Executive Wing.*

The Fourteenth Floor is peopled by the powers that be at General Motors, a group of mostly midwestern white males (only two blacks and two women ever attained Fourteenth Floor status). Perhaps the most satisfying moment in a GM lifer's career is the day he moves into an office on the Fourteenth Floor. It is as real a symbol of "making it" as one can aspire to in the city of autos. Once on the Fourteenth Floor, an executive has joined the elite. He has his own dining area, set apart from the lower-level executives and the workers. He has his own secretary, crisp and efficient. He even has his own high-level gofer—in GM lingo, this is called a "bag man"—an up-and-coming business school graduate who is at his beck and call.

The mystique of the Fourteenth Floor is heightened by the fact that it is physically so hard to enter. When the elevator arrives, you encounter two sets of electronically locked glass doors. First, you meet an imposing guard who demands a look at your credentials, then Hilda, the cheerful and efficient receptionist who lets you in by pressing a button on her desk. Whatever the fear—terrorist attacks? irate employees?—the executives are well protected.

Once inside, the first thing you notice is the deafening silence. There are no stray laughs drifting down the long hallway. No bustling workers racing by with reams of paper. No heated voices raised. As you walk along the corridor, you might not see anyone at all. Everyone on the floor—group vice presidents, executive vice presidents, and top management—all work behind closed doors, each of them laboring through a voluminous pile of paperwork in their own silent space. An elaborate protocol is observed for interoffice communications. If a conversation with another executive is desired, an appointment is made by phone through his secretary—even if he's right next door. There is no hanging out in office doorways shooting the breeze.

The ambiance of the seat of power has the same drab flavor as the rest of the building—as if to brag, "This is the Midwest. We don't care about fancy touches here." Everything blends together in a muted flow of beige carpeting and wood paneling. The pretty but bland paintings that line the walls would feel more at home in a private den than a corporate office.

The Fourteenth Floor has been this way since anyone can remember. Well-known auto industry maverick, John DeLorean, who did a stint as an executive in the early 1970s, recalls the Fourteenth Floor in his book, *On a Clear Day You Can See General Motors*. There is more than a hint of irony to his recollection:

> The atmosphere on The Fourteenth Floor is awesomely quiet. The hallways are usually deserted. People speak in hushed

voices. The omnipresent quiet projects an aura of great power. The reason it is so quiet must be that General Motors' powerful executives are hard at work in their offices, studying problems, analyzing mountains of complicated data, holding meetings and making important, calculated business decisions.

Once an executive reaches a level of prestige at General Motors, he hangs on for dear life. A visible change is likely to be seen in his demeanor. Gradually, he stops seeing the company's flaws and begins to develop a defensive posture toward critics and skeptics. Conformity is required, but an unbridled ambition also dictates his behavior. For, as a member of the elite corps, he understands that the "brass ring" of the presidency or even the chairmanship is within his grasp. His place in the corporate structure is so central to his personal identity and sense of worth that if the beige rug in his Fourteenth Floor office were to be pulled out from under him, he would lose far more than his job. He would also lose his comfortable life in the inbred suburban communities—Birmingham or Bloomfield Hills— where neighbors and friends alike belong to the GM family—or to the extended family of auto-parts and machine-tool manufacturers. Indeed, the sense of belonging is so great that many career GMers survive retirement poorly—statistics show that an unusual number of them die within two to five years of retirement. "For many people, there is no life beyond GM," an insider noted sadly. "They just die. There's no more purpose to their life. Just none."

This is General Motors today, securely fixed in America's heartland, designing the vehicles that will meet America's dreams. What kind of place is this *really*, behind the colorless scenery? It might surprise you to learn that it's the kind of place great novels are made of, full of drama, intrigue, and high adventure. What goes on here may well be the ultimate example of the heartbeat of American business. GM is a study in many of the things that are right about corporate America . . . and much that is wrong.

One cannot fail to give General Motors its due, for what a remarkable history it has had! What a tremendous influence it has been on this country and the world. Even today, in spite of the grave afflictions of recent decades, General Motors has an uncanny ability to rise from its deepest periods of sleep and, in a sudden stroke of genius, send the industry spinning. Indeed, there are signs as we approach the 1990s that change is once again on the wind for the unpredictable giant.

But a note of caution is indicated. For even if General Motors rises again to the lofty heights it once knew, the victory is bound to be short-lived unless change occurs at the very core of its corporate culture. Ultimately, it will be the company's ability to shift its fundamental assumptions that will determine whether it will maintain stature into the next century. GM must learn not just to *talk* about a corporate vision, but to implement it. It has been suggested that there have been four ailments festering beneath the rosy complexion of General Motors. It is for us to decide the extent to which these ailments are now being cured.

1. GOLIATH COMPLEX

General Motors started out to be big. From its birth it was a conglomerate, an empire in the making. To be sure, there have been lean years, but GM could hardly be called a rags-to-riches story. Some observers have argued that its very bigness has doomed it to a lumbering, unmanageable future. Even chairman Alfred Sloan, whose mission of structuring the giant into an orderly, well-oiled machine was successfully completed in the 1930s, agonized over the problems of bigness. "In practically all our activities we seem to suffer from the inertia resulting from our great size," he worried. "There are so many people involved and it requires such a tremendous effort to put something new into effect that a new idea is likely to be considered insignificant in comparison with the effort that it takes to put it across. . . . Sometimes I am almost forced to the conclusion that General Motors is so large and its inertia so great that it is impossible for us to be leaders."

In fact, Sloan's fears proved unwarranted. Thanks in large part to his skillful leadership, organizational ability, and total dedication, GM went on to become a phenomenal success story, establishing itself for a time as the leader not only in automaking but as a model to other American and international companies.

It would appear that GM's corporate crisis has not been due entirely to its bigness but, rather, to its belief that bigness is enough, even in a changing marketplace. Certainly GM's stature as the industry Goliath has not prevented it from being an innovative leader, especially in the 1950s, when styling and engineering innovation came quickly, yet GM dominated the marketplace. The problem might more accurately be described as its failure to appreciate the true power of the competition's "slingshot" attacks. It is the complacency of success that has given GM the most trouble. In its early years there were so many challenges, so much competition, that the burning drive to succeed kept the company moving ahead—it brought out the best in people. But when success was achieved, the absence of urgency led to stagnation.

Before he left General Motors, executive vice president Elmer Johnson stated the dilemma very well in a memo to GM chairman Roger Smith:

> The culture is based on a two-fold vision of reality or set of fundamental assumptions that became dominant in GM by the late 1950s. First, that we live in a very stable, reasonably predictable world; and second, that GM's overwhelming conceptual advantage lies to a large degree in its ability to achieve *monumental economies of scale.*
>
> For so long GM dictated our taste in styling and engineering. Because it built more of everything than its rivals, its costs were lower. In today's fragmented, competitive marketplace, it is impossible to achieve scale economies.

Peter F. Drucker, a highly respected management consultant, wrote in *Management: Tasks, Responsibilities, Practices,* a book published in the early 1970s, that companies like General Motors could run into trouble if they confused stability with standing still. Wrote Drucker: "Stability is not rigidity. On the contrary, organization structure requires a *high degree of adaptability.* A totally rigid structure is not stable; it is brittle. Only if the structure can adapt itself to new situations, new demands, new conditions—and also to new faces and personalities—will it be able to survive."

Gerald Hirshberg, now vice president of Nissan Design International in San Diego, and formerly a General Motors executive, remembers his experience of the company this way: "Everybody had a sense of almost genetically endowed superiority concerning the eventual victory of the company for all time, permanently. It was their place to win. I think it's a killing thing to deal with success that lasted that long. It was shocking to me that most of the people who succeeded and climbed the ladder really had never experienced in their careers the whole mechanism of fighting from second or third place or falling out of first place and doing what you had to do. So when a lot of us sensed that things were moving, that there were new opportunities, new challenges, new ways of looking at things to maintain the edge, it was met with a smug sense of security that simply obliterated new ideas."

Although American history is filled with examples of underdogs winning out over giants—most notably, the Revolution that brought our democracy into being—we have also carried on a long-standing love affair with bigness. As a nation, we are unabashedly in awe of things that are larger than life. Our ideas about who we are and the extent of our potential are often measured by our size. "Small in stature" implies lack of power. We are a big, bold, blustering nation; from sea to shining sea, our ideology is colored by the vastness of our landscape.

Indeed, so much did General Motors believe in its own greatness that in 1952, Charles "Engine Charlie" Wilson, former company president and major GM stockholder, couldn't imagine how his large holdings in the company might in any way compromise his ability to perform under President Eisenhower as secretary of defense—even though defense contracts were a key part of the industry's bread and butter. In Senate confirmation hearings, Wilson didn't hesitate to state his belief, no doubt shared by many: "For years I thought what was good for the country was good for General Motors, and vice versa." It is a sentiment that has become part of our vernacular.

In sharp contrast, the Japanese have a cultural affinity for things small—not in the sense of their being lesser, but in that they are more intricate and carefully designed. In *Thriving on Chaos*, Tom Peters calls this a "passion for smallness" whose time has come. Peters refers to the analysis of Korean writer O-Young Lee, who detailed this passion in his book, *Smaller Is Better: Japan's Mastery of the Miniature:*

> Lee does a thorough job of tracing the roots of Japan's attachment to smallness. Japanese fairy tales, for example, feature "little giants" who turn needles into swords and bowls into

boats, in contrast to such characters of Western folk legend as Paul Bunyan. But the language may provide the most important clue. For instance, the Japanese word for "craftmanship" is literally "delicate workmanship."

Peters illustrates the difference further in his description of an ad for Mazda—a soft, almost seductive piece that stresses the exquisite care taken in every detail, and the emphasis on craftsmanship. Compare that, he suggests, to the General Motors advertising theme, "No one sweats the details like GM," and the two are "figuratively and literally, worlds apart."

To avoid a superficial conclusion, the point is not that small is necessarily better than big. But GM's complacent bigness reflects a fundamental risk-adverse philosophy that is apparent in much of American business. Arrogance and aversion to risk seem unlikely foundations upon which to maintain an empire.

2. PAROCHIAL WORLD VIEW

Someone once defined General Motors as "a midwestern car company," an image that strikes at the heart of the parochialism that has plagued the company at least since the late 1950s. Having proven itself the leader, there seemed to be no need to look beyond its own internal mold to project future trends. Its absence of curiosity about the market (what the people "out there" were saying about their wants and needs) was so complete that it was not until *1985* that a consumer market research division even existed at General Motors! So, while mountains of market data were accumulated, the company had no means of integrating the information. Not only did GM lack sophistication in its understanding of foreign competition, it lacked any real sense of the public mentality beyond its own doors. As if to demonstrate this very understanding, a GM executive once created a map of the United States, which was widely circulated around the company. Ohio, Michigan, Indiana, Missouri, and Illinois were "our kind of guys." California was "the land of fruits and nuts." The Northeast was "the land of intellectual snobs." Texas was "gunrack and pickup truck territory." And so on. There was more truth in this exercise than most would care to admit.

Consider this scenario as a case in point: A General Motors

executive sees a citizen of Detroit driving by in a Japanese car. He feels hurt . . . angry . . . hostile. "How can people be so disloyal?" he asks. He returns to his office carrying a bit more resentment for the Japanese who have invaded his world and a bit more disdain for those of his fellow countrymen who have been seduced by the outsiders.

Given the economic crunch this executive has encountered in recent years, and the continuous barrage of books and articles about how the Japanese do it better, he might be forgiven for his initial emotional reaction. But since he cannot separate ideas like customer loyalty from the mechanics of sound business practice, he does not take the next logical step. He does not return to his office and *think about* why his Detroit neighbor is driving a Honda or a Toyota or a Nissan car. For him, it is reduced to an issue of loyalty—but what is the issue for the man driving the car? Why did he buy the car instead of a General Motors car? What list of priorities did he carry with him into the dealership?

These are simple enough questions. And although they lead to harder ones—such as, what can GM do to respond to the priorities on this man's list?—they follow a logical progression. One can get from point A to point B. And in a truly aggressive, innovative company, the executive would move even farther out on a limb to point C: What is the competition doing that is *right*? And point D: Why aren't we doing it? And point E: How can we do it better?

General Motors never understood their foreign competitors. They were viewed simply as opportunists who got lucky during the oil crises. To this day, there is still a reluctance to accept the fact that maybe the competition was building better cars, and are more than a temporary phenomenon. GM can't tolerate the idea that the Japanese had figured out something important that they might learn from and use. This animosity, coupled with a warped American "can do" illusion and a false assumption of consumer loyalty, prevented them from giving the competition due respect. It is hard to conquer an enemy one cannot see.

There was clearly an element of racism behind GM's initial inability to see the Japanese as viable competitors. The World War II veterans who held many of the managerial positions have struggled against a deeply rooted disdain for the Japanese—"we whipped their ass in World War II and showed them who was boss." It was hard for them to reconcile the memory of a defeated, humiliated Japan with the new reality of a rebuilt nation capable of playing as equals in a market GM virtually owned. The rare executives who recognized and warned about the Japanese threat early on were met with scorn. One executive recalls: "After Honda announced its first factory in the United States, I suggested that the people in the World Wide Product Planning Group should be looking at the impending invasion, because if Honda is coming, then others are going to come. The response I was met with was, 'Oh, don't worry about those little yellow Japs. They will never make a go of it in the United States. They are going to have to contend with high costs and they are going to have to contend with the UAW, and it's simply not going to work.' "

Another example of narrowness has been GM's inability to build a broad leadership base. Rather, the company has always been run by two distinct types. The first is the real power, the finance people. It is from their ranks that the chairmen have been selected since Fred Donner in 1958, with the single exception of James Roche, who became chairman in 1968. The second type is the product engineers. They are the real "car guys"— they know a lot about cars and they know that remaining as engineers precludes their ever getting the big money rewards at the top.

The finance staff is the circulatory system of the company, recruited from the best schools and compensated on a salary scale that is more lucrative than the rest of the corporation. They are responsible for coordinating decision-making and bringing information to the attention of top management. But they're not always sensitive to life in the real world of the factory or showroom. Finance people don't rise from the ranks of the product or production engineers, so they've never had hands-on experience in the making of cars. They are accused of having little sensitivity to the common problems that are encountered in production or design or engineering. They only know how things are supposed to look on paper. Since they work for GM, where company cars are a common executive perk, they don't even have to have the experience of shopping for, buying, driving, and maintaining a car.

Product engineers usually have never worked anywhere but

in the automotive industry, and their status increases with seniority—the more years they put in at the company, the higher
they rise within the ranks. Car guys have big garages that, for the
true loyalists, often house at least one classic car. Their offices
are filled with car memorabilia. They are fully conversant in
areas like acceleration, horsepower, and valves-per-cylinder.
They disdain talk of fuel economy or even crashworthiness. In
short, they live for cars—mainly fast ones. Over the years, many
of them have graduated from the General Motors Institute
(GMI), a good school that pioneered sound technical training
but offered limited exposure to liberal arts.

But knowledge about the design and engineering attributes
of a car, a diploma from a driving school, and fondness for
exceeding the speed limit say nothing about the competency of
individuals to run multinational, complex industrial organizations. They say nothing about ability to manage and lead. Nor
do they tell us about their abilities to inspire those who work for
them, make trade-offs on capital investments, establish cost objectives, implement correct pricing strategies, and commit to
product development programs in fulfillment of the company's
market goals—or even to be able to set those market goals in the
first place. Love of automobiles, or even the ability to engineer
one, may or may not mean that an individual understands the
diverse reasons consumers have for selecting cars, what buyers
will be looking for in the future, or the nature of the competition's strengths and weaknesses.

Missing from the power equation are the production engineers, who perform critical functions in the plant, and set out
the manufacturing systems by which parts and cars are made.
General Motors, like most of American industry, has accorded
little status to the very people who are responsible for the
hands-on creation of the product. Nor has there been status
given to the marketing people, a possible factor in GM's failure
to understand and address the needs of the changing marketplace.

Such narrow role definitions were not always the rule at
GM, and the finance staff has not always dominated policy. At
one time (often referred to by retired GMers as the "pre-Donner
days"), the general managers of car divisions were well-rounded
executives who had some responsibility for design, styling, engineering, manufacturing, and marketing the cars they sold. The
only thing they didn't do was control the finances of the opera-

tion. This was done by a comptroller who reported to the central office. His function was simply to oversee the profit and loss— not to pass judgment over the direction of the operation. But in recent decades, as GM's CEO has become more remote from company operations, the finance staff has emerged as something akin to his personal CIA. In the process, the powers that be at the company have learned to trust the insiders on the finance staff more than the operations people.

Sadly, the priorities often get scrambled when GM attempts to measure the *value* of its career professionals—a fact that is common in other auto companies, as well. For example, a top-notch drive train engineer is clearly of great worth to the company, but he is not compensated—either financially or with prestige—for his technical excellence. Rather, if he has any hope of earning good money, he must, by the time he is in his mid-thirties, become a manager. Apart from the fact that engineering talent does not necessarily translate into managerial talent and may result in a loss of technical talent for the company, the management track also involves a rapid turnover of jobs every two years. The intention is to give the manager broad exposure in the company. But the end result is that it fosters an environment where no one is responsible for or accountable to a project from start to finish.

Parochialism can cripple a business faster than anything. It implies that all the factors are known and that they won't change. It implies that the world will simply stop and wait for everyone to catch up. A former GM employee described the entrenched worldview that existed on the Fourteenth Floor. "They used to say, 'When we get going, we're going to be right up there with Honda.' And I'd say, 'Gee, that's great, but what is Honda going to be doing—sitting on their ass for the next four years waiting for you to catch up? Of course not. Honda is going to be improving their efficiency.' They didn't see it. They set a fixed target assuming that Honda was going to do nothing. I've sat there with the finance staff, the engineering staff, and the manufacturing staff and said, 'Guys, you've got a problem because the competition is going to be improving efficiency and they're still going to be ten, twelve, fifteen man-hours ahead of us by the time we get there. Why not set up a program of continuous improvement so we can keep with them as they grow?' And they'd just look at me like I didn't know what I was talking about and say, 'Bullshit. We're going to be the best there is.' "

Another executive echoed that view. "I used to carry that notebook full of myths that I had learned for twenty-two or twenty-three years. We all grew up with a lot of confidence that we were doing it the right way—that no one could teach us anything. There was no foreign competition then, so if you didn't like our cars, you went to Ford or Chrysler, but we were all playing in the same sandbox. Then, along come the Japanese and the competition is really heating up. But it took us a long time to even see them as a threat. Somehow we had the confidence that we would slug it out with them and not have to change."

In fairness, General Motors wasn't the only company in America that was resentful of the Japanese. The bunker mentality invaded much of American business. A story is told in *The Transformational Leader,* by Noel M. Tichy and Mary Anne Devanna, of a seminar that took place in the early 1960s to discuss the problems that industry was facing. The chairman of a major American steel company spoke out, saying, "We would have been better off if our mills had been bombed during the war just as theirs were." A voice from the back of the room expressed agreement. "I dare say, sir, that would be true if your management had been locked inside."

Jim McDonald, who was president of GM for most of the 1980s, told a joke in a speech he gave to company suppliers that reveals, beneath the humor, a basic cynicism about the competition, particularly the Japanese. As McDonald told it: "Three auto executives were sentenced to be shot by a firing squad. One of them was French, and when asked if he had a last request, he said he wanted one final bottle of Lafite Rothschild, 1938.

"The second was Japanese and his last request was a little different. He just wanted to deliver one last lecture on Statistical Process Control.

"Finally, they asked the American if he had a last request. And he said, 'Yes, shoot me first. I just can't handle another lecture on Japanese quality control.' "

3. LEADERSHIP BY THE NUMBERS

Financial people operate in a rarefied environment. For them, solving a problem means successfully juggling the numbers on financial statements. What happens when the numbers determine every major investment and product initiative? Reality gets distorted.

General Motors isn't like a mom-and-pop grocery store. In a small business, there's no juggling, no strategizing around the numbers. Things are pretty simple: You sell a certain amount of goods and you make a profit. Or you don't sell enough goods and you have trouble paying the rent. If your goods aren't selling, you don't sit up all night trying to add the columns a different way—the landlord doesn't care *what* your balance sheet says, he wants the cash. However, if you're smart, you try to figure out what changes you can make that will bring more customers into the store. You probably go around to other stores and notice the way they're doing it. Maybe you add some new inventory. You don't change the appearance of reality. You change the reality.

It's different in a large corporation, and that's why too much power in the hands of the finance people can be a tyrannical force. At General Motors, the finance staff is supreme; it exerts far too much influence over the company. In *The World After Oil,* Bruce Nussbaum makes a point about Ford Motor Company that is equally true for GM:

> The competing culture is one of statistical technicians, the numbers crunchers left over from the days of [Ford's] whiz kids, who believed that anything could be quantified. These people swarm over the company trying to knock off 50 cents from the manufacturing cost of a bumper and another 75 cents off the cost of a fender—cost savings that can mean millions of dollars to the company. But this process collides with the bettors who are trying to get out the best car with the newest features. Unless the company has a very strong system of overall values that encourage everyone to work for the same identifiable goals, these competing tendencies can easily turn into internecine wars. Where key people focus more on internal wars and less on keeping their organization in tune with the business environment, then it is possible for the market-place to pass them by.

The tyranny of the numbers crunchers has evolved, to a great extent, from GM's reluctance to hear bad news about itself. If the finance guys can present the right numbers, everyone breathes a sigh of relief, and the finance people look like heroes. There's no incentive for executives in finance positions to give bad news; the more facile they can be with numbers, the higher their fortunes rise. Such a mentality prevents long-term analysis; the focus is always on getting quick results and making the numbers look right.

A typical investment case at GM might look like this: An executive submits a plan that produces a 15-percent return on investment (ROI). Then something changes in the marketplace, such as the currency exchange rates. However, rather than evaluating the changes and adjusting accordingly, the numbers are reworked still to yield a 15-percent ROI. Over the years, operating people also have learned how to make the numbers "come out right." Usually their financial interrogators themselves lack the knowledge to evaluate programs on any basis except the numbers.

Another form of financial tyranny has been the frequent decision to pinch pennies at the expense of product content and design. Cars have often been produced that lack the exciting features once planned because original designs have had to be altered so many times to save money. Of course, the long-term results of penny-wise-and-pound-foolish car-building practices are legendary—as will be shown in later chapters.

Industry consultant Robert Templin recently recalled his experience with the penny-pinching mentality when he worked at General Motors. "I was the chief engineer at Cadillac from 1973 to 1984, a period of about eleven years," Templin said. "During that time, we shipped about a hundred billion dollars' worth of products. But also during that time we went through the '75 catalytic converter and the introduction of the electronic fuel injection on the new Seville, and a variety of other things which tended to overload the production system. And that's just like when you lower the water in a river, the rocks start to show—when you run the system at overload you start to see the weaknesses in it. I was always impressed with the fact that I was being pushed to reduce engineering costs by ten dollars a car, when the sales incentives and warranty costs totaled something like a couple of thousand dollars a car, and that we must have the pressure on the wrong thing."

A retired GM executive notes that the tyranny of the numbers crunchers began to take root under chairman Fred Donner during the 1960s. (Donner also happens to be current chairman Roger Smith's idol.) "An attitude started to develop that financial types could run things better than manufacturing or marketing people. And it got to the point where if you weren't in the favor of the financial people, you were just about dead. Everybody was catering to them and they got stronger and stronger."

The power of the finance staff is indicative of a deeper malaise at GM, which has been an overdependence on the way numbers look. Within divisions, there's a mad scramble to make one's own results look rosy—careers are built that way. A good example is how cutbacks were handled in 1986 and 1987, when GM was struggling. The word came down from the Fourteenth Floor that there would have to be a scaling down of staff. Many employees were retired early or received comfortable buyouts. But the more enterprising among those who left did not just sit home and lick their wounds. Many joined engineering contract houses—the very houses from which consulting engineers were hired by General Motors. In many cases, the engineers who were hired by GM—and paid a very high per diem rate—were the same guys who had been laid off from salaried positions to save money. A 1987 memo by a member of the GM audit staff noted a specific instance in which "an employee was offered an early retirement with special temporary benefits for five years; however, a month before his retirement, CPC arranged to rehire the individual through a contract agency on the date of his retirement. This transfer from regular headcount to temporary headcount resulted in CPC paying . . . an aggregate annual penalty of $21,000." Think about it: Not only were they receiving, in many cases, a year's salary and multiple benefits from their contract buyouts, they were also earning more as consultants for the company than they had earned while on staff—and often working on the same programs. But this didn't seem to matter to anyone, because those expenses showed up in a different column of the chart—the division managers could still show how much they had cut back on staff and reduced expenses. *Their* bottom lines looked better, even if overall company costs did not show the forecast improvement.

One executive recalls an early incident that demonstrates how ineffective managing by the numbers can be. Around 1960, the company decided to explore the possibility of establishing a standardized quality index to measure how GM plants compared with one another. At first, the index was simple. A score of 100 meant a car had no defects, 95 meant a car had five defects—and so on.

But this system ran into problems right away because too many plants were struggling only to rate above 60, which, in the grading system, was the line between passing and failing.

Everyone was very concerned with the rating system. No one said, "Wait a minute. Why are cars coming off the line with forty or more defects?"

Alex Mair, an engineer who started with Chevrolet in 1939 and retired as a vice president in 1986, remembers the system well. "Somebody started looking at a few more plants and decided that if we wrote down the number one forty-five and made that the perfect score, then very few plants would score below one hundred. The one-forty-five standard was adopted around 1968, and we began to give awards to people who made one thirty [fifteen defects] on this index." The system remained in force for twenty years, with plant managers and assessors haggling over paint drips and specks of dust and what counted as a defect. The focus was on the numbers.

In all those years, the focus never wavered: The goal remained to improve the numbers, not to improve the cars. By setting arbitrary standards that looked good on the books, the value of the standards became meaningless. In theory, if the quality slipped, the setpoint could be adjusted again.

4. CONTEMPTUOUS PATERNALISM

In the past, one of the best things about working for General Motors was the job security, as long as you played the game and didn't rock the boat. The company's nicknames were Mother Motors and Generous Motors. The workers were treated as though they were the vast extended family of benevolent parents. And you can't fire a member of your family, even if he or she is ineffective. One always had the sense that the protective mother stood in the background soothing ruffled feathers— "Now, don't be too hard on Cousin Bill. He's doing the best he can." For many years, it was almost impossible to get fired, or even demoted.

A former employee recalls the day she was summoned to her boss's office to discuss a "sensitive" matter. She couldn't imagine what it could be, and she was taken aback by the funereal mood in the office as her boss ushered her in. He told her in a sad, hushed voice that he had very distressing news and he wanted to tell her before she heard it from someone else; one of her coworkers was about to be fired for incompetence.

Perhaps her boss expected her to collapse in dismay, but she took the news well. As she later recounted about the co-worker: "He was rated an unsatisfactory performer during his probation period at the company, and was continually rated poorly in his evaluations. But it took them sixteen years to work up the courage to let him go!"

Nevertheless, firing a worker—even when incompetence was irrefutably proven—was a traumatic event at GM. Short of committing a crime, it was almost impossible to get fired, and only about one hundred salaried employees were involuntarily let go each year. Usually what happened if you performed poorly on a consistent basis (say, over a period of sixteen years) was that you got moved around a lot or were retired early with generous benefits. Even the company's rating system had no category for someone whose performance indicated that he or she should be shown the door. The ratings went from "superior" to "very good" to "effective" to "marginally effective" to "needs improvement." In theory, one could "need improvement" for the life of his or her career, then retire happily and go fishing. With compensation linked to seniority, tenure has always been the primary criterion for promotions and salary increases.

One policy long practiced by the automotive industry in general was to automatically grant salaried employees comparable salary increases, holidays, insurance coverage, and other benefits whenever new gains were negotiated with the United Auto Workers. This policy (which is no longer practiced) helped create a work force whose compensation was not directly linked to their performance or to the company's bottom line.

Yet this very benevolence was ultimately a show of contempt. One might argue, "Hey, the workers had it good. They didn't *have* to excel." But for those who were conscientious and wanted to perform well, it was discouraging to find that it didn't seem to matter from a compensation standpoint whether they performed well or not. Ironically, this has even been a problem for the bonus-eligible executives. For example, in 1987, those new bonus-level executives who performed in the top 3 percent averaged only about $2,000 more in stock grants than those who performed in the next 16 percent. That's not much of a difference for superior performance. There was a much larger gap in bonuses when they were compared according to age.

Recent restrictions and limitations on salary increases and promotion to bonus-eligible status have demoralized the Grade 7 and Grade 8 employees, who are being told that good performance will not necessarily be rewarded. Ambitious individuals are often attracted to other employers where their financial reward will be more directly tied to performance. In truth, it is just such paternalism that is most demoralizing to a work force. Given time, it is bound to backfire. In recent years, when the company tightened its belt and chose to let go or retire large numbers of workers, the shock waves reverberated throughout the company. Former executive vice president Elmer Johnson remembers how tough it was. "I would sit in meetings and say, 'I think we have to learn to say good-bye to people.' I would guess that's true in most organizations . . . but in this company above others, because there's this ethos; it's been so prosperous, so successful, so strong—and people have a sense of cradle-to-grave security and a sense of community."

Johnson describes a common scene. "I went to a retirement party where some people were leaving, and a lot of retirees came back. This has been their whole life. And it's a wonderful thing, in a way, but you can understand how it's so hard on people now. These retired secretaries were at the party. They'd come up to me and start talking . . . 'I remember back in '76,' and start recounting old times. And they'd sigh, 'General Motors has sure changed, hasn't it?' And it's hard to have to make these decisions about people in a company that has this sense of community. It's a lot of pain."

Tom Peters offers a scathing evaluation of GM's corporate contempt in *Thriving on Chaos:*

> We insult employees with executive parking spots, heated, no less; with executive dining rooms; with bonuses and "strategy meetings" in lavish settings for the top 100 officers and their spouses even after lousy years. Roger Smith announces eleven plant closings and 27,000 more potential layoffs—then retreats behind double-locked glass doors to contemplate the wasteland he's created. . . .
>
> Stop! I want to scream. It's dumb. I don't say this for human-

itarian reasons, much as I believe in such reasons. My point is
pragmatic: How do you humiliate and demean someone and then
expect him or her to care about product quality and constant
improvement?

Elitism within the system was inevitable. Over the years it
has become easy for executives to buy staff loyalty; everyone
knows that's how you get on the fast track—in GM lingo that's
called being a HI-POT, a high-potential employee. At General
Motors, the road to the corporate dining room is paved with
occasions of looking the other way, of saying yes, of supporting
the team, of keeping one's opinions to oneself. Those chosen
few—about four thousand in number—who have achieved
bonus-eligible status continue to be yes-sayers, their huge
bonus earnings buying their loyalty.

GM executives—even those in middle management positions—learned to heighten their prestige by surrounding themselves with the trappings of importance and power. Though less
common today, the practice illustrates GM's traditional power
complex. One executive recalls how dazzled he was in his early
days at Chevrolet about how important the executives were
made to look—not just those on top, but those in the middle as
well. He remembers one in particular—an assistant general sales
manager.

"When he would fly in from the Chevrolet Central Office
in Kansas City, I was assigned to stand outside the door of the
Muehlenbach Hotel in a snowstorm and I was not to move
because whenever he showed up, I had to be there to open the
door. We bought the elevator and blocked it off so he'd have an
elevator to go to. We had somebody assigned to stand outside
his room all day to take his shirts to the laundry and perform
other tasks. And—this is true—we had learned that he had to
have his morning orange juice a certain temperature, so we had
somebody in the kitchen every day who tested the orange juice
with a thermometer!" Another former executive was legendary
for his vast consumption of soft drinks, which necessitated that
he travel through Europe with an American-size refrigerator—
even if that meant breaking down a hotel room wall to accommodate it.

The trappings of power are less splendid today, but they
still exist. The executives who enjoy them are often unaware that

they too are victims of corporate contempt. Eventually, the quality of their lives at General Motors may seem thin because a heated parking space is small compensation for the compromises.

A savvy observer inside General Motors uses an analogy that would surely make top management shudder. "In a way it's like communism. Keep them fed, clothed, and in a house. Give them their security, but don't let them ask what's going on here, don't let them achieve, don't challenge them."

One retired executive rails against a system that creates vertical thinkers and cautious leaders. "The whole system stinks once you're in it. You continue to want to make vertical decisions: 'What is it that I should decide that will be good for me. Never make a horizontal decision based on what is good for the company. I want to get promoted.'

"So you get promoted because you're sponsored by someone; you get promoted before they catch up with you. I can go through a litany of those clowns. They go from this plant to that complex and then, all of a sudden, they've got plaques all over their walls that say how great they've done—but the plant's falling apart and the division's falling apart."

Finally, it all boils down to the *people:* How does a company motivate its people, handle the breakdowns in morale, give every worker the sense of having a voice in the operation? Neither the condescension of a benevolent parent nor the hard-boiled, bottom-line toughness of a corporate giant accomplishes the ultimate goal. Alfred Sloan had the kernel of a good idea when he established an employee bonus program, saying, "The interests of the corporation and its stockholders are best served by making key employees partners in the company's prosperity." Yet his plan eventually became a source of divisiveness and negative productivity. Financial incentives for a select few—or even for many—workers do not address the primary quality-of-life issues that are the soul of every corporation. The bonus incentive, which included a broader base—some sixteen thousand workers—in Sloan's day, has today been narrowed to include only an elite four thousand.

If one were to ask W. Edwards Deming for his prescription to cure the ills that have afflicted General Motors in recent decades, the eighty-eight-year-old management guru would reel off his solution in clipped, unclouded prose. During the 1950s, Deming was instrumental in catalyzing the masterful development of Japanese industry. His tenets, simple yet undeniably logical, stressed management processes as an independent factor, separate from product innovation. He has been called "the father of the postwar Japanese economic miracle."

Ford Motor Company was eager to utilize Deming's advice in the early 1980s, and General Motors, after trying and failing with a number of other approaches, has followed suit—albeit with less trust in the master. Time will tell whether or not the General Motors culture can assimilate concepts that are so foreign to its historical management philosophy. While the current management might nod agreement with Deming's precepts, the question remains whether they can make the spiritual leap that is required for true transformation.

Deming is not a wizard so much as he is a man of abiding common sense and simple logic. It is this simplicity that is reflected in his fourteen points for management transformation:

1. Create constancy of purpose toward improvement of product and service, with the aim to become competitive and to stay in business, and to provide jobs.

2. Adopt a new philosophy. We are in a new economic age. Western management must awaken to the challenge, must learn their responsibilities, and take on leadership for change.

3. Cease dependence on inspection to achieve quality. Eliminate the need for inspection on a mass basis by building quality into the product in the first place.

4. End the practice of awarding business on the basis of price tag. Instead, minimize total cost. Move toward a single supplier for any one item, on a long-term relationship of loyalty and trust.

5. Improve constantly and forever the system of production and service, to improve quality and productivity, and thus constantly decrease costs.

6. Institute training on the job.

7. Institute leadership. The aim of leadership should be to help people and machines and gadgets to do a better job. Leadership of management is in need of overhaul, as well as leadership of production workers.

8.   Drive out fear, so that everybody may work effectively for the company.

9.   Break down barriers between departments. People in research, design, sales, and production must work as a team, to foresee problems of production and in use that may be encountered with the product or service.

10.   Eliminate slogans, exhortations, and targets for the work force, asking for zero defects and new levels of productivity.

11a.   Eliminate work standards (quotas) on the factory floor. Substitute leadership.

11b.   Eliminate management by objective. Eliminate management by numbers, numerical goals. Substitute leadership.

12a.   Remove barriers that rob the hourly worker of his right to pride of workmanship. The responsibility of supervisors must be changed from sheer numbers to quality.

12b.   Remove barriers that rob people in management and in engineering of their right to pride of workmanship. This means, *inter alia*, abolishment of the annual or merit rating and of management by objective, management by the numbers.

13.   Institute a vigorous program of education and self-improvement.

14.   Put everybody in the company to work to accomplish the transformation. The transformation is everybody's job.

Deming has never been interested in flattering corporate giants. He is stern and uncompromising. "Management must understand their jobs. If they don't, just forget it," he says. "Management must not just be in favor of quality. They've got to know what it is and what they have to do about it. The greatest management problem is that management doesn't *realize* its problems or face up to them."

Deming is the first to admit, with some regret, that he will probably not live to see his management points fully operating in American corporations. In the case of General Motors, there is a feeling that change is in the wind, but one only has to review Deming's fourteen points to see what a long, long way the company has to go. As recently as the summer of 1988, Roger Smith, the chairman of GM, was reading a summary of Deming's book, *Out of the Crisis,* for the first time. It was prepared for him after

Smith continued to argue that the best price was attained by having several suppliers bid against one another, rather than developing a long-term relationship with a single supplier- "partner." To his credit, Smith is now one of the converted.

It has been said that "revolutions are not made with rosewater." Clearly, achieving cultural change at General Motors is a tremendously complex and deeply uprooting process. The company is the size of many small countries, its influence more sweeping than any corporation in America.

To be sure, the 1980s have witnessed great change within the company. It has reached out across the ocean in an attempt to understand and utilize the business sensibilities of Japanese industry. It has attempted the first massive reorganization since the 1930s. It has invested more than $40 billion in plants and machinery in a desperate attempt to better the Japanese in productivity and flexibility. It has acquired EDS and Hughes Aircraft to diversify and expand its technological prowess. It has created Saturn—a project aimed at surpassing the Japanese, not only in product and manufacturing process, but also in employee and dealer relations. But one wonders: Have the dramatic events of the last decade constituted a revolution? Or have they merely laid a new mask atop an old visage? In telling the story, perhaps the answer will become clear: Has General Motors learned how to execute the vision it so often talks about? Have all of these initiatives furthered that vision, or diverted attention away from it?

2

In the Beginning:

For the Love of Cars

General Motors could hardly be imagined to exist anywhere but in this country, with its very active and enterprising people; its resources, including its science and technology and its business and industrial knowhow; its vast spaces, roads, rich markets; its characteristics of change, mobility, and mass production; its great industrial expansion in this century, and its system of freedom in general and free competitive enterprise in particular. Adapting to the distinctive character of the American automobile market has been a critical and rather complex element of General Motors' progress. If in turn we have contributed to the style of the United States as expressed in the automobile, this has been by interaction.

—Alfred P. Sloan

Magnificent inventions are not the work of small dreamers. Nor are great successes born from those with eyes too carefully trained to the bottom line.

Billy Durant was a man with big dreams, a master stock market manipulator, a brilliant charmer whose slender, 135-pound body bristled with energy and enthusiasm. Unlike most of the early pioneers in the auto business, he was not himself a tinkerer or an engineer. He was just a wealthy entrepreneur and salesman who fell in love with a Buick in 1904 and never looked back.

Durant's vision, in the early years of the twentieth century, was to become a car baron, with the same kind of dominance he had seen exercised in the banking and railroad industries. His plan was to create a group of independent car companies that, by cooperating with one another, would rise to power and take control of the industry. He was an empire builder in the classic mode, for though he did not himself have the resources to foster his dream, he possessed the ingenuity to engage the imaginations of the powerful and the monied.

In turn-of-the-century America the automobile business was one of the most exciting places to be. While few may have visualized quite how important automobiles would become (in the late nineteenth century, statisticians were predicting that by 1940, New York City would be six feet deep in horse manure, from the projected increase in horse carriages), the technological edge rested in the hands of the automobile pioneers. Billy Durant, who himself had made his wealth in the Michigan horse-drawn carriage business, was completely enamored of the possibilities. Given the chance to direct the course of Buick, he jumped in with both feet, moving the operation to Flint, Michigan, and within four years, building it into one of the major forces to be contended with in the industry.

In 1908, the four leading car manufacturers were Ford, Buick, REO (Ransom E. Olds), and Maxwell-Briscoe. In the midst of rapid sales growth, a concern was being expressed by Wall Street kingpins, among them J. Pierpont Morgan, that the industry was far too fragmented and a plan of consolidation should be pursued. Morgan had his own dreams of controlling the auto industry, and he set up a meeting of the top four's leadership to discuss a plan.

Henry Ford, Ransom Olds, Benjamin Briscoe, and Billy Durant met in a frigid Detroit in January of 1908. Ford chilled things further by immediately saying he wasn't interested in consolidation. Durant countered by suggesting a holding company that would set only the broadest policies, leaving the individual companies essentially autonomous. A tentative agreement was reached.

The second meeting was held in New York with representatives of the House of Morgan. But Henry Ford once again pulled the plug on an agreement, surprising everyone by saying that he would not accept stock as payment in a consolidation—only cash. Olds agreed. It was cash or the deal was off. Morgan's people were shocked. This was simply out of the question. The talks collapsed.

At that point, Durant, who had all the Buick stock in his pocket (he either owned it or had proxies for what he didn't own), offered to deal directly with Benjamin Briscoe. With Morgan agreeing to underwrite the plan for $5 million, the genesis of a new company began. It was to be called International Motors.

But Morgan's budding auto empire fell apart before it ever reached the paper-signing stage, when the companies were unable to reach an agreement on the terms. Durant decided to go it alone, and on September 16, 1908, he incorporated General Motors Company, capitalized at only $2,000.

Billy Durant didn't hold a title in the infant corporation, but there was no question about who was in charge. Durant's new company picked up steam fast with the acquisition of Buick, followed in short order by the acquisition of Oldsmobile, Cadillac, and Oakland (which later became Pontiac). These acquisitions led to the development of a national distribution network and a diversity of product lines. In 1909, Durant even flirted briefly with the idea of buying Ford, but it was decided that the $8-million price (cash, of course) was too high.

During the first two years, the acquisitions continued with a number of auto-parts concerns; the McLaughlin Motor Car Company in Ontario, which would later become GM of Canada; and Bedford Motors of Britain, GM's first European acquisition. By the end of two years, GM had swallowed up thirty companies, including eleven automakers.

But although Durant excelled in sales savvy, he lacked organizational skills, and by 1910, the company was broke. There had been no financial controls placed on Durant's spending spree. He'd been lost in a feeding frenzy, bidding for companies big and small, and haggling with bankers for loans. The early profits were insufficient to stem the flow of red ink when the economy went through one of its predictable recessions.

Dreamer Durant took the blow personally, retreating into brooding about how he could save his "baby." He was indignant at the way the financial vultures were circling, and deeply frustrated that he seemed to be running out of time when he'd just barely started. A reporter from *The Flint Journal* recalled the day he was sitting in Durant's office listening to a phone conversation between Durant and an eastern banker. The banker seemed to be unconvinced by Durant's grand vision of the future, and apparently suggested that the automobile might have a more limited influence in America than Durant had projected. The reporter recalled Durant's huffy reply: "No, sir, there is no such thing as a saturation point—not until every man, woman, and eligible child in the country has an automobile."

By the time John H. McClement, a GM stockholder, proposed a plan to save the company, most people—Durant aside—had already given up hope. Actually, McClement's plan, to form a consortium of eastern bankers to bail the company out, was not really a plan to save the GM empire. From the start, the bankers were more interested in pieces of GM, such as Buick, that promised to be profitable. They had to be convinced that the entire package was worth saving. The bankers recognized that even though the company was in disarray, Durant had put together enough high-quality, profit-generating assets to make the deal worthwhile.

Eventually an agreement was reached, with Lee, Higgins and Company of Boston and J. and W. Seligman and Company of New York agreeing to underwrite the business. The banks provided $15 million in the form of a loan secured by GM property at rates that generated an exorbitant $9 million in interest over five years, plus $6.2 million in GM stock. It was agreed that Durant's control had to end if GM were to survive, so while his "baby" was saved, Durant was, in essence, thrown out with the bathwater. He maintained a vice presidency, but General Motors was now controlled by the banks.

This turn of events hurt Durant deeply. In the months to come, he could not reconcile himself to new management directions that were sterile in their concentration on the bottom line. Durant's actions had always been fueled by his deep love of the automobile and the thrill of bringing a new era into being. GM's new directors lacked the spirit that had driven him; the business had lost its fun. Impassioned with frustration, he wrote:

I had been given a title and a position, but the support, the cooperation, the spirit, the unselfishness that is needed in every successful undertaking, was not there. In a way, it was the same old story, "too many cooks"; a board of directors comprised of bankers, action by committees, and the lack of knowledge that comes only with experience. I saw some of my cherished ideas laid aside for future actions, never to be revived. Opportunities that should have been taken care of with quickness and decision were not considered. The things that counted so much in the past, which gave General Motors its unique and powerful position, were subordinated to "liquidate and pay." (From *Billy Durant*, by Lawrence R. Gustin, Craneshaw Publishers, 1984.)

But it was not Durant's nature to stay beaten for long. In the course of the next four years, he mollified himself by founding five motorcar companies, most significantly Chevrolet Motor Company of Michigan. He used his profits to buy GM stock—and he urged his friends to hold on to their GM stock and buy more, even though the price for shares was rising. In an almost superhuman show of resilience, Durant was setting the stage to take back his company.

His ace in the hole was the close friendship he had developed with a man named Jacob Raskob. Raskob was cut from the same cloth as Durant—ambitious, charismatic, a risk taker. As CFO at the Dupont Company, Raskob had the ear of the more conservative Pierre du Pont, and he convinced him to invest in General Motors because he realized the Dupont Company could profit by selling paint to the carmaker. Pierre du Pont would eventually invest $50 million in the company, and he would reluctantly become president during its later financial crisis.

In 1915, with car sales booming, the bankers met to vote on whether to renew their arrangement with GM. Before the meeting, GM president Walter Nash told Durant that a majority of the board was prepared to vote to renew the trust. "Let's not have any trouble," he warned Durant. Durant called the bluff. "There won't be any trouble," he replied coolly. "We won't renew the agreement, but there won't be any trouble. It just so happens that I own General Motors."

It was a bold stroke made by a man who knew how to stage a dramatic moment. It was unclear whether or not Durant really controlled the majority of GM shares, but he had found an ally in Pierre Du Pont, and the bankers trusted du Pont. By the time the smoke from the meeting was cleared, Nash was out, and Durant was once more in the driver's seat—this time with the title of president. By 1916, the bankers were purged from GM's board and replaced by car company managers. And Durant went back to buying. In the coming years, he would take over Pontiac Body Company and incorporate it into Oakland, and buy 50 percent of Fisher Body, the pioneer in *closed-car* engineering.

Durant saw that for the car to realize its potential, it had to be comfortable in all seasons.

Durant also created the General Motors Acceptance Corporation (GMAC), the industry's first company set up to provide loans for car buyers, car dealers, and would-be dealership owners.

Although Durant never tried to assimilate his acquisitions into a cohesive organization, Fisher was more separate from the corporation than the others. From the start, Fisher would remain staunchly independent from its parent, both physically and culturally. (The Fisher building, taller and more impressive than GM's, is often mistaken for GM headquarters across the street.) And the fierce loyalties of Fisher workers would later become an enormous stumbling block when the company tried to reorganize in its fight against foreign competition.

Alfred P. Sloan was as different from Billy Durant as night from day. Tall, thin, and almost dour in appearance, he surprised those who didn't know him with his heavy Brooklyn accent. Sloan was a businessman in a more traditional sense, an organizational problem solver. Where Billy Durant built his plans on dreams, Sloan was more inclined to build from reality. This is not to say that Sloan didn't possess a brilliance of his own. In fact, his administrative genius was such that to this day his words are quoted more frequently than those of any other man associated with GM. Durant may have given birth to the baby, but it was Alfred Sloan who nurtured it to healthy adulthood.

By the middle of 1919, GM's common stock was valued at more than $1 billion. But members of Durant's Executive Committee, among them Sloan (then a vice president), were warning him that foreboding factors were at work in the economy that might threaten GM. Indeed, in 1920, farm prices began to fall, the bond markets went into a slump, and GM couldn't sell debt. Cash reserves of $100 million had vanished, factories were closed, and inventories of unwanted cars were beginning to mount and rust in storage yards.

At the time, GM was a sprawling, unwieldy empire of seventy-five factories in forty cities, all under the personal direction of Durant. Alfred Sloan recognized that the empire was too big for one man to direct, and in any case, Durant's strong suit was acquisition, not management. Sloan drafted a reorganization plan he titled "Organizational Study," a concise corporate constitution whose intention was to render GM manageable in spite of size, and profitable in spite of the state of the economy. Sloan's mission was to bring discipline to GM's finances and coordinate the operating units to eliminate waste.

But even as Sloan was penning a new direction for the faltering company, Durant was resorting to his old tried-and-true ploys. As GM stock slid, Durant began heavily buying shares, hoping this would create greater demand in the market. Not only did the ploy fail, but it left Durant in personal financial trouble, because he had purchased the stock on margin. Durant's debt—estimated at about $38 million—posed an even greater threat to the company. If Durant was left to fail personally, he would take a number of bankers and brokers with him and set in motion a stock market panic. Seeing a crisis at hand, J. P. Morgan and his bankers formed a company to bail Durant out, and he resigned as president in late 1920. It was Durant's last stand at General Motors, and, ironically, his leave-taking saved the company. News of his resignation and the rescue abruptly halted the GM stock slide.

He was nearly sixty years old at the time, and it appeared that the old master had run out of steam. His effort to start a new car company—Durant Motors—floundered, and ensuing business efforts were unsuccessful. He died at the age of eighty-six, in a New York apartment he shared with his wife. They would have been penniless, were it not for donations from Sloan and others at GM, paid in gratitude to the entrepreneur who created, but could not manage, the world's largest industrial concern. Although Alfred Sloan chose a wholly different course of action from Durant's, he held the founder in high regard and even some awe. As Sloan would later write in *Adventures of a White-Collar Man:*

> I was constantly amazed by his daring ways of making a decision. Mr. Durant would proceed on a course of action guided solely, as far as I could tell, by some intuitive flash of brilliance. He never felt obliged to make an engineering hunt for facts. Yet at times he was astoundingly correct in his judgements.
>
> Durant's integrity? Unblemished. Work? He was a prodigious worker. Devotion to General Motors? Why, it was his baby!

With Durant out, Pierre du Pont was convinced to take on the presidency. He was a reluctant leader, whose experience in the automobile industry was nearly nonexistent. But the financial community believed du Pont's stable, no-nonsense style was exactly what the company needed. One of his first moves was to quickly approve vice president Sloan's concept of reorganization, with only minor changes. He also appointed a young man named Donaldson Brown vice president of finance. Brown was to become the first of the new breed of financial specialists who would ultimately dominate the power structure of GM. He was the creator of the concept of "cost-plus" accounting—pricing cars to recover costs, plus some.

Billy Durant probably would not have enjoyed life at GM very much once Sloan's plan took effect. This was a decidedly unromantic program that turned the company from one of boys-playing-with-cars to a more adult world, where planning was designed both to manage the present and prepare for the future.

Sloan's plan was ingenious because it balanced the important values that had to be considered by a company of GM's size and stature. He set out to end the chaos created by a lack of centralized control, while at the same time avoiding the choke-hold of a rigidly centralized organization. The overall direction and strategy of the company would be articulated by a central staff, while division managers would be free to set their own strategies to accomplish corporate goals. Sloan's plan might be termed a corporate democracy, a system of committees staffed by inside and outside board members and executives to oversee such functions as finance, product planning, executive compensation, and leadership succession. Sloan wanted a system that would make it difficult for absolute power to rest in the hands of any one individual; he believed that too much power in the hands of Billy Durant had nearly ruined the company. Most important, Sloan's plan called for the parent company to coordinate "corporate" matters, while the business of engineering, manufacturing, and selling the cars remained hands-on functions, performed by the people who knew best how to accomplish these tasks.

Alfred Sloan, who didn't actually become president until Pierre du Pont resigned in 1923, went on to become chairman in 1937. He was the company's longest-reigning leader and is widely considered to be the man who built GM into the company it is today.

He dealt effectively with GM's vast size by making its subsidiaries autonomous profit centers, and tying the decentralized staffs into a cohesive whole under the direction of a corporate management team. As management expert Peter Drucker would later write, Sloan's genius was that he recognized that big business was more than simply a personality cult or what he called "anarchy tempered by stock options." Noted Drucker, "Everyone before Sloan had seen the problem as one of personalities, to be solved through a struggle for power from which one man would emerge victorious. Sloan saw it as a constitutional problem to be solved through a new structure; decentralization which balances local autonomy in operations with central control of direction and policy."

Alfred Sloan was a dedicated worker and brilliant leader who surrounded himself with high-quality people, from whom he was not reluctant to solicit advice. He was also a natural manager who understood the process, people, and product. Rather than isolate himself from the operation, as later leadership would be prone to do, Sloan remained close to the workings of the company, visiting the proving grounds regularly, and holding frequent meetings with employees. He recognized that "pride of ownership" was at the heart of corporate incentive. He created a managerial compensation package based on the premise that employees were, in effect, "partners" in the goals of the organization, and they should be rewarded in conjunction with their contribution. He believed that when an employee's personal interest coincided with the corporate interest, he would be more effective. (The strategy of management incentives was considered revolutionary, and the system remains basically unchanged, except for the reduction of the number of eligible people and the escalation in the size of the payments.) But while the premise was sound, even Sloan didn't recognize the dangers down the road. Eventually, the annual incentive program was one of the factors that prevented GM management from taking the necessary risks; managers were reluctant to forgo profits and bonuses in the short term to take steps that would only pay off in the long term. Divisions would work against one another to bolster their results and garner a larger share of the pie.

What Sloan lacked in Durant-style fire and charisma, he more than made up for in his mastery at controlling the massive corporation and his intuitive grasp of the business and the marketplace. To Sloan, the mandate was clear: Find a way to structure the giant so that it could hum along as smoothly as a mom-and-pop concern. In this task he largely succeeded. For decades, under Sloan and his successors, GM would grow to become practically impervious to the ups and downs of the economy, and would never suffer the financial crises that afflicted Ford and Chrysler.

It was certainly never Sloan's intention that General Motors would turn its prominence into a form of fat-cat arrogance that would leave it vulnerable to the competition. Sloan's management doctrine evolved during a period of tremendous challenge within the industry. Eventually, as the company gained in stature and actually succeeded in becoming number one, the adrenaline rush of striving for a competitive edge sputtered and died. No longer was GM battling against a surge of competition. It had attained its status as the leader, and the headiness of this success took hold and eventually became ingrained into the corporate philosophy: *General Motors could do no wrong.* A confrontation with reality was inevitable.

By the 1950s, General Motors was a monster, a smug and secure empire. The company's executive ranks were replenished by aggressive, ambitious young men who were lulled into feelings of superiority, seeing only that their personal access to power could be guaranteed within the sanctity of GM's executive ranks. There was a comfortable hum to the way GM operated, and the leaders were colorless company men, with few interests outside GM. Fred Donner, who became chariman in 1958, epitomized the conservative, low-profile, bottom-line-oriented manager. But he was to see more of the glare of the cameras than he expected.

By the end of the 1950s, small cracks were beginning to appear in the empire. Irritants rose from all fronts—the most aggressive in the form of a struggling law school graduate named Ralph Nader. Nader possessed the fire of conviction and, like a nagging insect, he couldn't be batted away. His campaign against the automotive industry and its lack of commitment to vehicle safety was sparked by an unforgettably horrifying personal experience—he saw a child beheaded by a glove compartment door in a fifteen-mile-per-hour car crash. Nader began his crusade against built-in car defects. And he singled out GM's inexpensive new "import fighter," the Corvair, as his primary target.

Nader was like a bloodhound in pursuit of his prey: the overblown fat-guy capitalistic company who would slice off the heads of small children to satisfy its bottom line. He had three main allegations against the Corvair:

1. It was unstable on turns.

2. The cooling system leaked deadly carbon monoxide fumes into the car.

3. In a front-end crash, a driver could be lanced by the steering column.

With Nader and others prodding the industry, small steps were taken to mollify the public in its emerging concern for auto safety. For example, in 1964, seat belts became standard equipment.

In July 1965, Senator Abraham Ribicoff of Connecticut opened Senate hearings on auto safety, concerned that the cars the federal government was purchasing might not be sufficiently safe. Fred Donner and president James Roche were summoned to testify. A week earlier, GM had announced a $1-million grant for a study on auto safety.

In the hearings, Senator Robert F. Kennedy began by asking Donner and Roche what the company's earnings had been during the previous year. The executives hedged. "I will have to ask one of my associates," Donner answered finally. A huddle took place amid cynical snickers that surely the chairman of General Motors should have such a number on the tip of his tongue. Roche finally piped up with the number—about $1.7 billion.

Perhaps the reluctance of GM executives to state the extent of their profit was due to the startling juxtaposition of that number with the meager $1 million it had committed to the study of safety. If this was their fear, it was warranted. Kennedy immediately expressed indignation that a company with such huge earning levels would spend such a miserly sum to ensure public safety.

Enter Ralph Nader. His book, *Unsafe at Any Speed,* blasted the Corvair for its safety defects. Nader pointed a particularly damning finger at Ed Cole, chief engineer and general manager of Chevrolet. He said of Cole, who would later become GM president, "No man in the last twenty years had the authority and the knowledge to make safe cars, and didn't use it, like Ed Cole." After the book's publication, Senator Ribicoff called Nader to testify before the Senate committee investigating auto safety. GM executives were livid. Nader was even offering to help motorists sue the giant! In a rash, emotional frenzy, it was decided by GM executives that Nader himself should be investigated.

But General Motors was an amateur player in the spying game. A company employee contacted a friend to hire a former FBI agent to tail Nader, and Ribicoff quickly learned of the effort. The senator was furious over this sleazy attempt to harass one of his witnesses; he called for an investigation of GM.

A deeply humiliated General Motors admitted that indeed it had tried to investigate Nader. It was later revealed that the investigation was focused on an effort to substantiate completely false rumors that Nader was anti-Semitic and a homosexual.

The end result was that the committee pulled in the unsophisticated James Roche (he had earned his accounting degree from a correspondence course) to make a public confession: Yes, GM had tailed Nader. Yes, GM had then lied about it. No, it had not intended harassment. Yes, the company was very sorry.

A senator on the committee echoed the public dismay. "Everyone is so outraged that a great corporation was out to clobber a guy because he wrote critically about them," he said. And perhaps GM paid the price for its indiscretion, because a torrent of federal auto safety regulations followed, beginning with the passage of the National Traffic and Motor Vehicle Safety Act. By the end of 1967, recalls for safety defects had risen to one in three cars, and warranty payments became a substantial cost factor.

Meanwhile, GM settled out of court on hundreds of Nader-inspired Corvair suits—the result of death and injury. The publicity crippled Corvair and ultimately led to its demise, but in spite of the public setback, General Motors thrived during this period, solidifying its leadership position in the market and moving its share back up over the 50-percent mark.

But there were other rumblings on the horizon at that time. Since the 1950s, General Motors had been the subject of controversy because of its size, and talk of a breakup was always in the air. Fearful of antitrust action, Donner looked around for ways to protect General Motors from breakup action. Although it has never been confirmed by the company, it was widely believed that the creation of General Motors Assembly Division, in 1965, was part of an antibreakup strategy. The establishment of GMAD essentially removed most of the assembly plants from the control of the car divisions and consolidated them under GMAD—making it nearly impossible to break up GM into free-standing companies. It also had the effect of creating another autonomous bureaucracy in GMAD and another hurdle in the tedious process of getting a car from the design studio to the showroom. And it was the first major reorganization of GM that slowly bled away the individuality of GM brands. GMAD was testimony to the collapse of Sloan's concept of divisional identities.

GM's arrogant we're-number-one posture, buttressed by a corporate culture that could not stand to hear the bad news about itself, set the company up for a fall as foreign competition began to make inroads.

GM hadn't understood the appeal of the dumpy little Volkswagen "Bug" that gained popularity in the 1960s; nor did it understand that the popularity of the Honda represented far more than customer whim. In the early 1970s, while GM was concentrating on keeping Americans in big, cushy land-yachts and gas-gulping muscle cars, Honda took the nation by storm, selling 1,300 cars in 1970—by 1975, that number would swell to 100,000.

The Japanese, who were producing lightweight, fuel-efficient cars, were poised to take advantage of the trend, while General Motors refused to acknowledge its problems.

One former truck executive recalled a lesson from his first report to the Executive Committee during the Roche presidency in the late 1960s. "I had made a study and I told them, 'If anybody buys a GM pickup truck, it's impossible for him or her to stay out of the dealership during the first year.' Mr. Roche looked at me with surprise and said, 'Why is that?' I said, 'Well, it's because we build so many defects into the car, he *has* to go to a dealership.' There was dead silence in the room—nobody said a word. After the meeting, my boss came up to me and said, 'We don't talk about things like that in the administrative meetings.' I asked him why not and he just shrugged, 'We're supposed to solve those problems ourselves.' Management was afraid to hear controversy or get involved in something that needed to be worked at. I don't know why."

GM's numbing habit of ignoring the competition—domestic or foreign—was a dangerous one. The only competition recognized in those days was that which existed inside the company. Pontiac, for example, never looked at Dodge or Mercury—only at Buick and Oldsmobile. And *nobody* looked at the Japanese.

The shape of the world in the early 1970s—and particularly the world inhabited by the auto industry—was changing at a dizzying pace. Perhaps the most futuristic thinkers could see what was ahead. But Detroit was mostly oblivious to the changing times.

The oil embargo, announced by Saudi Arabia in late 1973 to punish the United States for supporting Israel in the Yom Kippur War, and the unilateral OPEC agreement that followed dealt a tremendous blow to the domestic auto industry. Not only were consumers paying two to three times more for gasoline, they were having a hard time finding it. Lines snaked around gas stations all over America; desperate car owners were topping off tanks and hoarding gasoline in their garages. The greatest fear was not so much that prices would rise. Although that was certainly a consideration, the real fear was that the country would run so low on gasoline that rationing would be permanent. Considering that the post-World War II suburban communities had grown up around a reliance on the automobile, to be stranded miles from commerce, schools, and work was a horrifying prospect indeed.

The crisis hit General Motors, with its large, gas-guzzling cars, hardest of all. Traditionally loyal customers were now demanding compact, fuel-efficient cars, and the sudden market shift rattled the company to the very roots of its big-car, cheap-gas heritage. People were speaking a new language—a foreign language that GM didn't understand. It was called "miles per gallon."

At the time, General Motors executives believed the problem would be short-lived. As Thomas Murphy would later say: "The Arabs were sitting on that pot of oil over there and they were trying to punish the United States for favoring Israel. I think the people in this country felt, well, okay, they're having their fun. But it was not a real serious concern. It was a concern about the fact that they were dictating to us and were raising the price of oil. But I think people felt it was a phase and we'll get it behind us." Not only did GM executives believe the change in buying habits was short-lived, they also possessed a smugness about the consumers' choice of foreign cars. "They'll be sorry," was the expressed sentiment. "These little crackerjack boxes haven't got the quality—wait until they start falling apart." While GM was partly right and the panic buying of econoboxes subsided, the company failed to appreciate the importance of the beachhead the Japanese had established on American shores.

The immediate impact of the energy crisis appeared in GM's sales and profits. Within five months of the oil embargo, car sales were already down more than 35 percent, the worst slump since the 1958 recession. Plagued by swollen inventories, GM temporarily closed as many as fifteen of its twenty-two assembly plants and three of its four stamping plants. General Motors was guilty of two errors at this point. First, they made small-car development a low priority since the Japanese had set a pricing standard at which GM could not be profitable. Second, they believed it would be foolhardy to lure big-car buyers to smaller cars by making them too good. Captive to the big-car strategy of the past, GM failed to notice the lion charging until the company was locked in the grip of its paws.

In the panic that ensued during the latter part of 1973 and early 1974, executives at the company could not accept the possibility that economical cars were more than a stopgap response to the energy crisis, even though many in the industry (including GM's own former vice president, John DeLorean) called it a lasting trend. They held their corporate breath and waited for the oil embargo to be lifted, confidently announcing that the oil crisis was solely responsible for the decline in sales. This stubborn adherence to outdated strategies and arrogant disregard for trends that did not fit the company's worldview set GM on a path that came close to fatally crippling the giant. As one executive lamented, "Once President Nixon announced in December 1973 that people should turn down their thermostats to save energy, we couldn't sell a big car to save our ass from first base."

But the energy crisis was not the *only* cause of the small-car surge, merely another element in a long-term trend toward smaller, less expensive cars. Other factors in the marketplace had emerged to set a clear precedent for the gradual increase in small-car sales. And for so long GM had been a trend shaper, it did not understand that sociological factors outside its dominance might turn the tides. Awesome as it might appear in today's market-driven culture, in the late 1960s, the largest employer in the world was not conducting market research to determine what the public wanted or needed. Its philosophy was well articulated by a top executive who once said, "A company doing forty-five to fifty percent of the business can make an aspect of car appearance a necessary earmark of product acceptance by the public. Familiarity," he insisted, "breeds acceptance."

On a fundamental level, GM missed the point of what was happening around them. And they were locked into narrow concepts about what customers found desirable in their cars. They defined small as cheap, uncomfortable, underpowered, and Spartan. In fact, when GM tried to build small cars they were just that. They were afraid of making good, desirable small cars for fear it would cut into their big-car business. What they failed to appreciate was that the Japanese were prepared to design small cars with big-car quality and features—and good mileage to boot.

The energy crisis merely pushed an already emerging trend over the edge. Even as General Motors complacently continued to design its "family" cars, the shape of the American family was changing. Women were returning to the workplace in droves, creating the demand for a second, more economical family car. The first generation of suburban youth were coming of age; they got driver's licenses and needed to have cars to get around, and parents were discovering that it was cheaper to buy their teenagers and college-age children new gas-efficient imports like the Volkswagen than to spring for larger, used cars that would cost more to run. The energy crisis merely deepened an already existing consumer sensitivity to car economy—both in purchase price and operating costs. The GM leadership could not grasp the very simple fact that the small car was here to stay—with or without an energy crisis.

At the start of the oil embargo, the only conceivable defense GM had to offer was in the form of the Chevy Vega. The Vega had been introduced in 1971 as a challenger to the Volkswagen "Bug," but it had all the attributes of a born loser. When James Roche first announced the project in 1968, shortly after becoming chairman, he had promised it would be a 2,000-pound car priced at the level of the Volkswagen—$1,800. But the research that preceded the announcement was based on computerized studies; there wasn't even a prototype. The Vega debuted 382 pounds heavier and a foot longer than the Volkswagen. And not only did it cost $311 more than its foreign rival, but that price was only reached after compromise upon compromise; numerous styling touches were removed and cheaper tires were substituted for those that would have delivered better mileage and a classier look. In the vernacular of the day, the Vega was a lemon. It couldn't even compete with the Pinto, Ford's far-from-perfect response to foreign competition—the car that would eventually tarnish Ford's reputation because of its tendency to explode in rear-end collisions.

Rather than face the fact that the Vega wouldn't achieve its targets, GM executives chose to ignore it. They didn't fix the car. They just changed the targets, and justified the higher cost and heavier weight by saying that the car was American-made and therefore had higher quality standards. This wasn't just public relations talk, either. They really *believed* that made-in-America meant higher quality, and this factor was enough to compensate for weight and price. But the condition of the Vega lent faint support to the argument, since it was quickly revealed that the car had numerous mechanical problems. In the 1971 model year, Pinto outsold Vega 316,700 to 245,000.

The company might eventually have pulled the Vega out of its hole, were it not for the decision, in late 1971, to cut costs and escalate production in the Lordstown, Ohio, plant where the Vega was being built. High productivity was a noble goal, but GM had no idea how to do it except to make people work harder and faster, and this method doomed the effort to failure. Lordstown was taken over by GMAD, which was well known for its ironfisted policies and its use of line speedups to increase production. GMAD immediately slashed seven hundred workers from the payroll and invested in twenty-six high-speed welding robots whose job was to fast-forward work on the production line. These speeding robots required *humans* to feed them sheet metal panels, and since human beings are not "designed" to

operate at breakneck robotic speed, there was tremendous resentment among workers. Some told stories of plant managers
who had secret switches in their offices that they pulled to speed
up the line. After four months of working under almost impossible conditions, a rebellious rank and file cried, "No more!" and
walked off the job.

The three-week strike captured the imagination of the press
and no doubt hurt sales of the car. It was a classic confrontation
between the dedicated but beaten-down *human* worker and the
unfeeling, job-stealing robot. Automation, it was suggested, was
a ruthless direction; it created a salt mines environment, sapping
dry creativity and pride from the American labor force and leaving workers deadened with boredom and unmotivated. The
striking workers fed the press's hunger for examples of just this
eventuality by complaining about the myriad of quality control
problems that existed in the automated environment, and the
many compromises that had been made on the Vega's structure.
By the time the strike was settled, the Vega's reputation was
unsalvageable.

Sad to say, the lesson learned by GM as a result of this
disaster was slightly askew of the mark. The company correctly
concluded that the heavy use of robots didn't necessarily translate into higher productivity or higher quality. But they failed to
take the equation the next logical step and ask themselves *why*
this was so. The problem wasn't with the robots, per se. The
problem was designing a system that integrated humans and
robots in a compatible work environment. GM thought it could
reduce the number of workers by replacing them with robots;
instead, the workers had to stay on the line because of frequent
robot breakdowns. The human supervisors were poorly trained
to handle the problems, and both humans and machines failed
to produce. With the lesson left unlearned, similar problems
would return to haunt GM once again in the 1980s. They stem
from an inbred management belief that workers are expensive
nuisances who can be replaced.

Furthermore, the company never laid the groundwork that
would allow workers to psychologically accept the introduction
of robots. Workers could hardly have been expected to welcome
their mechanical "buddies" with open arms when they had just
seen seven hundred family members and friends laid off. Robots, after all, didn't have families to feed or mortgages to pay.

The implication that twenty-six machines could replace seven hundred humans was very disturbing indeed. Concern for worker security started the UAW on a quest for job protections, and led to a paranoia about automation.

The oil crisis landed in the lap of Richard Gerstenberg, a traditional GM workhorse, who had moved up the ranks from his first job as timekeeper at Frigidaire and eventually through the finance division—he referred to himself as "Old Gerstenberg the bookkeeper." In the wake of the oil embargo, he made the decision that General Motors must do something quickly to build efficiency into its cars. He inaugurated GM's major "downsizing" program—taking the traditional hulks and making them shorter and substituting parts so they were lighter in weight, while persuading the public that they were worthy of a higher price than their bigger, heavier predecessors.

Downsizing was a brilliant, stopgap measure for a company caught off guard by the energy crisis and inflation. It was a savvy financial move because the public was willing to pay more for the leaner, stylish cars. Compared to Ford and Chrysler, GM looked like a genius. The company was very successful with its seven-hundred-pound-lighter, foot-shorter big cars. The first small Cadillac, the Seville, proved to be very popular. GM was able to stabilize while Ford and Chrysler were suffering mightily at the hands of the Japanese. GM's downsized models elevated the company's market share while Chrysler's condition worsened and Ford was being scrutinized for faulty transmissions and exploding Pintos.

But there were two major hurdles facing the company. The first was that the Japanese were gaining sophistication as they evolved from econobox producers to manufacturers capable of building compact-size cars with big-car features and performance.

The second was the continued interest in fuel economy. When fuel-economy standards were enacted in 1978, a new burden was placed on the auto industry: If you build gas guzzlers, you pay the price in taxes. GM chairman Thomas Murphy was determined that the company would never pay a penny in gas-guzzler taxes, and he put in place a program to shrink virtually every GM car and transform every GM assembly plant by the mid-1980s. Front-wheel-drive and smaller cars, as well as diesel engines and electric batteries, would be GM's answer to the new government standards. Unfortunately, many of the models failed in quality and price. But in the beginning, the impressive high-tech direction of the company made GM once again appear invincible, especially against its floundering domestic rivals.

GM's initial strategy was a plan to build two small-car models. The first was the X-car—with transverse mounted front engine, front-wheel drive, and engine refinements designed to deliver both lower emission levels and higher gas mileage. Front-wheel drive was a logical solution if cars had to become smaller. It allowed for a roomier interior, a lighter car, and better handling. The innovation required a vast investment— one that GM's American competition could not afford. The X-car was widely viewed as having great potential, although it would not debut until April 1979—as the Chevrolet Citation, Pontiac Phoenix, Oldsmobile Omega, and Buick Skylark. Initially, GM got lucky with the X-car, because it hit the market right in the middle of the second energy crisis, which developed when the Shah left Iran and oil was once again being held hostage. If there was any complaint, it was that dealers didn't have enough X-cars available to meet the demand. Only later would the problem of poor quality rear its ugly head and lead to the model's demise.

The second design plan was the J-car, scheduled to debut in 1981. Like the Vega, it was defined as an "import fighter," this time against the Honda Accord. But it was an underpowered flop at launch, and complaints began to surface about look-alike cars.

By 1974, when Thomas Murphy began his chairmanship, GM's traditional methods for strategic planning were being put to the test by the unfamiliar new imperatives emerging from inflation and the energy crisis. Both Murphy and his president, Elliott "Pete" Estes, were lifetime GM employees, who had been with the company during its golden era. They believed in the big-car strategy, and felt that the core of the problem GM was facing was the onslaught of government regulations and fuel-economy standards that made it increasingly difficult to produce cars profitably. They continued to ignore the long-term implications of the energy crisis, and Estes would even declare, "The fuel economy standards are not necessary and they are not good for America."

But it was becoming increasingly clear that the external

environment could no longer be ignored, and the market changes could no longer be considered short-term problems. One executive at General Motors saw this more clearly than most. His name was Roger Bonham Smith.

A true-blue General Motors corporate man, Smith had been moving steadily up the ladder in the organization, and it was well known that he had the ear—and the affection—of the new chairman. When Murphy became chairman, Smith was promoted to executive vice president, finance. It was commonly expected that Smith would become chairman himself after Murphy's tenure was over—and indeed he did, in 1981.

In 1974, Roger Smith was hard at work trying to pave the way for that future. He saw that one of the company's greatest stumbling blocks was its lack of comprehensive, futuristic strategic planning.

At the time, several groups within the company were involved in planning activities, but these groups were ineffective in developing broad, long-range strategies. For the most part, the groups operated as separate, divisional entities, with narrow loyalties. As such, they were heavily influenced by their own departmental goals—not the least of which was to provide favorable year-to-year financial forecasts.

Smith recognized the need for planning on a larger scale— the kind that could carry General Motors into the next century. He used to say, "I don't want to run a buggy-whip company when somebody is inventing the automobile." So a cadre of four group executives, with Smith at the helm, was established to develop a master plan for the corporation's future. It was called the Corporate Directions Group.

"The name is significant," Smith says today in a rare display of corporate self-deprecation. "Our mission was corporate strategic planning but the top management did not want to call it that for several reasons. First, they didn't want GM people to think we were just starting to do strategic planning. In fact, this was true. GM for years had great product planning (run by operating people) and strong capital and financial planning (run by the financial people), but the strategic planning, such as it was, was done informally by the CEO and the Executive Committee. I'm sure that the CEO knew where he wanted the corporation to go but it was communicated to the organization through the product programs and the action of the various policy groups. Nowhere could you find a master plan for the corporation's future."

At the outset, Smith's group was uncertain of the nature of its task and less than enthusiastic about being involved in planning. "Strategic planning was not really held in high regard—it was in its infancy then," recalls Smith. He quickly found out just how *little* it was regarded when the members of his group offered to let him carry the ball. "They advised me that they would try to help me if I needed help, but that they all felt I was better prepared to take on the task of strategic planning than they were."

Smith moved fast to jump-start the reluctant planning group, enlisting Mike Naylor, a British-born engineer in the Transportations Systems division, who had a solid reputation for his facility in brainstorming key long-range issues and developing strategies. For example, Naylor created a plan for his division called Scenario 2000, an unprecedented piece of futuristic work in GM circles.

Smith asked Naylor if he could take Scenario 2000 and convert it into something that could be used for overall company strategy. "He said, 'Put a presentation together for me, and when you've got it done, let me know,' " Naylor recalls. "I asked him, 'How soon do you want this?' and he said in the next couple of weeks.

"I called him back ten days later and said, 'Okay, I've got a first draft done. When would you like to see it?' and he said, 'How about twenty minutes from now?' I thought, my God, this guy is really serious."

Smith was dead serious. He recognized that without a corporate strategy, GM might not survive the shifting tides of a global automotive market. And he had reason to strongly suspect that *he* would be the chairman who could put in place the strategy to take GM into the twenty-first century. The idea, he would later say, was to be prepared for anything. "I don't like people running into my office saying, 'Jeez, this just happened. What do we do next?' I want to have a plan for just about everything. I don't have one for a nuclear attack, but of course we have all the usual security precautions for that, too."

Within twenty-four hours of presenting his draft to Smith, Mike Naylor was standing in front of the Executive Committee, outlining the plan. It was fast work, and the EC bought it.

Smith's corporate strategic planning group was a formal reality.

Roger Smith's initial instincts called for a three-prong goal: (1) Identify and eliminate the businesses where GM didn't belong; (2) get the domestic car divisions to think globally; and (3) identify the new businesses in which GM should get involved.

"Our early efforts weren't all that successful," Smith remembers ruefully. "One occasion sticks out vividly in my mind. Mike and I were convinced that we needed to know more about the fundamentals of strategic planning. We organized a symposium and invited the top thirty experts from all over the United States—corporate people, academics, consultants, and so forth—and asked six of them to present papers on various aspects of strategic planning. At the end of the day, all the experts departed, congratulating themselves on the fabulous symposium. Mike and I simply looked at each other and said, 'My God, they don't know any more than we do!' So we rolled up our sleeves and went to work.

"Three tries and many gray hairs later, we came up with what I believe is the best strategic planning system in the country, if not the world. It is complex and requires a lot of effort and honest self-analysis. It was an analysis of the business plans that convinced Jim McDonald (then executive vice president, with jurisdiction over group operations) that we could not be successful if we continued with our present organizational structure. The car division–Fisher Body–GMAD setup was too cumbersome, costly, and slow to be competitive."

This was the genesis of Smith's sweeping vision for General Motors. He and Naylor were asking the kind of futuristic questions that were rarely on the lips of GM planners: What would the world be like in ten, twenty, even thirty years? How would the marketing environment change? And what should GM do to take full advantage of that changing environment?

It would later become painfully clear that the task of strategic planning should not have been so dependent on the talents of abstract thinkers like Smith and Naylor. For, while they were effectively targeting the external battlefronts, neither man concerned himself with the vast internal culture of General Motors. Both believed that with the right formula, the organization (including its 800,000 workers) could be convinced to go along with the plan.

Naylor's planning group consisted of Ph.D.'s and computer

jocks—an elitist element held in faint regard by the company regulars. They worked in the basement of the GM building, where they developed a giant computer model of General Motors. The basement location was chosen for "security" reasons, since the group was dealing with highly confidential information about the company's operations. But symbolically, the fact that the small band of elite computer types were being hustled off to the basement to build their plans made it easier for other executives to ridicule them. Most people believed the group was merely performing meaningless "intellectual exercises." The skepticism of the operating people was not surprising, considering that the staff and operating functions were perceived as spinning in two separate orbits. Operating people felt the staff could not possibly understand the practical day-to-day logistics of building and selling cars, and this attitude led to great resistance when Smith and Naylor tried to convince people of the necessity of strategic planning.

A New Era Begins at GM:

An Old Boy Breaks Ranks

We're up to our ass in trouble and we've got to start doing things differently. We're behind our foreign competition right now in quality, in technological design, in plants and facilities, and, yes, even in our own management . . . in 1980, the little girl with the lemonade stand down the street made more profit than all of us—GM, Ford, Chrysler and AMC together.

—Roger Smith

Roger Smith's first public reaction to the announcement that he had been elected chairman of General Motors was to say that it would be business as usual for the 1980s. Reported *The Wall Street Journal:* "Mr. Smith says he envisions no break with GM's philosophy or operating policies. 'I'd be very surprised if there are any dramatic changes,' he said."

Looking back to that day in September 1980, one might conclude that Smith was a master of understatement. But at the time, most industry insiders—including many within GM's own ranks—were inclined to agree with the assessment. Even in an era of dramatic change in the auto industry, Smith's tenure promised to be, as one columnist put it, "a yawner." There were several reasons for this perception: First, for many years, Smith had been practically joined at the hip with Thomas Murphy, the outgoing chairman, so most of the policies of the preceding years bore Smith's signature. Why should he change now? Few, if any, recognized a portent of things to come from Smith's vague statements in the following days. "I have been close enough to watch the chairman's function. I know how it works," he said in one interview. "I'll have ten years on this job, the good Lord willing, and I'll have an opportunity to leave my mark. Our team will be plowing new ground." But, he added, that "new ground" was a ways down the road, when they "ran out of things past management has done." Such statements didn't exactly establish Roger Smith as a world-beater, much less hint at his concerns about the status quo at GM.

Everyone had known for several years that Roger Smith was the heir apparent to the chairmanship, so the announcement itself hardly took the industry by storm. In the GM corporate tradition, new chairmen were handpicked by their predecessors; given Smith's careful grooming by Thomas Murphy, there was little doubt that the baton would be passed to him. For nearly twenty years, Smith had been Murphy's closest adviser and primary implementer. And Murphy loved the guy. One insider recalls that the day John Kennedy was shot, Smith was scheduled for an appointment at the Sloan-Kettering Institute for Cancer Research in New York to be checked for melanoma. Murphy was said to be so despondent at the prospect of a GM without Smith and the news of the Kennedy assassination that he wondered if his own life could continue without Smith around. (For the record, Murphy hotly denies that Smith's election was inevitable, describing the lengthy review of many candidates that preceded Smith's selection. But most industry watchers agree that the process is merely a formality—and that the outgoing chairman taps his successor.)

Another reason for media inertia at the prospect of a Smith chairmanship was that his demeanor seemed to deny the possibility of strong leadership. To put it mildly, Roger Smith was no Lee Iacocca. Flamboyance of any kind seemed anathema to him. Neither was he a match for his mentor, Thomas Murphy, whose personal warmth and public spirit made him one of GM's best-loved chairmen. Smith was uncomfortable in public forums, and incapable of easy humor. Even his physical characteristics seemed at odds with the role of the most powerful corporate chairman in the world. With his diminutive stature, cherubic cheeks, sandy hair, and high-pitched, almost squeaky voice, Smith appeared, at first blush, to be better suited for the role of cheerleader in the stands than for star quarterback. Behind his back, many in the company referred to him (with some degree of sarcasm) as Jolly Roger.

But with Roger Smith, things are not always as they seem. He is a man of contradictions, hard to get close to, a chameleon, who can rapidly shift moods from iron fist to folksy handshake. Examples of the paradox that is Roger Smith are numerous:

- He is a man of vision, yet his passion is tightly controlled. He is brilliant, but he often lacks both the charisma and the sensitivity to motivate others to see his vision through to completion, or to understand when the vision is flawed. He speaks often of the importance of "communication," but for him that term has not always implied a two-way street, an interchange of ideas. Having formulated his vision, he is married to it until death. He has been described as rigid, demanding, stern, and inflexible by those who have worked for him. His loner's stance reflects an attitude that *"I* have the vision, *you* do the work."
- Although he can be quite charming in a one-on-one setting, his public persona is stiff and humorless. He dislikes truly personal encounters, and this makes his folksiness appear inauthentic. Once, when a television interviewer pressed him to talk about the effect cancer had on his life, he could not answer and, indeed, looked mystified about what point she was trying to make. "Well," he said finally, "I missed a month of work."
- Although he has often demonstrated a cool lack of concern for the human implications of his policies, he can flip the mask and appear as a caring, concerned human being who considers his family the most important thing in his life. He is a devoted husband and father—when his youngest son went off to college, he openly showed his feelings of loss.
- Insiders will report that Smith has a blistering temper and a needle-sharp tongue that can cut subordinates down to size. But in public his conversations are peppered with expressions like "Gee whiz" and "Holy Toledo!" In Smith-speak, "Hey" is a common prefix; "Darn!" is the way one expresses grave disappointment.
- He is the consummate company man, yet he disdains many of the activities common to executive gamesmanship. He'd much rather go fishing than engage in corporate entertaining.

All in all, Smith seemed an odd choice to become GM's Rambo on the international front. But then, there was always something more to Roger Smith than met the eye.

* * *

For those who expected to doze through Smith's tenure, the awakening came almost the moment he took charge in January 1981.

From the start, Roger Smith made it clear that he intended to run a one-man show. There would be little team play with president-elect James McDonald, and McDonald, whose most notable quality appeared to be that he was a nice guy, seemed unlikely to complain. While his predecessor, Elliott "Pete" Estes, had been viewed as a strong president, McDonald (who some said was in awe of his promotion) seemed unlikely to rock the boat—much less stand up to the aggressive new chairman. McDonald played the "George Bush" to Smith's "Ronald Reagan." (In behavior uncharacteristic of Bush, however, McDonald would later resist pressure to retire early and become the scapegoat for GM's troubles.)

Smith was the boss and he made the decisions—not just on corporate strategy, but also on the insignificant details of daily corporate life. (It would astonish many people to learn that the chairman of the greatest company in the world took responsibility for deciding how the parking spaces in GM's executive garage should be allocated, or assigning secretaries to top executives and determining their salaries, and deciding which offices on the Fourteenth Floor executives would occupy.) Almost immediately, he began to put in force changes that ultimately led observers to describe his tenure as the building—or rather, rebuilding—of an empire.

On the surface, Smith appeared to be the kind of leader who might welcome an energetic exchange of ideas, and the same spirit of team play promoted by Alfred Sloan. But Smith didn't like being challenged. His idea of team play was that executives support his plan without questioning it. In truth, by the time Smith was elected chairman, the days of Sloan-style democracy were a thing of the past; the idea that one could be opinionated, overly creative, or a freethinker had long since died a natural death at General Motors, not just at the level of chairman, but throughout the organization.

"The bad news syndrome just wasn't acceptable," recalls a former executive. "If you raised a problem, you got labeled as 'negative,' not a team player. If you wanted to rise in the company, you kept your mouth shut and said yes to everything."

During the late 1970s, a writer for *Fortune* magazine set out on a quest for a dissenting view at General Motors, and found it hard "to find a top executive at GM who does not evidence enthusiasm for what he or the company is doing." One view might hold that GM had achieved a state of management consensus that would be the envy of any company. But more likely, the lack of dissension was motivated by self-interest. It was managerial suicide to be the person who got labeled as a naysayer. There was also an element of denial; in the same way that children of alcoholics often refuse to accept their parents' addiction, GM employees refused to admit the truth about their corporate parent. They didn't want to believe.

Thomas Murphy once complained that "one of the biggest dangers for a chief executive is that communications dry up. People no longer tell you, 'The emperor has no clothes.' " But why should they? There was little incentive to take on the mantle of the antiestablishment. One has only to review Roger Smith's career to understand that.

Roger Smith is fond of saying that there was no great secret to his success. "I guess some of it was luck," he demurs. "And there's no substitute for hard work. It's easy to say, 'Ah, heck' and give up, but you just have to keep going."

What Smith fails to communicate is the *way* he worked. For thirty-one years, Smith moved up through the ranks of GM as the consummate corporate player—the GM culture coursed in his veins. Admiration for and loyalty to the organization was at the core of his being. He was one of a new breed of corporate politicians whose success depended on their ease in wearing the corporate mantle. Translated, that meant, "Above all, be loyal to your superior's agenda."

Roger Smith quickly developed the reputation for being particularly adept at the game. Not only would he enthusiastically support the task on the table, he would also make certain that he got it done faster and more masterfully than anyone else.

"Whatever the senior people wanted done, he did it," a former colleague told *Fortune* magazine in a 1984 profile of Smith. "In the '50s, there was a little joke that if you asked Roger Smith to move the GM building across Grand Boulevard, the only thing he would say was, 'Which way do you want it to face?' " It appears that this was the "company joke," used to distinguish those with an uncharacteristic degree of loyalty—the true "yes men," if you will. For example, the same story was told about Ed Cole, the company man–car nut who was GM president from 1967 to 1974.

But Smith was no corporate zombie. He was smarter than that. There was a certain brilliant cunning to the way he managed the tricky balancing act between obedience to the corporate dogma and personal initiative.

To hear Smith describe it, each time he was told he'd been promoted (and there were nine of these occasions), he'd look up from the work he was buried in, blink a couple of times, blush a characteristic beet-red, and say, "You mean *me?*"

"I guess I really liked every job I ever had at GM," he said once. "I would have been happy to keep doing it. I never knew I was getting a promotion until they told me."

But clearly Smith had a plan—and the genius to execute it. He was an eager beaver, capable of outworking everyone around him. He put himself at GM's service and developed the reputation of a young comer who would go anywhere or do anything for the company.

Smith knew how to make his presence known without ever appearing to steal his bosses' thunder in the process. It was this instinct for being the "good old boy" in the corporate game that first brought him to the attention of Thomas Murphy, then in New York, who learned, like others before him, that he could depend on Smith. "It wasn't too long before I realized that if you wanted to get something done and you had to be sure it got done on time and accurately, Roger was the guy who could do it," recalls Murphy, who shares Smith's admiration for the old-fashioned work ethic. "I know guys that could have gone very far at General Motors if they had been willing to work. But they weren't . . . and if they were frustrated by not getting ahead, they should have looked in the mirror and made one or two decisions: Either get in and get with it, or get out. Roger never really thought about doing anything else *but* staying with it. He was a guy who was willing to work at whatever you gave him, whenever it was there, and do well at it. I don't know what would have happened if one of the jobs wasn't appetizing to him. I think he would have found a way to make it so."

Smith has always presented himself as an ordinary guy—a *car* guy, if you will. He meets some of the criteria for being a car guy—for one thing, he is a great lover of classic cars and his

1959 Corvette is his pride and joy. But Smith makes no pretenses about having grease under his nails. He was strictly a numbers man who rose to power through the financial staffs, not the product side of the business.

Roger Smith credits his father with being the primary force in his development. Quimby Smith had a love for business and an entrepreneurial spirit that fashioned his approach to parenting. He ran his household like a well-oiled company machine, with every moment organized for optimum results. His style could verge on iron-handed discipline; like the recent fictional character, "The Great Santini," he was said to wake the household by blowing a bugle. It is telling that Roger Smith describes his father in much the same way one would describe a good boss, admiring how effectively he organized the family and established projects and incentives. "He had high expectations," Smith once said, citing the example that most stuck in his mind, a system of financial incentives. "We were given five cents for an 'A' on our report cards, two cents for a 'B,' and nothing for a 'C.' "

More than any other quality, Quimby Smith stressed the importance of discipline, and his son Roger was not inclined to rebel. His upbringing stuck. In adulthood, both the strong work ethic and the importance of family became the primary elements of Smith's identity. This was not exactly atypical in Michigan, the heart of the Midwest, where family values and honest work were fundamental cultural themes.

In 1954, Roger Smith met and married Barbara Ann Rasch, a pretty young woman who worked as a clerk in the GM public relations department. He was a well-mannered and serious suitor, and even—though he'll blush today at the suggestion—something of a romantic, who enjoyed whipping up gourmet candle-lit dinners of decidedly nonmidwestern fare; crepes suzette and cherries jubilee were two of his favorites.

Smith always says that his family has been the most important consideration in his life, and, in spite of the long hours he devoted to moving up the ranks at GM, he worked hard at being deeply involved in the lives of his four children, patterning himself after his own father—especially in his close relationship with his youngest son, Drew.

In both his career and family life, Roger Smith followed a seemingly unremarkable path. He blended well into the GMstyled community, worked tirelessly, and had the correct priorities. And yet, beneath his plodding, middle-manager facade, he kept an inner eye trained on the big picture, avoiding the parochial worldview that was characteristic of General Motors management during the 1950s and 1960s.

Roger Smith pounced on the chairmanship with a gung-ho enthusiasm. And he would need it, since the challenges he inherited were complex ones. The company was in the midst of a new product and investment program, designed to put it in the forefront of the auto industry. But the costs were high and, in 1980, GM posted its first calendar-year loss in sixty years—a sum of $763 million. Even though the sentiment inside GM was that the loss was a mere drop in the bucket compared with the staggering problems Ford and Chrysler were facing, there were signs that stress was building in the company. Could it cope with the massive technical challenge of modernizing aging factories, changing virtually all of its cars from rear-wheel- to front-wheel-drive, meeting a slew of new government regulations, and introducing automation into its assembly plants? These were the issues that Roger Smith faced. And the cracks in GM's armor were beginning to show.

The launch of the J-car, GM's so-called import fighter, was a disaster, and it was becoming increasingly clear that anyone who lusted after the features of a Honda Accord—tight-fitting panels, five-speed manual transmission, a quiet but powerful four-cylinder engine, 30 to 32 miles per gallon, a list price below $4,000—wasn't going to take the J-car very seriously. Contrary to popular belief within GM, most consumers now expected good performance and high quality to be standard features on their cars. The Japanese had taught them to demand that.

But the status of the J-car as an import fighter was hampered from the start by an edict from the finance staff: "Keep costs down." In other words, conduct a form of plastic surgery on X-car parts to make the look technologically advanced without actually advancing the technology. Surely the consumer would not be sophisticated enough to recognize that the J-car was an X-car in sheep's clothing. Little did they know.

The J-car would end up being only four hundred pounds lighter than the X-car, and its structure was essentially a cannibalization of the former. Specifically, it was outfitted with the following X-car features:

steering system
front suspension control arms
front-wheel-drive axle joints
wheel bearings
starter motor
generator
power steering pump
radiator and air-conditioner compressor
automatic and manual transmissions

But perhaps the greatest compromise of all occurred in the engine design. Despite the fact that high-revving engines were a major attraction for imports like the Accord, GM decided to go with a four-cylinder version of the V-6 power plant built for the X-car. The Chevy four-cylinder push-rod engine—the modification of a design established in 1955!—seemed a poor choice to match the J-car's decidedly unsluggish billing. President Pete Estes pushed for the use of the Opel's far peppier 1.8-liter overhead camshaft four-cylinder, but the bean counters of the finance staff couldn't pass up the opportunity to extract more profit by putting in place an engine that could borrow pistons, valves, and valve springs from the X-car V-6. (The Opel engine was used in European models; thus the J-car became a great success in Europe and enhanced the operations image, as GM Europe began a long period of revival.)

To defend the use of the modified X-car engine against the argument that consumers might prefer their cars to have more oomph, GM engineers conducted their own Keystone Cops–style "scientific" test. According to project center manager Bill Brewbaker, the test was designed to find out whether Americans really wanted a high-revving engine like the Opel's. "We attached hidden recorders to the engines of a few prototype J-cars, fitted with manual transmissions, and loaned them out to a bunch of employees," Brewbaker explained. The engineering division's "research" showed that very few of the GM employees revved the engines past 3,000 rpm, compared with the nearly 5,000 rpm that Europeans traditionally approached. Verdict: Americans didn't want high-revving engines.

It was the result of this simplistic in-house test that carried the most weight in the company's decision not to use the Opel engine for the J-car.

Alfred Sloan was undoubtedly turning over in his grave, for it was he who had shifted the negative paradigm of "planned obsolescence" into the consumer-sensitive concept of exciting, ever-changing car evolution. In *My Years with General Motors,* Sloan warned:

> The changes in the new model should be so novel and so attractive as to create demand for the new value and, so to speak, create a certain amount of dissatisfaction with past models as compared with the new one. . . . Each line of General Motors cars produced should preserve a distinction of appearance.

If J-cars and X-cars were not much different, there was also little difference among the J-car models themselves. This time Cadillac was included because its dealers were the most battered by the energy crisis and they sensed the need for a small, peppy car to attract affluent young buyers who were flocking to BMW. Unfortunately, GM misread the market; its interpretation of the peppy new Cadillac appeared as the Cimarron—nothing more than a Chevrolet Cavalier with leather seats and a luggage rack. The public wasn't fooled, and Cimarron made a mockery of the Cadillac heritage and name.

In all, GM assembled five J-cars, all of them virtually identical except for cosmetic elements. In addition to Cimarron, there were the Chevrolet Cavalier, the Pontiac J-2000, the Buick Skyhawk, and the Oldsmobile Firenza.

But while GM was trying to cover all of its bases and respond to dealer pressure, the dealers were not entirely happy with the end result. Dealers wanted distinctive small cars; they got an inventory of stultifying sameness. Their customers wanted variety, and it was becoming harder and harder to provide it from a single car manufacturer like GM. Formerly loyal dealers were being forced to become megadealers. Some acquired Toyota, Datsun, and Honda franchises and featured the Japanese cars in their showrooms right alongside the Buicks, Oldsmobiles, Cadillacs, Chevrolets, and Pontiacs.

The source of GM's look-alike problem was the declining individuality of the car divisions. Initially, Alfred Sloan had given each division primary responsibility for a piece of the market—from the least expensive to the most expensive models, and for many years these divisions retained the character of their founders. With this system, there was very little overlap. But over time, the general managers of divisions began to view themselves as competitive with one another. GM grew so large that the only way a division could expand was by crossing into the product territory of a sister division. Since the objective of each division was to sell more cars, each division began to produce a wider variety of models, so overlap became inevitable, and the distinctive image of each division was lost in the process. By the 1970s, every division had small, medium, and large cars; in order to maintain some control over investment, they had no choice but to borrow parts from one another—hence the look-alike problem, referred to as "badge engineering." But, as finance-driven companies often do, GM had cut off its nose to spite its face; in an effort to enhance the bottom line on the manufacturing side, they were losing customers in the showroom. Dealers were stuck with the monumental task of figuring out how to sell these sluggish, bland-looking, poor-quality, diminutive cars to a populace whose more sophisticated tastes were effectively being met by the foreign competition.

The J-car was a victim of "badge engineering"—changing the nameplate and a few decorative features. And the consensus was that badge engineering was a method whose time had come and gone; it was poorly suited to the aggressively competitive nature of the 1980s. But GM could not alter the product programs well under way. To the later dismay of GM dealers, the look-alike problems worsened with the H-cars, the E-cars, and the C-cars.

However, design handicaps were the least of the J-car's problems. Even many employees privately acknowledged that the car had serious quality problems as well. "I get into a J-car," said one former GM employee, "and I see the fake stitching and the chrome that peels on a company car that's only been out for two months, and I say, 'How can anyone ever like this?' "

Paralyzed with production problems, GM introduced the J-car with only three thousand Cavaliers for nine thousand Chevrolet and Pontiac dealerships, at prices that were higher than the competition. Formerly loyal customers were getting disgusted. They couldn't get the cars and when they did, they were disappointed with the performance and quality.

Smith weakly defended the car with typical bravado. "I always live in deadly fear of the day the light turns green and you don't get across," he said. "This one, before that light gets warmed up, it will be across."

Thomas Murphy would defend the car, too, using the shop-worn GM excuse for poor car quality: too much government interference. The need to spend time and money to comply with government regulations, he complained, made it impossible for the company to spend any time trying to make the cars look attractive and distinctive. Murphy failed to explain why the Japanese, who were obedient to the same regulations, were not hampered by them. The Japanese carmakers were applauded, not only for the operating efficiency of their vehicles, but also for their trouble-free performance.

Theodore Louckes, retired Oldsmobile chief engineer and now an executive at an automotive engineering firm, has suggested that the problem may go deeper than look-alike—to *feel-alike*. "The use of common parts across the car lines," said Louckes, "impairs the ability of GM to make products that are truly distinctive in terms of drivability and character—the things under the skin that make the personality of the car so important. Developing uniqueness in the *feel* of a car was much more straightforward when all the components were different."

Indeed, in the early days of the Smith-McDonald administration, GM was hit by one blow after another regarding the quality and styling of its cars. The notion that individual GM cars were distinctive from each other was dealt a blow in the late 1970s when owners of 1977 Oldsmobiles discovered Chevrolet engines under the hoods and sued—the press dubbed the vehicle the "Chevymobile." At the time, the revelation shocked the public, for even though the cars had ceased being unique years before, the brand image was so strong that the public perception was that they were different. Now, in April 1981, the *Detroit Free Press* published a report that the initially popular X-car had serious product problems. According to the report, the quality at one plant that assembled X-car models was the lowest of any GM plant. McDonald admitted publicly that the X-car had problems: "It isn't good enough to overcome the competition."

McDonald's frankness stood in stark contrast to the usual GM aloofness in the face of criticism. In fact, when analyst Steve Soderberg asked vice chairman Howard Kehrl, at a meeting in the GM building in New York, whether the X-car would receive a high rating from *Consumer Reports,* given their bravado about superior quality, Kehrl replied that GM didn't pay much attention to *Consumer Reports.* Analysts were dumbfounded. How could it be that a top GM executive could so blithely write off the bible of the consumer? McDonald, who was no doubt criticized internally for his honesty, must have seen that it was pointless to ignore the truth. By the summer of 1981, GM was forced to recall all of its 1980 and some 1981 standard transmission X-cars (about 245,000 cars) to fix clutch and rear-brake systems. About 47,000 of the 1980 vehicles were being recalled because the rear brakes were suspected of locking and causing the car to lose control.

At Cadillac, the V-8-6-4 variable replacement engine was turning into a nightmare. It was fraught with mechanical problems, and the ensuing complaints and lawsuits alleging design defects were widely publicized. It was almost unthinkable to GM that its all-important Cadillac could have its prestige image tarnished.

The V-8-6-4 engine was developed in an attempt to reduce the "guzzle" of GM's luxury cars. Its principle was that gasoline would flow to all eight cylinders only when it was needed, but would be cut off to some cylinders when full power was not required. Unfortunately, the V-8-6-4 was introduced before it was really ready for market. The electronics weren't perfected, making the car a nightmare for its owners and for the mechanics who tried to fix it. It followed the diesel engine, also a disaster, and caused massive defections from the Cadillac brand.

As the upscale market turned increasingly away from Cadillac to Mercedes and BMW, the division desperately tried to reclaim the high-class image.

The Cimarron debuted in May of 1981 to a hostile dealer environment. The "compact Cadillac" was an oxymoron. *Cadillac* implies big, roomy, powerful, unique styling, plushness, opulence. The Cimarron was a small, boring, poorly performing car—only distinguishable from the Chevy Cavalier by a luggage rack and leather seats. This was not a car designed for the BMW-Mercedes market, although Cadillac's advertising copy compared it to these models. The press raced to point out that BMW-bluebloods shouldn't bother to shop the showrooms for the new Cadillac. "Cadillac is about to take the wraps off what it hopes will restore its injured pride," reported *The Wall Street*

Journal. ". . . the Cimarron, a front-drive, high-mileage little car that will bring gasps from the bluebloods who have driven big Caddies for years."

Ultimately, GM would see the J-car selling a respectable volume, after much investment and effort to correct mechanical defects. But, for Cadillac, it was nearly the last straw in a string of affronts to the nameplate that had always stood for the highest standard of quality. In the past, Cadillac had produced the most powerful, dependable engines in the world. This tradition of superiority was established by Henry Leland in 1902. Leland was a fanatic about quality because he understood that engineering and manufacturing precision were essential to building the best cars. It was Leland's genius that made Cadillac the symbol of excellence for so many years. The engineering developments that secured Cadillac's reputation included the V-8 engine in 1914; the V-16 with hydraulic valve adjusters in 1929; power steering in 1933; automatic transmission in 1935; factory air conditioning in 1941; and finally, after World War II, the 331 V-8 high-compression, short-stroke engine.

Until the late 1960s, a Cadillac dealership was a gold mine. The volume was modest, but the extraordinary quality made the high ticket price worthwhile. But the struggle with quality control that began in the 1970s, when the division began to increase volume and forsake prestige, would nearly cripple Cadillac. In his 1988 report, *Cadillac—The Heartbreak of America,* James P. Musselman traced the decline of Cadillac during the 1970s and early 1980s. During that period, the high-sticker Cadillac cars were rife with defects, many of them severe enough to make the cars inoperative or dangerous on the highway. Some of the most dramatic defects included:

- Ashtray designs in the Cadillac de Villes, Broughams, and limousines that caused vehicle components to ignite.
- Accelerator pads in the Cadillac de Ville, Brougham, and commercial chassis vehicles that were easily displaced and wedged under the pedal, increasing speed at unexpected times. (This problem led to the largest recalls in Cadillac's history—372,466 1978 and 1979 models.)
- Brake problems in a variety of models, including the new J-car, the Cimarron. These included "phantom brakes" that sometimes worked and sometimes stuck.

- The notorious diesel engine, introduced in 1978–1979, whose problems included oil leaks, head gasket and crankshaft failures, and engine block defects.

In all, Cadillac models suffered more than fifteen major defects during this period. According to Musselman, Cadillac's response to the problems was more infuriating than the defects themselves. "GM frequently denied the existence of many of these malfunctions, instead of acknowledging them and taking immediate action on behalf of the consumer—despite the fact that, many times, its own internal memorandums and documents showed knowledge of these flaws." Musselman published letter after letter from angry consumers who had shopped Cadillac for quality and ended up with automobile nightmares. This letter from the owner of a Cadillac Eldorado is typical:

> This is a story concerning a little boy's dream of having a Cadillac when he grew up to manhood, only to have that dream shattered by shoddy workmanship on the part of the American Automobile Manufacturer. I was patriotic and bought American, but I lost lots of time and money on my Cadillac Eldorado. I remember in 1926 on my 10th birthday when a 1924 Cadillac passed me on a country road. I looked up to heaven and prayed to myself that when I got older I could afford to buy a Cadillac. Sixty years later I finally had enough to buy a Cadillac which fulfilled my dreams for eight days when problems began. My dream shattered, I realized that maybe the little boy of today should dream of owning a Honda, Toyota, Lincoln or Mercedes-Benz.

In 1981, the J. D. Power survey, which measures a consumer satisfaction index (CSI), ranked Cadillac number fifteen out of twenty-two brands, far behind Mercedes-Benz and BMW, as well as Isuzu, Mazda, Datsun, Volkswagen, and Mitsubishi. *Consumer Reports* ranked three 1981 model cars—the Cadillac de Ville, Eldorado, and Seville V-8—"much worse than average" in both its "trouble index" and "cost index." GM was getting clobbered from two fronts. Whereas Chevrolet was getting beat by the Japanese, Cadillac was being slaughtered by Europe.

For Roger Smith, salvaging Cadillac's prestige was an early priority, since much of GM's credibility as a producer hinged on the now-fading Cadillac image.

Cadillac turned to Pininfarina of Italy to bid on a design

against a design prepared by in-house staff, the object being to build a car to compete against Europe's best. The European company emerged with a design concept that appeared competitive with the Mercedes 560SL convertible two-seater. GM bought the plan, though not without causing much internal turmoil among Cadillac people who favored the domestic version. It was hoped that the Pininfarina name would lend mystique to the car and give it credibility in competing with models like Mercedes 560-SL and Jaguar X-JS. This car program, Callisto, later dubbed Allanté, would be completed in Detroit, but instead of the once proud "body by Fisher," it would have a "body by Pininfarina."

Even before Smith became chairman, plans had been under way to close two aging Detroit plants that built Cadillacs. According to Thomas Murphy, who was chairman at the time: "Back in 1978, the Cadillac and Fisher Body plants were a disaster. They were built in 1915 and 1919, at a time when there were two separate corporations. Fisher was not a part of General Motors back then. So the plants were not physically located together and you had to truck the bodies through the city of Detroit in order to put cars together. Also, the plants were multistoried and inefficient. They had to be modernized if we were going to use them. We would have spent two hundred million dollars just to modernize the paint systems to meet the plant emission requirements. So, it was obvious that we were going to have to build a new plant." It was hoped that a modern, automated plant could eliminate some of the fit-and-finish and quality problems that plagued Cadillac.

The plant, which was eventually built in the Hamtramck section of Detroit, would become a public relations nightmare in the early period of Roger Smith's chairmanship.

"Probably what we should have done," Murphy says in retrospect, "and what all the operating people wanted to do, was to take a green field site someplace else and build a plant with the space that we needed. And I said no, these people are working for General Motors in Detroit. We are in Detroit and we ought to try to find a Detroit location. I went to Coleman Young, the mayor, and I said to him, 'Mr. Mayor, if you can find a site in the city of Detroit that will meet our needs with acreage where we can lay out a plant as we could if we went to a green field, we'll stay.' The city of Detroit selected the site."

Mayor Young had been enthusiastic about the project, hoping that the new plant within city boundaries would help with the struggling revitalization efforts in Detroit. Since GM was planning to close two aging plants in other parts of the city, Young believed the new plant was the only way to hang on to the jobs that would be lost. Young and the City Council voted to tear down a neighborhood in Detroit for the plant, using a Michigan statute that allowed the government to take over an area for revitalization purposes. Nobody expected the community uprising and the subsequent publicity that would make GM look like an insensitive corporate giant that carelessly trampled the lives and dreams of ordinary citizens. Such accusations might have made company management bitter. After all, they would have preferred to build the plant in a more rural setting. The choice of a city location was based on GM's commitment to take responsibility for jobs and inner-city growth, but it was being thrown back in its face as a decision motivated by greed.

Hamtramck was a section in eastern Detroit, dubbed Poletown because of the influx of Polish immigrants who settled there in the late nineteenth century. In the early 1980s the area was an integrated lower-middle-class community. Its citizens became outraged after they learned that their homes were to be bulldozed to make way for a General Motors plant.

Viewed from a balance-sheet perspective, the move was very good for Detroit's economy and just okay for GM. It was probably good for Poletown residents, too—they would be fairly compensated for their property. But General Motors has always lacked the ability to grasp and address the deeper human issues surrounding its decisions. Had Roger Smith been a more charismatic and sensitive leader, he might have avoided the public relations fiasco that ensued. He might, for example, have spoken directly to the community, urging the people to support the future of Detroit. He might have said, "Look, General Motors isn't abandoning the cities to run to the suburbs like so many other companies." He might have engaged the public relations department in displaying more sensitivity to the loss of roots and community that concerned people more than money. But his silence as the controversy built only allowed the anti-GM voices to gain the spotlight.

The Poletown Neighborhood Council was formed to block the takeover of their land by the Detroit City Council, but the community refused to back down. Its rallying point became a fight to save the Church of the Immaculate Conception. Catholic hierarchy had already agreed not to oppose GM's plan, but the church made the perfect symbolic point of resistance. How could General Motors demolish the community's most important place of worship to make way for a parking lot?

According to Thomas Murphy, himself an ardent Catholic, the implications of demolishing the church were blown way out of proportion. "I think the figures showed that there were something like fifty or seventy-five people attending services there on Sunday. People came in from outside and they were the ones that raised most of the fuss. But Roger was shown as a villain. He was the one who was displacing all those families. He was taking down the church and martyring the pastor who had only been put there because the archdiocese didn't have anyplace else to put him."

When the wrecking balls finally slammed into the side of the Immaculate Conception Church, the press had a heyday showing parishioners behind police barricades collapsed sobbing against one another. Embarrassed police were forced to place elderly citizens under arrest when they tried to stage a last-minute sit-in. The dramatic coverage only solidified GM's image as the bad guy. Roger Smith didn't understand the power of symbols and he let it happen.

The Poletown incident left a sour taste in the community's mouth. And the prospect of new jobs was little comfort—the Poletown plant would not be completed until 1985. In the meantime, thousands of jobs were lost as GM closed two plants in south Detroit.

This was not an auspicious start for the new chairman. His first annual meeting in 1981 might have been a brawl, were it not for the tight control Smith exerted during the proceedings. Community members who had cashed in their savings so they could buy stock and speak at the shareholders' meeting were given two minutes each to speak. A large illuminated clock ticked off the seconds; those who went over their allotted time had their microphones cut off.

Roger Smith stood in the tense, packed room and offered no solace. Instead, he railed against the United Auto Workers, calling on labor to dip into its pocket to help in the fight against foreign competition, with concessions in pay and benefits.

"Our U.S. auto workers earn eight dollars an hour more

than their counterparts in Japan," he said. "Put together with the pay for time not worked here in the United States, this is too great a differential to overcome—even with our new plants and products. All our great technology and even the magic of robots can't make up the differential." Smith announced that a new wage structure must be negotiated, suggesting that wages might be reduced in exchange for profit sharing.

Of the community protesters, Smith said, "We knew it would be difficult for some people living in these homes to move. But most of the people were delighted to be rescued from homes they couldn't sell. A few were not, of course."

Roger Smith received mixed reviews in the early period of his chairmanship. The media continued to puzzle over the many contradictions in Smith's policies and style. He was a chameleon, changing moods with dizzying speed. An aggressive, take-charge leader on one hand, he could seem maddeningly conventional on the other. As one executive recalls: "One day Roger could look like a hero, the next day a bum. Nobody really knew which was the real Roger." But the most controversial action of all occurred the day Roger Smith decided to climb into bed with Japanese carmakers.

Small Car, Big Strategy:
Regaining the Competitive Edge

They tell us we're number one in the world. So why are we getting into bed with the Japanese?
—Disgruntled GM executive

Within months of taking office, Roger Smith was to prove that he was an unconventional chairman. Perhaps he saw that the new challenges required a more dramatic approach. There was a lot of distressing news in the air. The U.S. Department of Transportation was publishing a report that amounted to a scathing indictment of the domestic carmakers' ability to compete in the international marketplace. The report, titled "The U.S. Automobile Industry, 1980," noted that between World War II and the 1973 oil embargo, the United States auto industry had been unchallenged in the domestic market. But, the report went on to say, the embargo changed that "permanently and dramatically." Concluded Transportation Secretary Neil Goldschmidt, "It will take a minimum of five years for our industry to return to full competitive strength. That time is needed to accomplish the structural changes required to meet the market demand for new generation autos at competitive prices."

There had always been the blanket assumption in the American car industry that it was hard to compete with Japanese pricing because their labor costs were so low. But Goldschmidt's report startled the industry by pointing out that only about one half of Japan's $1,500-per-car cost advantage was attributable to wages. Goldschmidt wrote, "The greatest source of Japanese advantage is structural: process and product technology which yield major productivity gains. U.S. management must commit major resources to matching these productivity accomplishments if our industry is to regain competitive health."

The report spared neither management nor labor in its criticism. Management was accused of tolerating production inefficiencies, poor quality, and shortsighted product development. Labor was cited for expecting pay increases, regardless of the competitive consequences of high wages and the impediments thrown in the way of higher productivity. Even the government was criticized for imposing environmental and other regulations on the industry without regard for the cumulative impact on the automakers.

Goldschmidt saw the domestic auto business as the single most important factor in the industrial health of the United States economy. He believed that if it were permitted to decline, it would pose a severe threat, and he based his thesis on hard statistics:

- Roughly four million American jobs were connected to the auto industry.
- Some $40 billion worth of equipment and new materials were purchased by the industry each year.
- Nearly 34 percent of the oil consumed in the United States was used to fuel the country's autos.

Smith seemed almost invigorated by the challenge of knocking the irritating foreign interlopers out of the market, and reestablishing GM's dominance. He even managed to put a brave face on GM's gloomy profit picture. "When have we always done our best?" he asked in an interview with *Forbes* magazine.

It's when we're coming off a bad year and we're mean, lean and tough and running so fast. It takes us a while to fatten up and slow down once the volume hits us. Our record years have always followed downturns, and it isn't because the volume came up. It's because we've got the organization so hungry and lean that they're running like hell.

In his burst of new administration enthusiasm, Smith might have exaggerated the extent to which the lumbering giant could be considered lean and hungry . . . much less "running fast." In truth, the company was losing the race to compete in the small-car sector. Model after model was plagued by sluggish perform-ance, mechanical defects, and a stunning lack of originality. The truth was clear to anyone who was looking: GM couldn't seem to build a good small car to save its life, and it dawned on Smith that a new generation of car buyers might be lost forever. Chev-rolet, the brand aimed at the first-time buyer, had nothing to offer to an increasingly sophisticated car-buying public.

Roger Smith was looking, and he didn't like what he saw. The company's newest attempt, the S-car, was scheduled for launch in 1985, but Smith was beginning to question whether GM could realistically hope to make money on it—or would this be yet another small-car program that failed to deliver the pro-jected return? He commissioned a comparative study to find out how much it would cost Isuzu to build a comparable car, as opposed to GM. One ought to wonder why it took so long for GM to investigate Isuzu's costs, considering it had owned a large stake in the Japanese company since 1971. In any event, it was the outcome of this six-week study that convinced him of the fact that the S-car could not be built profitably by General Motors in North America. And more than that, he faced the hard reality that his company was not even "in the game" when it came to building subcompacts. The total cost of the S-car came to $5,731, compared to Isuzu's comparable model at $2,857, a difference of $2,874.

Smith must have spent many long, painful hours facing the truth. And his ultimate decision to explore a partnership ar-rangement with Japanese car companies amounted to a para-digm shift in his own soul and the soul of General Motors. He was forced to confront the doubters in his own ranks who ar-gued that the analysis was flawed. But according to Tom McDan-iel, a member of the task force, Smith stood his ground against an immediate barrage of criticism from other members of the

Executive Committee, who were inclined to find flaws in the analysis.

Smith was as locked into the anti-Japanese mentality at the time as anyone at General Motors, and it took a quantum leap in imagination and honesty to recognize that perhaps they could build better cars at lower costs. But he could no longer afford to deny reality.

His decision to kill the S-car and go into partnership with the Japanese was met with a storm of criticism, but Smith says now of that decision, "It was terrifying when you saw what gasoline was selling for—and everybody saying it was going to be three bucks a gallon. Our market study said that if you asked the average housewife, she didn't care if she went to the store once in the Cadillac . . . what she wanted to be able to do was go to the store *three* times. We all of a sudden said, 'Boy, are we in a big pile of trouble here.' There's only a certain amount or number of gallons—people wanted to get the maximum mileage. And we were not in that game, so we said we better find out what to do, and that's where our Japanese strategy came from."

Roger Smith anticipated the outcome of the study and began to develop a plan to broaden ties with the Japanese even before the S-car was terminated.

At a January 1981 meeting, which took place in a dusty conference room at the Biltmore Hotel in Los Angeles, Smith, Jim McDonald, and Jim Waters met with T. Okamoto, chairman of Isuzu Motors, and Jay Chai, executive vice president with C. Itoh and Company, who served as interpreter and adviser to Isuzu and GM.

Okamoto was completely unprepared for Roger Smith's request that he assist General Motors in affiliating or acquiring Honda. Smith informed Okamoto that Isuzu lacked the critical mass in auto production to be the kind of international partner GM needed. (In a December 1980 presentation, concern had been expressed that Isuzu might not make it as a passenger-car company. That same presentation suggested that Honda appeared vulnerable to what GM analysts saw as mounting excess capacity in Japan.)

Okamoto was petrified because he appreciated the importance of GM to Isuzu and feared the prospect of GM getting a stake in Honda. In spite of this, he agreed to make the overture to Honda. Honda rebuffed the company, and Okamoto then became the emissary in GM's unsuccessful bid to acquire

Toyota's 8 percent interest in Daihatsu, and finally, GM's successful bid to buy 5 percent of Suzuki.

While GM was engaging in small deals with small Japanese auto companies, Ford was heavily involved in talks with the largest and most profitable Japanese carmaker of them all, Toyota. According to Chai, Toyota felt they could "kill three birds with one stone" by hooking up with an American company.

"First, they felt that a joint alliance was politically desirable. Toyota was concerned about the anti-Japanese sentiment in America. Second, the company felt that an alliance would mitigate against the protectionist pressures of the time. And third, they saw it as a way to learn how American companies dealt with labor and management situations."

But the talks with Ford never came to fruition. As Chai explains: "Toyota were very proud people; their headquarters is two hundred miles outside of Tokyo, so they're very independent. They have a very great sense of *us*. They know they can build cars in Japan, but they were very cautious with Ford, because they wanted to be sure they could do the same in a different environment. They weren't willing to accept any situation." Ultimately, the talks broke down when the two parties failed to agree on a location and which products the joint venture would be building.

One of their problems," notes Chai, "is that they had no go-betweens, no matchmaker. They dealt head-to-head. And you know, a go-between is a beautiful thing. If things go well, you can claim the credit. If they go screwy, you can blame the go-between."

As Chai watched the Toyota-Ford talks sputter and die, he realized that an opportunity might be there for the taking: a General Motors-Toyota collaboration. Chai tells how the match was made:

"It's very much like a matchmaker who brings the parties together, but makes them both think it was their idea. I began to plant the seeds in Toyota's mind over lunch with a friend who was senior managing director. By the end of the lunch, he was saying, 'Ford is going nowhere. We prefer GM, anyway.'

"And I knew the helplessness GM was feeling, the despair that they didn't know how to build the small cars. So I suggest to Roger that we have a meeting with Toyota.

"The meeting took place two days before Christmas, in

1981. Seisi Kato, the chairman of Toyota Motors Sales Company, met with Roger and John McCormack, the vice president of GM Asia-Africa. I did not attend this meeting—there are times when you need to let the parties talk without you.

"Mr. Kato brought his interpreter, but he chose to speak English during the meeting—and his English was poor. Roger was behaving like the no-nonsense American executive—you know, let's get down to business. But Mr. Kato apparently had worked in a GM office in Tokyo forty years ago, and he wanted to reminisce and talk about his experiences. Roger and John McCormack couldn't understand him. They sensed the meeting was amicable, but no business was discussed.

"So McCormack called me after the meeting and he said, 'Nothing happened—we didn't understand what the hell this nice old gentleman was talking about.'

"I had to put a positive translation on the meeting. I explained to John about body language and how it sounded to me like it was an extremely positive meeting. I had no idea what Mr. Kato was talking about, either. But I cannot say, 'Let's just forget the whole thing.'

"I went to Detroit to meet with Roger, and I could see how excited he was. He had several reasons for wanting the deal to happen. First, he wanted a car made by Toyota. And he wanted to find out about Toyota's cost structure and how they ran their plants—he was very interested in that. And he was already thinking that a partnership with Toyota might be a way to deal with his own excess plant capacity—using a plant in California to build the cars that would come out of the deal."

It was decided that Chai would take a team to Japan to further explore the possibility of a GM-Toyota partnership. Bill Larson and Jack Smith headed the delegation that accompanied him. It was on Chai's shoulders to convince Toyota management that GM was a suitable partner. Before they would even meet with the Americans, S. Hanai, chairman; Eiji Toyoda, president; and H. Tamura, senior managing director; spent three hours grilling Chai—in what he compares to "a freshman applicant being interviewed by the admissions officer of a university."

Chai passed the initial test, and the group went on to visit Toyota City. But the meeting went badly—the GM team found Tamura to be very arrogant and combative. After the meeting, Bill Larson wanted to return home, but Chai interceded. He called his friend Kamio, who was senior marketing director for Toyota Motor Sales, and told him how badly the visit had gone. Kamio obviously passed Chai's concerns along to Toyoda, who invited the team to dinner at the Nagaya Castle Hotel the following evening. At the dinner, Toyoda took pains to soothe the ruffled feathers. He urged the team to be patient and keep talking, and conveyed his personal interest in the deal to his subordinates. From then on, the talks warmed up. By the end of their stay, the signals were clear that the Japanese company was interested in having a third date. "This time," Chai remembers, "Eiji Toyoda said it was time for the two top managers to confront each other directly. He arranged to come to the United States and meet with Roger Smith in New York."

It was to be a dinner meeting with Toyoda and his interpreter, Roger Smith, Jack Smith, Jim Waters, and Jay Chai. Smith arranged for it to take place at the Lincks Club, a very old, somewhat grubby private club, not known for its good food. But it served Smith's primary purpose, since it was a discreet setting where the unusual meeting could take place privately.

Chai remembers that when he picked up Toyoda and his interpreter at the Helmsley Palace to take them to the Lynx Club, "Mr. Toyoda was very quiet. I could feel the tension in his body. But once we were in the dining room, he relaxed, because Roger Smith was in a very good mood—very talkative. Roger is an interesting person in this way. He can be the coldest person you've ever met, and he can make a meeting *miserable*. But sometimes he can be the warmest, most charming host, and that is the way he was that evening. As a result, he and Toyoda formed more than just a business relationship; they formed a personal relationship, as well. That personal relationship still exists today, although it's been somewhat tarnished by subsequent events, such as GM's handling of the acquisition of Lotus. The basic proposal was outlined at that dinner, and on the way back to the hotel, Toyoda was very talkative, very pleased with the way things had gone."

Chai and the GM team returned to Detroit to report their findings and outline a working proposal that could be discussed at the next meeting. For the second visit to Toyota, Jack Smith, now director of worldwide planning, headed the team. Jack Smith remembers how enthusiastic they were on the flight home. "It was the first time we really had a clear understanding of how they ran. Coming back, I had a Fisher engineer sitting next to me. Between the two of us, we were able to marry up the Toyota plant by body shop, trim, vinyl, paint shop, stampings, and so forth—and the data was just unbelievable. Right there on the plane I put the charts together."

But he was so engrossed in the possibilities that he forgot the culture of the company for whom he was working. Armed with his data, he marched into the Executive Committee the following Monday morning, anxious to show everyone what had been learned. "It was one of the great mistakes of my life," he remembers wryly. "I had no intention of embarrassing anybody. It was just the data I had. But it was such a shock for the system. I had more people mad at me than I have ever had in my career—no one likes to get their noses rubbed in it. They don't like to get news that way and I should have done it differently. I learned a lesson, but, of course, the data was there and eventually it stood up."

Thanks to Roger Smith. Smith *believed* the data. He may not have liked it, but he believed it. While other executives were trying their best to disprove the data, and making excuses for why Jack Smith was wrong, he knew it was true, and that partnership was the best solution. Of course, Smith never saw this as a permanent match—just a plan to tide GM over until it could do something spectacular on its own. He often spoke of it being a "learning experience"—why not take the opportunity to get an insider's view of how the Japanese do what they do?

In March 1983, Toyota and General Motors reached an agreement in principle for a joint venture. At the same time, Jack Smith formed another joint venture for GM with a Japanese concern—this one a fifty-fifty deal with Fujitsu Fanuc to develop and produce industrial robots in the United States, many of which would be destined for GM's own factories.

"When Roger Smith started making deals with Japanese companies, it was very controversial," says Chai. "It was a very emotional issue, because the auto industry was at the pinnacle of American society, and now they're saying General Motors needs the Japanese. I give a lot of credit to Roger. It was very creative and courageous."

The climate in the early years of Reagan's "morning in America" contributed to a deeply felt protectionist sentiment. Reagan preached the gospel of America believing in itself again.

In this time of homespun pride, Roger Smith was saying, in effect, the foreign competition can do it better.

His first move was to kill the S-car program. But he didn't spell out the reasons too specifically; the cost data were worse than anyone suspected and he didn't want the press to get hold of them. So the decision to kill the S-car, buy cars from Isuzu and Suzuki, and enter a joint venture with Toyota was announced without a clear context. Not surprising, the announcement was met with anger by labor, the General Motors staff, and many American politicians. Even the board members privately believed Smith was making a mistake. It seemed that Roger Smith had laid down the gauntlet in the fight for the small-car business. Smith's response was cool. "Yes, we're giving up building in the small market with domestic content and losing our shirt on it." It was a thinly veiled criticism of high wages paid in the United States—in Smith's view, the major cause for the problem.

His argument was not convincing to his critics, whose numbers were growing. In fact, the controversy was so heated that a year after his election to chairman, there were rumors on Wall Street that the board of directors would ask for Smith's resignation. While this never occurred, the very fact of the rumors demonstrated just how controversial Smith's policies were.

On one hand, the midwesterners were afraid of the Japanese. They didn't understand them, but suspected they possessed a secret strategy that went far beyond technology. In fact, when GMers toured Japanese plants, they could not find the *tangible, technological* evidence of mastery. Usually they would return from these fact-finding missions secure in the knowledge that the Japanese weren't harboring any mysterious high-tech weapon. Alex Mair, a company executive who would later be instrumental in conceptualizing GM's own car of the future, was one of the most vocal skeptics about Smith's collaboration with the Japanese. Now retired, Mair recalls how he felt at the time. "I personally said to everyone, 'We already know what they do. Why would we have to have them come to California and do that?' It was to prove that it could really be done here."

Another executive grumbled, "They tell us we're number one in the world. So why are we getting in bed with the Japanese?"

If it wasn't a matter of plain and simple technological superiority, what *was* the edge?

A few GM executives recognized signs of the Japanese flexibility and broad-based training in the attitude of the employees.
One executive recalled meeting a public relations director for
one of the Japanese automakers and being impressed with how
deep the director's knowledge was about the arcane engineering
details of both American and Japanese cars. This was minutiae
that only the most technically oriented car-buff magazines might
bother mentioning. When asked how a PR director acquires
such knowledge, the Japanese man replied, "In my country, to
be in my job, you must know all about the products."

Another GM employee shakes his head in frustration when
he remembers how many cues the people at GM missed about
the Japanese methods. "The Japanese just kept bringing out
another one and another one and another one. And they were
wonderfully designed—they weren't just boxes with wheels that
were cheap. And we weren't asking ourselves what might have
been behind the success—what was the Japanese brilliance. I
remember a couple of us doing some research on how the competitors were designing their automobiles—what the process
was, what kind of team makeup existed. And I don't remember
the exact vehicle we were looking at, but it was a real sporty
semivan wagon kind of thing that they had targeted for a specific
segment in the market. And they put together a design team of
people who matched the profile of the people in this segment.
They were between twenty-five and thirty-five and they were
beach people—very athletic. And the company said, 'Go build
yourself a car.' "

One executive admitted with a grudging respect that the
Japanese understood an element that American car companies
knew little about—*surprise.* "You couple the performance and
quality with some surprises in the performance of the engine, or
surprises in terms of some of the features on the car—a place
to put your glasses, a coin tray. People start saying, 'This *exceeds*
my expectations.' "

By early 1983, the nuts and bolts of the joint venture were
set. Toyota would contribute $100 million in cash. GM would
contribute the equivalent, mainly in assets, including its plant in
Fremont, California. In addition, a new stamping plant would be

constructed adjacent to the assembly facility. Roger Smith announced that some three thousand workers would be employed in the operation of the complex, in addition to an estimated nine thousand American jobs that would be created around the operation of the plant. They would build a small Chevy model, which would be called Nova, the same name used in the early 1970s on a Chevy compact car with an undistinguished history.

The new venture, later called NUMMI (New United Motor Manufacturing, Inc.), would be run by its own board of directors, half appointed from each company. Toyota would select the president and chief executive officer. It was planned that about 200,000 cars would be produced each year for a period of twelve years—to be marketed through Chevrolet dealers in the United States. The first NUMMI-made car—the Chevy Nova—was slated to roll off the line by the end of 1984.

Public reaction continued to be hot and heavy in the days following the formal announcement. The United Auto Workers union was cautiously optimistic about the joint venture, seeing it as a way to rehire laid-off workers—but some union officials wondered aloud whether or not the move would ultimately lead to a further displacement of American workers. There was also the sentiment, expressed time and again, that the Japanese had achieved success on the backs of their workers. Sure, they could build cars faster and more economically—all those people over there were working like slaves for no money. Who wants to live that way? In America, people cared about the quality of their lives. But NUMMI accepted the UAW and wrote a precedent-setting contract that guaranteed job security with a no-layoff clause.

GM's American competition was scared by the idea that two such powerful companies would be teaming up. In 1984, Chrysler would receive clearance from a federal judge to enter a lawsuit against Genral Motors. In its suit, Chrysler claimed that the venture would violate antitrust laws by attempting to limit the competition's access to the market and establish a monopoly. Chrysler would chase GM through the courts until early 1985 before finally agreeing to settle out of court. There seemed little chance that Chrysler could actually win the suit, since the Federal Trade Commission had already approved the venture. The settlement (which had little real effect on NUMMI) was considered a face-saving way for Chrysler to bow out of the suit.

When Chrysler realized it couldn't stop the joint venture, it quickly formed its own collaboration with Mitsubishi. Ford was also busy making deals. By 1989, Ford would have basically given almost all its small-car development to Mazda.

It didn't matter that from a sales standpoint, the deals amounted to a small percentage of business. GM's partnership with three Japanese companies—Toyota, Isuzu, and Suzuki—was considered heresy by those who held fast to the protectionist view that the best way to fight foreign competition was to "push it back across the ocean" by erecting trade barriers. Protectionist instincts were very strong at the time, and already Japanese car companies had been pressured into voluntarily limiting imports. Why bother working with them when they could simply be sent back?

But at the Third United States–Japan Automotive Industry Conference at the University of Michigan in March, director of worldwide planning Jack Smith presented a position against protectionism that must have seemed downright radical coming from General Motors. "Protectionism is not a good answer," he said. "Legislation is inflexible and often results in more problems than solutions. Instead of trying to hide behind laws and regulations, U.S. auto companies must catch up with their foreign competition—and catch up as quickly as possible."

Jack Smith went on to defend GM's matchup with Toyota as a first practical step in the direction of growth. "New management strategies are required. And among those strategies are the expanded use of cooperative business arrangements among automotive manufacturers—more specifically, between U.S. and Japanese companies.

"We have been faced with difficult choices," he said bluntly. "GM could abandon the small-car business and build only larger cars. But that would mean deserting many customers who have relied on GM for small cars. The Chevrolet Chevette, for example, has been the best-selling car in its class during four of the last six years. Since its introduction, we've sold nearly two million Chevettes—we're not going to walk away from that.

"We could wait until we develop additional new small cars of our own, of course—*American* cars. Built in an American way. By American workers. To American standards. To appeal to American tastes and preferences. But in today's competitive marketplace, such a car would have to be more than just a new car. It would have to be built in a new way. A way that makes use of new product technology and manufacturing efficiency to help narrow our current cost disadvantages. And, as you know, that takes time. So we decided that business arrangements of various kinds presented a sensible interim solution—ways of working with the Japanese in constructive and mutually beneficial arrangements, ways to preserve jobs here in the U.S. while improving the foundation for future expansion."

The Toyota deal put GM and Roger Smith on the defensive. Was it a cop-out, a sellout, an admission of defeat at the hands of the Japanese? Not at all, insisted Smith. While it was true that GM was relying on the Japanese *for now,* this was only a temporary measure until GM could cut costs, boost efficiency, and develop the necessary quality to go it alone.

Roger Smith never gave up on the idea that General Motors would eventually invent its own trademark small car—a car that defied anything the imagination could fathom, a space age vision, a model for the next century. Saturn was born of this vision, and something more—that GM would not only build the car of the future, but design the car-building company of the future, too. Smith's speculation: "Given a clean piece of paper, how would you build a high-quality, low-cost car aimed at committed import owners and how would you manage a company to ensure a high probability of succeeding by tapping the resources and talents of every employee and supplier or dealer-partner?"

As stated, it was an astonishing goal for General Motors, one more example of how this new chairman could shake up the system. This was a break with tradition unlike any the company had ever seen. He called it "the factory of the future."

The genesis of Saturn is an interesting departure for General Motors, and for the domestic car industry as a whole. Throughout the 1970s, it had combated the rising influence of foreign competitors by throwing money and new car models at the problem. Every competitive effort turned into a frightful reduction of the global reality. If customers wanted small cars, the company would chop a foot off big cars; if customers wanted economy, it would eliminate luxury features such as air conditioning; if customers loved the Honda, it would build a model that was its interpretation of what a Honda was. Ultimately, these methods were unsuccessful because they were the result of a tunnel vision. Even Smith's collaborative efforts with Japanese car companies would only suffice as relatively short-term strategies to place GM at the starting gate in the subcompact market. But the inescapable fact was that the company desperately needed to generate its own leading-edge product if it hoped to stay on top during the next twenty years. It was unthinkable that GM would simply abdicate its leadership position.

The Saturn project became Roger Smith's bold symbol of GM's intention to launch an aggressive fight for its future. And it was by no means a sudden inspiration. The project's beginnings can be traced back to a "skunk works" project directed by Alex Mair, who was determined to show that GM could build the best small cars without help from the Japanese. In May of 1982, Smith quietly created a new staff, under the leadership of Alex Mair, called Advance Product Manufacturing and Engineering Staff. The group took people from both the manufacturing and engineering sides of GM. Its mandate was to develop a program for producing small cars competitively in the United States, using the long-range strategic plan as an overlay. So quiet was the group that when Smith first mentioned it to the press, the Toyota negotiating team was caught off guard. Toyota representatives, stunned by the news of the small-car program, peppered the American team with questions, which they were unable to answer. The program was news to them too.

As Neil De Koker, the director of business systems for the project and now an executive with Magna International, remembers it: "We looked at all the disciplines to find out what we needed to do differently to become competitive. And the bottom line was that it wasn't just design, engineering, and manufacturing that needed to change, but *the entire business of running the business.*"

According to De Koker, the first step in this process would be to radically change the nature of the relationships between labor and management. "The adversarial relationship was just no good. There was no way that the Japanese, who work together for a common goal, could ever be beaten by people who were trying to kill each other—and here, internally, we were beating each other up."

In order to do this, De Koker involved a group of ninety-nine people representing the UAW, the plants, management, and other divisions to provide the necessary input. "At first," he

says, "Alex Mair, our group leader, was resistant to the idea of
the ninety-nine. He wanted it to be a very small team of people
and he was upset that we had let this thing grow, and especially
upset with me for having these ninety-nine outsiders from the
UAW and other divisions doing something that maybe ten or
fifteen people could have done. But what we understood was
that the way you gain a commitment in an organization represented by a union is to have a large number of people involved
and becoming committed, rather than a small sophisticated
group of people writing a report."

In addition to the ninety-nine, the team utilized the expertise of more than three hundred others, representing all disciplines within the company.

The project was named after the rockets that had propelled
the first space vehicles. The name signified the group's intention
to launch a futuristic plan in the automotive industry that would
be comparable to the space program.

Memories of the team's closeness and its dedication to such
an important mission literally bring tears to De Koker's eyes. It
was, in the early 1980s, a rare experience in corporate America,
and almost unthinkable at General Motors, to set a group of
people free to run with their vision. "The emotions, the tears,
the whatever it took to really create a team and a culture and a
commitment . . . I could never fully describe it. I get emotional
now, just thinking about it. It was like being part of an evangelis-
tic organization—we were the Bible-wielding 'southern Baptists'
carrying our Saturn philosophy around."

The final report recommended that General Motors pursue
some very dramatic new directions:

1. The establishment of a car-building project that was not just
a vehicle program, but an integrated business process.

2. To operate the project as a wholly owned subsidiary of GM,
with a separate union-management relationship.

3. The creation of a separate dealership franchise to operate in
conjunction with the project.

4. The development of a new car for the 1990s that would be
completely unique in design and structure.

It is likely that Smith didn't intend to announce the Saturn
project until the team had gone the next step to create the

tactical outline of its operation. But by late 1983, he was feeling the heat over his decision to do three deals with the Japanese. He needed a way to say, "Look—we're not selling out the U.S. car industry to the Japanese. Our arrangement with Toyota is part of a grander strategy, an *American* strategy. And here it is, the Saturn project."

Smith was caught in a squeeze play. On one side were his domestic competitors, accusing him of a collusion with Japanese companies that would render American carmakers impotent. He had to show that it wasn't so—that all along, his intention had been only to learn from the Japanese so he could build his own all-American market leader, and in the meantime give Chevrolet some cars to hold on to the customers it was losing.

On the other side were the heightening tensions between labor and management—a stalemate that did not appear to be solvable by traditional means.

An earlier than planned Saturn announcement could mollify both sides, but Smith might later regret having spoken too soon.

In November 1983, Roger Smith held a news conference to formalize Project Saturn with a $5-billion investment. Saturn, he told the media, was not just the design of a new product, but also the creation of a new manufacturing, engineering, and assembly system to produce it. It was, Smith said, a project of "cosmic proportions." The end product would be the car of the future, scheduled to roll out in 1990. And to build it, GM would design the factory of the future. The more Smith spoke, the more magnificent his vision appeared. The press was dazzled, and they rushed to tell the world about this wonderful new idea being conceived by Roger Smith. For this reason, Saturn became a focal point for GM-watching throughout the 1980s. It represented Roger Smith's dream come true for the corporation, the first entirely new nameplate for GM since the days of Billy Durant. But the nuts and bolts were still to be worked out, and there would be times in the coming years when Smith might have preferred less publicity. For the process of Saturn's birth would be more traumatic than he could ever have imagined in the heady days of its conception.

By now it was clear that Smith's chief strategy was to introduce irritants into the company that, like a virus, would cause a rash of upheavals. In this way, Smith hoped to create an environment that was primed for change over the long haul.

In 1983, he would introduce yet one more irritant in the form of Elmer Johnson, the first "outsider" to be granted an executive office without a General Motors portfolio.

Elmer Johnson wasn't a car guy. He wasn't even a finance guy. Rather, he was a corporate lawyer. When Smith sought him out, he was a managing partner of Chicago's Kirkland and Ellis. Smith approached him about moving to General Motors as general counsel, with the promise of expanded responsibilities every two years and, ultimately, consideration for the chairmanship.

Once Smith decided that Johnson was the man he wanted, he courted him vigorously. Johnson told Smith that he was flattered, but not interested. He suggested a couple of other people GM might consider. "I'm not giving up on you," Smith warned him, and Johnson laughed. It was nice to be courted, but he promptly forgot about it.

Two months later, Johnson was in Detroit on other business and his secretary reached him to say that Roger Smith wanted to see him for a few minutes and would send his driver.

When he walked into Smith's office, the chairman was cheerful. "I heard you were in the neighborhood and I just wanted to let you know that my search is completed. I found the man. I'm really happy."

"Well," said Johnson, "it's very nice of you to call me over. Who did you get?"

"You!" Smith announced.

Johnson shook his head. "Roger, I told you, I just cannot—"

Smith waved him into a chair. "Would you just sit down and listen."

Recalling that day, Johnson said, "The man is very agile. He had organization charts and a description of my initial responsibilities. But, if I didn't like this, we could do that, and change it every couple of years or so. And how many guys, at age fifty, get a chance to do something totally different with their lives?"

As Roger Smith remembers it, he was only interested in finding the best person for the job. If that meant hiring an outsider, so be it. But Elmer Johnson's arrival on the executive scene gave some people at GM a queasy sense that maybe the rules were changing and that long years of faithful service would no longer be the criterion for advancement.

There was something else uncomfortable about Elmer Johnson's presence. He wouldn't conform to the culture. He asked questions that others had long ago stopped asking. He was, in other words, an irritant.

Only later would GM staff—and Roger Smith himself—see exactly how much of an irritant a bright, independent thinker who had not been corralled by the GM culture could be.

Come the Reorganization:
Massive Musical Chairs

The reorganization of General Motors was like swallowing
a pill to cure your fever . . . except the pill was the size of
a baseball. The swallow is the problem. Once it gets down
and does the work, it will help you.

—A GM executive

Imagine taking a company the size of General Motors and saying, "Every person should pack his things and be prepared to
move to a new location. Once you get there, you'll have a new
office, a new boss, new job responsibilities, a new product to
create—and your division will have a new name. There won't be
one single thing you'll recognize as being familiar. Everybody
ready? One . . . two . . . three . . . *move!*"

This might be a fair description of the vast reorganization
that General Motors began in 1984. In retrospect, it was a phenomenal undertaking for the normally sluggish company. But
over the years, the organization had become unresponsive to the
needs of a rapidly changing competitive environment, and a
reorganization was urgently needed. The surprise was that it
happened on such a large scale.

The reorganization was president Jim McDonald's brain-
child. McDonald is a steady, unpretentious man, with none of

Roger Smith's grandiose vision. It would be out of character for McDonald to use words like "vision." He was straightforward and practical; very simply, if something didn't work, he figured he'd better think about fixing it. And whenever he embarked upon a big job, he admitted that there were butterflies in his stomach. One might chart the major events in Jim McDonald's life by the butterflies. It's an endearing quality in a company where arrogance usually prevents anyone from openly admitting doubts and fears.

McDonald never appeared to be a driven corporate man, just a hard worker, well liked and considered smart. "I don't ever remember having a burning desire to be president," he said once. "But I *always* wanted to be an engineer."

Because McDonald had risen up through the production engineering ranks, and had more manufacturing experience than most GM presidents, his ear was closer to the ground when it came to recognizing trouble. "It was the X-car experience that really motivated me to think, our systems aren't right . . . our organization isn't right to make good decisions from a quality standpoint," he said, referring to the quality and performance problems that plagued the model. "In one sense, the failures in the early eighties might turn out to be some of the best things that could have happened—they jolted the organization and put people in a position to accept change."

The major glitch in the system appeared to be that General Motors did not operate as one cohesive corporation but, rather, as seven separate and distinct operations, each with its own insulated empire. It took three separate operations—a car division, Fisher Body, and GMAD—to build a single car. And at no time did they interface, except through the president. They were entirely vertical organizations.

Think about it. A car division would approve the design of the car and turn it over to Fisher Body. Fisher would engineer the body to conform to the design, sign off, and send it to GMAD. GMAD would then modify plants and equipment to prepare for the new model. Later, GMAD would be responsible for assembling the car. At no point was there interaction among lower-level people. All divisions reported ultimately to the president, who was responsible for arbitrating disputes.

There were myriad problems with the way the system worked. Created during simpler times, when there were fewer models, less engineering complexity, and no urgency about keeping costs down, the system had become a dinosaur. The structure of autonomy that separated the car divisions, Fisher Body, and GMAD was ill-suited to the building of the new uni-body cars, or to addressing the new imperatives of getting cars to market faster and at lower cost.

How much more logical it would have been for representatives of all three divisions to sit down together in the beginning and design the car as a single project, rather than grunting through this unwieldy and often unworkable process! But by the 1980s, such interaction was virtually impossible, since each of the three viewed itself as a separate entity with the necessity of protecting its own autonomy.

As Roger Smith once described the process: "Guys in Fisher Body would draw up a body and send the blueprint over and tell the guy, 'Okay, you build it if you can, you SOB.' And the guy at GMAD would say, 'Well, Jesus, there's no damn way you can stamp metal like that and there's no way we can weld this stuff together.' "

In contrast, the Japanese had known for decades that when designers, engineers, and manufacturing personnel are all working together during the early stages of a vehicle's conception, problems could be anticipated and corrected before they became impossible (or very costly) to fix. They could also plan for steps to be taken from the outset, while the car was still in the design stage, that would cut costs and improve quality.

"I really didn't like the process," McDonald said. "If this had been a flash that occurred in 1981, I would have said, 'You're just trying to do something dramatic to put your nail on the wall.' But I'd been thinking about it carefully for some time."

What occurred in 1981 and 1982 with the GM-10 program might have been an important catalyst—if not for McDonald himself, at least for many others in the organization. The GM-10 experiment demonstrated very clearly that the bureaucracy and outdated organizational structure had become so strangled that it was virtually impossible to achieve a cooperative working environment.

Bob Dorn was the chief engineer at Pontiac in 1981 when he was asked to manage a program called GM-10. GM had approved $7 billion to produce a new line of midsize cars that would replace its aging rear-wheel-drive midsize models and the yet-to-be-launched front-wheel-drive A-cars.

When Dorn learned that he had been selected by the five

car division managers to be the GM-10 program manager, he told the executives, "The only way I'll go down to run the GM-10 is if I'm responsible for developing the car and I've got all the resources. And I don't mean just the chassis. I mean the chassis *and* body."

The division managers assured Dorn that it was the plan that people from each division would be assigned to work together as a team on the new car, under Dorn's direction. Unfortunately, the division managers never passed the message to their staffs, so Dorn's project was seen as crossing over the boundaries of appropriate responsibility.

William "Bill" Hoglund, then general manager at Pontiac, recalls the devastating—but totally predictable—turn of events.

"He went in to the executive who ran the body and assembly side, and that guy said, 'I'm not going to give you my resources.' "

That was only the beginning of Dorn's headaches. Next, he was assigned to work out of Chevrolet Engineering. Because of its size and dominance within the company, only Chevrolet had enough clout to be the home of a project the size of the GM-10 effort.

"So Dorn goes into Chevrolet Engineering," Hoglund remembers, "and he brings a couple of other guys with him, but there are no resources made available to him outside of Chevrolet Engineering to engineer the car. You laid this guy into an organization that was bound to fail. The GM-10 screwed around for two years in that kind of environment.

"And Dorn was absolutely devastated. It almost ruined him." Dorn later became general manager of operations at Cadillac, but he admits today that the GM-10 experience "almost sent me over the brink of going stark raving mad.

"I approached the formulation of the proposal to my bosses as a technical solution on how you organize to get this job done. And I think I entirely underestimated the organizational difficulties of trying to do that. It just evolved as it went along into being a more and more difficult situation for the people who were being asked to do something they didn't think they should be doing."

Dorn's attempt to build a car as a cooperative effort among the three divisions was comparable to asking hostile nations to dissolve their borders. "They kept saying, 'Gee, this

is really out of our definition, our boundaries and guidelines.'
The divisions just didn't like it at all that we were starting to
step into their areas.

"The original plan was for us to borrow resources from
Chevrolet Engineering and Fisher Body and clearly whatever
was supposed to occur to have that happen didn't. I don't believe I really know who prevented it or didn't do it. But as we
tried to get the program done, there was more and more pressure from the outside—and people threw up more and more
roadblocks."

As Dorn's small group continued to get slammed up against
brick walls, his frustration grew to the breaking point. Not only
was the organization physically unprepared to allow for such
interaction, but within GM's every-man-for-himself culture, cooperative endeavors such as this one were close to impossible.
"People could see the struggle, and they'd say, 'I can help,' and
some of them did," he says. "But not enough did. Clearly there
wasn't enough support for the idea in enough places with all the
resources to make it happen. I'm not sure this is a problem with
individuals—it's more of a *cultural* problem that we had. You
have to ask, Who wanted the project to happen? Analyzing it
now, it appears that not all of the top executives had the same
vision of what should be done and why. And simply ordering
people to do something didn't work. Even vice presidents with
a lot of power couldn't make that happen. We got to thinking
that there was actually insubordination going on for a while and
that people were purposefully trying to stymie the program
. . . I got to the point where I *hated* people I used to like a lot.
But as time went on, I realized it wasn't a problem with a *person*.
It was a problem with the system we were working in."

In the end, it would take seven years—two more than the
traditional GM product cycle and three more than the Japanese
product cycle—to get the first GM-10 cars into dealerships. And
even then, only the two-door cars would be available. It would
take another year and a half before the four-door versions would
be ready. The station wagons were killed, and the cars were built
in only four factories rather than in seven as originally planned.
This lapse in time allowed Ford's Taurus and Sable to have the
midsize market to themselves. In fact, even though GM began
the GM-10 project earlier than Ford, its cars eventually had to
be modified because they looked too much like the Taurus. In

every respect, the project would have been a complete fiasco were it not for the fact that it alerted the leadership of General Motors to the awful, deadly truth: *The organization simply did not work.*

It was clear that the two biggest obstacles to change were GMAD and Fisher Body, naturally autonomous companies that had become so powerful that they could literally change the direction of a vehicle program at whim. Legitimate progress was impossible in the face of such a hardened structural reality.

"The issue," Jim McDonald would say later, "was how do you get the responsibility level *down here,* not *up there.* We needed a full-time person to work on this and that's when we decided to bring in John Debbink from the component operation."

In late 1981, Debbink, then general manager of the Delco Moraine subsidiary, received a call from Donald McPherson, group executive of the car divisions. Debbink was sympathetic to the issues raised by McDonald. Twenty-five years at Chevrolet, the most powerful of the car divisions, had proved to him that GM's structure no longer worked in the contemporary auto world.

McPherson asked him, "Is it possible to organize all the engine plants and the engine engineering into one organization?" Debbink agreed to give it some thought and draft a plan for president McDonald.

"Let's take a broader approach," suggested McDonald, when he had reviewed Debbink's work. "Let's look at how we could do a better job of bringing passenger cars to market in North America."

"All right," Debbink agreed. "How long do I have?"

McDonald told him to take the time he needed, and Debbink went to work to study the problem, using two of his brightest people at Delco Moraine, Ken Clayton and Don Pais. In December, they submitted a concept paper to McDonald that would become the preliminary plan for reorganization. Top management moved cautiously to evaluate the plan; it wasn't until the fall of 1982 that Roger Smith and Jim McDonald formalized the assignment to Debbink to direct a special task force to study reorganizing the North American car operations. The reorganization of the central office staff was not to be included in the plan, so the proposal failed to address the vast empire that had developed in the headquarters building—to the increasing resentment of employees. "We decided not to try to do it all at once," said Debbink. "Do the part that's most vital immediately, then work on the rest."

Before they began, Debbink and Clayton visited half a dozen other major United States corporations that had undergone similar internal renovation. "It kind of put things in focus early on," said Debbink. "We were talking about a lot of different things. We were talking about a structural change, systems changes, and what we'd now call *cultural* changes. If you had to do it in ideal order, you'd create the culture first, then you'd make your systems match the job that had to be done. The last thing you'd do would be to change the structure because if you did the first two things the right way, almost any structure would work." Debbink's team defined cultural change as having several components. It implied the following shifts in emphasis:

a move from hierarchical to participatory structure
a move from a no-risk to an entrepreneurial philosophy
a move from an auditor's mentality to trust and responsibility
a move to teamwork and mutual respect
a move to open communication without risk

In other words, major brain surgery for GM. The challenge facing Debbink's team was to see if a cultural shift could happen in the process of making the urgent organizational changes that were needed. They began by asking McKinsey and Company, a research and consulting firm, to help evaluate the options. McKinsey provided the logical format for analyzing GM car operations and formalizing what had already been decided. Their final approach differed little from Debbink's original concept. The basic objectives were that General Motors had to have an integrated organization, eliminate the redundancies, and create the opportunity for systems that worked across the divisions—in other words, tear down the divisional barriers. And it had to be done in a way that was institutionally valid.

As part of its study, the McKinsey team interviewed the top sixty-five executives and eight hundred employees in the company and asked them, "What organizational problems do you see, and what are the areas for improvement?"

According to Debbink, the list was long. "They pointed out the barriers between divisions. They pointed out the conflicting goals of different divisions. They were concerned with the timing of programs. They were concerned with the decision-making process. They were disturbed that decisions went almost to the top before they could be resolved. Those were all complaints that, when you dissected them, pointed to more fundamental areas that needed to be addressed."

The Debbink team reported once a month to a steering committee that consisted of McPherson; Alexander Cunningham, vice president in charge of the body and assembly group; and Dave Collier, vice president in charge of the operating staffs. Every three months, the team reported its progress to the Executive Committee.

The team did one other thing. It analyzed every function necessary to take a car from concept to production. "It was taking us longer to bring a car from concept to market than it took us to win World War Two," observed Debbink. It was a line that was to be often repeated by H. Ross Perot in his criticism of GM.

A large part of the reason, the consultants found, was that the bureaucracy was a virtual quicksand bog of procedures. One consultant reported an incident where a simple design solution was found to fix a clutch problem. Finding the solution was the easy part. Getting it implemented was another story entirely. It might take years. In a well-organized environment, the engineer on the project should have been empowered to contact the supplier and order the change. But not at General Motors. "You have to produce *fifty thousand* studies to show that it's a better solution," the consultant said. "Then you have to go through *ten* different committees to get it approved."

The complaints rolled in. Too much oversight by top management. Too many people assigned to the same programs. Too little accountability. Too much resistance to letting middle managers run with the ball.

Many of the problems were tangled up in GM's no-risk management environment, where individuals were not held accountable for the decisions they made. Since the high potential managers were frequently rotated from one assignment to another, there was little continuity. This was devastating to the company and to the staffers, who were constantly subjected to new personalities whose private agendas included making themselves look good so they could move up the next rung on the ladder.

The company was a lazy, permissive parent to its out-of-control children, and the consultants found case after case of the company sheltering its people from the hard knocks of the real world. It might have expected them to work hard (and more often than not, they *did* work long hours), but they were generally left unchallenged; in spite of the fiercely competitive nature of the industry, the employees were not prodded to be more efficient or more innovative. The structure of the company and the corporate culture which valued conformity more than creativity prevented that from happening. The reward system functioned on automatic pilot. Put in the years, support the party line, and you'll be protected from harm.

Providing for the needs of executives isn't a bad policy, but at GM it served to distance key people from the real world of the customers they were trying to serve. A telling example is the story told by Mary Rabaut, a strategic planner who started with the Detroit Diesel Allison division in 1980. Rabaut described the company car benefit.

"I never put gas in the car," she said. "I never washed it or cleaned it. I never did anything to it. Every three thousand miles there was another clean car, with a full tank of gas in my spot. Now, I knew how unusual this was because I had come from the other world.

"Once I was in an automobile accident and I smashed up the car. I mean, I *totaled* this car. I was taken to the hospital—I was okay, I stayed home for two or three days. And when I went back to work, there was a new car waiting for me. It was like, 'You smashed up the car . . . no problem.' There was an accident report which someone else took care of getting. There were insurance forms that somebody else took care of filling out. I swear to God, it was like the car was disposable—absolutely disposable."

Roger Smith was not surprised to hear the feedback that was emerging from the bowels of his company. And he knew that GM could never be nimble enough to outperform the Japanese unless people began to work more effectively. He understood that the joint pressures of government regulation and the oil crisis had pushed the company against a wall and contributed to its becoming more centralized. "How in heaven's name, in Alfred Sloan's company, do you become too centralized?" he asked. Well, no matter—it was time to change, to chop off some of the layers.

Smith recognized that the inefficient structure was capable of crippling General Motors. And he glimpsed the truth that, beyond just the physical organization, the fundamental understandings of the company might be to blame. But he didn't really grasp the depth of the cultural issues; indeed, he seemed to believe that a tighter strategy and a loud rallying cry were enough to change attitudes that had solidified over many decades.

On April 18, 1983, about seven hundred of GM's top executives gathered at the sprawling Greenbrier Hotel complex in White Sulfur Springs, West Virginia, for the triennial management conference—Smith's first as chairman and chief executive.

The theme of the conference was borrowed from the military: Mission/Objectives/Strategies. It was to be unlike any conference GM had ever held. Smith wanted to get the executives thinking about change—real change. He wanted to jolt them out of their complacency—shove the future in their faces and make them look. "We don't have what you might call a typical Greenbrier agenda where all our top executives give presentations," he told them. "For this one, we threw out the organizational chart. The *message* of this conference is more important than the people who deliver it." The executives sat up in their seats. This was different.

"Today GM is going through a period of critical change," the chairman said. "The automobile market has become a *global* market. Demand has shifted away from our traditional strengths into areas where foreign manufacturers now hold significant advantages. To meet the intense competition we face from abroad, we need to do things differently. We need a greater emphasis on strategic planning—and, even more important, on strategic business management."

Smith went on to outline the mission, objectives, and strategies of General Motors.

"The mission reads like this: 'The fundamental purpose of General Motors is to provide products and services of such quality that our customers will receive superior value, our em-

ployees and business partners will share in our success, and our
stockholders will receive a *sustained, superior* return on their investment.' "

Next, Smith outlined eight primary objectives:

1. Achieve superior product quality.

2. Strengthen employee relations.

3. Improve asset utilization and cost structure.

4. Improve our competitive position.

5. Expand our business opportunities.

6. Increase our technological capabilities.

7. Increase our market share.

8. Improve management effectiveness.

The remainder of the three days, Smith told them, would
be devoted to programs to outline the strategy that had been
devised. And one last thing. "More than ever before," he said,
"we are laying everything on the line. But I'm not going to say,
'It's for your eyes and ears only,' as we always used to say.

"In fact, I'm going to say the opposite. I want you to take
what you learn here back to your people, back to your own unit.
Tell them about our corporate mission, objectives, and strategies. Relate our corporate goals to those of your own unit.
Involve your people." That was new for the secretive GM.
Against the backdrop of a surging auto industry and record
earnings at GM, the executives enthusiastically welcomed the
challenge of Greenbrier. But soon after they returned to work,
it became evident that it was business as usual. Nothing had
changed except that now they had to spend time preparing
strategic plans that ended up on the shelf gathering dust.

The results of the McKinsey investigation yielded no particular surprises. The consultant's conclusion: GMAD and Fisher
Body had become powerful, bureaucratic fiefdoms that stood in
the way of efficiency and progress. For Smith, the handwriting
was already on the wall. "We got together," he recalled, "and
said, 'Hey, we've got to push this decision making back down to
where it was. We've got to get the market responses faster.
We've got to decentralize.' "

The final plan that McDonald presented for reorganizing the company was a radical one: Reslice the corporate pie and create two fully operative groups, incorporating the functions of GMAD and Fisher Body into each. McDonald remembers being fully aware of the major implications of the move. "It's like Gordie Howe said—practice is fun, but when he goes into a game, he has butterflies in his stomach. Well, the exercise of looking at the company was interesting, but when you start to execute a plan, you really do have butterflies because you could screw up the corporation forever."

Before the final organizational structure was decided, the planners kicked around the idea of structuring the company into five separate car companies. "The question," John Debbink said, "was how many ways could you slice Fisher Body? We thought, 'Why not have five car companies and slice Fisher Body five ways?' But as we got to looking at the individual areas of expertise within Fisher Body, it was clear that you couldn't cut them up into fives without losing your critical numbers in any one of the capabilities. We finally concluded that two was as many as you could do." McDonald himself had the walls of an empty office lined with fabric. He spent much time in there, moving around small markers on the wall that represented various functions and departments, in a dedicated effort to understand and create the right organization structure. It was a task that consumed him for several months, and may have diverted his attention from what was happening to the new cars and factories GM was developing.

In January 1984, Roger Smith made the formal announcement of what had been rumored for more than a year, and the most ambitious reorganization program ever attempted in a major company was under way. As one executive described it, "It was like taking a car apart and putting it back together again while it was hurtling down the highway at sixty miles per hour."

The plan called for the "integration of Fisher Body and GMAD into the two new car groups." A more appropriate description might have been *disintegration*.

The first group was composed of the Buick-Oldsmobile-Cadillac car divisions. It was dubbed BOC.

The second group included the Chevrolet-Pontiac-GM of Canada car divisions and was dubbed CPC.

Although to this day all GM executives deny it was ever the

case, the 1983 annual report clearly stated that the difference between the two groups was that BOC would develop and produce regular-size and large cars (GM's traditional base) and CPC would focus on small cars. Whether or not this was really the intention, each group ended up with both big and small cars when the specific projects were assigned.

Robert "Bob" Stempel, an engineer, was named vice president and group executive in charge of BOC. Stempel, a tall, well-spoken fast-tracker who would later become GM president, had been Chevrolet general manager for less than two years prior to the assignment. Stempel had been close to former GM president Ed Cole, and was regarded as a capable engineer. Before that, he had spent almost two years as managing director of GM's Adam Opel AG unit in West Germany. In traditional HI-POT fashion, Stempel had skirted up the ladder so quickly that he had never had a chance to fully make his mark in his previous few jobs, but he would have that chance at BOC.

Lloyd Reuss, assigned to head up CPC, was a rising executive whose management style was more traditional than Stempel's. His fortunes appeared to result from his close relationship with McDonald. Like Stempel, Reuss had moved quickly through the ranks, spending little time at any one assignment. He had been general manager of Buick for only three years when he was called upon to head up the new group.

Alex Cunningham was appointed executive vice president in charge of North American car operations; Stempel and Reuss would report to him. And Charles Katko, general manager of Fisher, was assigned to the "undertaker's" job of overseeing the disintegration of Fisher and GMAD. His primary task would ultimately be to prevent revolt within the ranks as executives saw their empires crumbling, and staffers found themselves in new roles with no idea where they were going.

The method by which Stempel and Reuss were assigned is an example of how intent McDonald was on achieving *true* change, not just the appearance of change.

"Originally, my thinking was that since Stempel was general manager of Chevrolet and Reuss was general manager of Buick, Stempel should head up CPC and Reuss should head up BOC," he recalls. "But one day, before the announcement was made, John Stewart, a McKinsey man with an excellent mind, called me up. He said, 'Think about this. Big changes are tough on people and there are winners and losers. You should do everything you possibly can to minimize the losers. If you put Reuss in as head of BOC, the Oldsmobile and Cadillac people are going to feel like losers because Reuss came out of Buick. The same thing will happen if you put Stempel in CPC—the Pontiac people will feel like losers. If you switch them, you cut their loyalties.' " McDonald accepted the wisdom of Stewart's proposal.

Debbink, Stempel, Reuss, Katko, and their staffs took six months to prepare for the reorganization process, setting up a transition headquarters in the Renaissance Center a few miles from corporate headquarters. The task that would confront them was great. It wasn't just to move all the employees into new positions on the company chessboard. The chessboard now had a different configuration and there were no directions for how to proceed to reabsorb the displaced Fisher and GMAD people, and simultaneously achieve the stated mandate of creating an organization that was more market driven.

The first step was to write job descriptions for each of the key spots to be assigned within BOC and CPC. Then the group took all the people in Fisher, GMAD, and the car divisions and tried to fit them into the job descriptions. If there were too many people that fit a particular job description, they narrowed it down to four or five candidates. Then they each voted on their preferred choices. In this way, the group felt they were putting the best people into the best spots.

When they were done, they had a list of people with no jobs. What could be done with them? Some they talked into early retirement; others they talked to about transferring to a different position.

But having done this, a new reality began to enter into the employee picture. In order to have two fully integrated companies, it would be necessary to beef up the engineering staffs with people from outside. The plan was that each of the two groups would be fully self-sufficient so that, in theory, the company could shut down one form of operation and open up the next day with the new one. General Motors became like Noah staffing his ark—they needed two of every species of worker. In this way, the reorganization, which was devised as an overall efficiency measure, also touched off a hiring spree that would add tens of thousands of professionals to GM's payroll.

A second unpleasant task was in store for the reorganization team. They had to wade through the enormous roadblocks that resistant employees were busily putting in their way. Across the board, small corporate power brokers were hanging on for dear life to the vestiges of their control. Their fingers had to be pried loose one by one.

One of the first things the group discovered was the severity of the lack of integration; not only were GMAD and Fisher operating as independent companies, but *within* the two companies there existed many other layers of independence. They were startled to discover, for example, that Ternstedt, a maker of trim which Fisher acquired during the 1970s, was still operating very much as a separate entity. "Those Ternstedt guys were alive and well within Fisher Body," Debbink said. "It was natural, because they were responsible for a specific part of the body of the car, and they had a pride in their organization. When they were absorbed by Fisher, they simply circled their wagons and did their own thing. The Ternstedt people were still *Ternstedt people*, even though they were being paid by Fisher Body."

Katko had spent much of his career at GMAD and Fisher— he knew better than anyone the problems posed by the two divisions. Katko realized that although the car divisions were the closest to the pulse of the market, they constantly encountered resistance from the two superpowers. "The car divisions couldn't simply take the designs down the hall and work out the designs with the engineers," Katko said. "They had to be able to *sell* their thinking and their timing to Fisher Body and Fisher Body had to deal with GMAD. You had too many chains of command for a fast response, and you didn't always have the right kind of coordination because you not only had a problem of coordination between Fisher and the selling division, you also had to deal with coordinating between Fisher Body and the assembly plant." Lack of coordination between body design and assembly plant inevitably led to disaster. If the assembly people were left out of the design process, there was the very real danger that cars would be designed that could not be built. It was a *core* problem—to say the least!

His experience on the other end gave Katko a clear insight into another problem the reorganization team faced. "When I was general manager of the assembly division and then general manager of Fisher, there's no question that I was looking to see how I could make them the most profitable and productive.

Certainly if I saw things that were going to affect my area of responsibility, I had my objections."

Fisher Body proved to be tougher to break up than GMAD because it had been so autonomous since its acquisition in 1926. The team was surprised to find out how strong its ties to the past were. Fisher was like a crotchety old man who was very, very set in his ways.

Loyalty at Fisher proved to be a major obstacle to the smooth dismantling of the division. People at Fisher never saw themselves as working for General Motors. They worked for Fisher Body, never mind who paid the bills. Many Fisher employees viewed the reorganization as being comparable to a hostile takeover of an independent company.

"Right from the start, we knew that GMAD would become part of the vehicle business unit," Katko said. "But it wasn't quite clear where Fisher Body would be." As word filtered down through the ranks at Fisher, resistance heightened, and Katko had the thankless task of soothing employee fears and helping determine which people would be sent to each of the two new-car groups.

More consultants were hired to evaluate people, and over and over they encountered a stubborn refusal on the part of employees to believe this was really happening. As time went on, it became harder and harder to pry the fingers loose.

John Debbink admitted that some of the issues being raised by Fisher were quite legitimate. "They pointed out some of the things they did for the corporation that we've since lost," Debbink said. "Fisher Body commonized many of the body components. And it was true that all radio switches looked the same, but it wasn't all bad. They were very quick to point out that those areas where they had particular expertise were important and some things were going to be lost. They were concerned that we would fragment expertise in the stamping area, for example."

But finally, Debbink said, "the thinking people at Fisher knew things couldn't continue forever the way they were. We had to deal with a car as a car—and not as *chunks*. And when you get right down to it, a big part of the problem with doing it the old way was that you couldn't assign responsibility. Somebody always had somebody else to blame. They could say, 'It isn't my fault if it doesn't ride right—the structure of the body is wrong.' Or, 'They didn't follow the specifications.' It can go on and on.

One of the major intents was to be able to assign accountability and responsibility for the total vehicle."

A consultant at United Research Company, a consulting firm hired to help with the reorganization, described the headache of the move. "Any little thing that came up became a reason that breaking up Fisher between BOC and CPC wouldn't work," he said. "And the whole Fisher organization would seize upon it as a way to stop this thing and roll it back. So in many cases, we were going two steps forward and one and a half steps back."

The consultant recalled one point where the pocket of resistance was deeper than usual. He asked Skip LeFauve, general manufacturing manager of the Chevrolet Motor division to help out. No problem, LeFauve told him. "I've always been successful in being able to be up front and logical and make these things happen."

So LeFauve went over to Fisher Body at the GM Tech Center to talk to the people. He never expected to find the anger, hostility, and frustration he encountered.

"It was traumatic for him," the consultant said. "He walked up and down the halls of this huge engineering place, stopping and answering questions and talking to people, and trying to be reasonable. But the people were so up-to-here with what they perceived to be threats to their well-being that LeFauve was in serious jeopardy. I mean, emotions had gotten that hot and people were saying, *'Hell no, we won't go!'* "

The day after LeFauve's fire walk at Fisher, he met with the consultant and shook his head in amazement. "I've never had an experience like that in my whole career," the executive told the consultant. "Those people are really angry . . . they really are."

In classic fashion, General Motors had been unprepared for the storm of protest, had never considered the depth of passion and loyalty that employees felt for their divisions, especially Fisher. It was a serious flaw in the management style—the tendency to put the cart before the horse. Roger Smith himself has admitted this is true. "One of the problems we had, and still have, is miscommunicating what we're doing. The top management was all for us—all for the program. They thought it was great. So, we assumed that, hey, when we go charging up San Juan Hill, the rest of the troops are going to come whizzing along behind us. Only, we got halfway up and turned around and looked, and they're still down there at the bottom trying to decide whether to follow us. We hadn't sold the bottom ranks thoroughly enough on the necessity of what we were doing. So we had to run back down the hill a little bit and say, 'Hey, do you understand what happens if you don't do this? And do you understand what happens if you *do*—where we'll be in the twenty-first century?' "

But even these comments reveal a failing in the understanding Smith and McDonald had of the true meaning of communication in the corporate culture. Their view was simply another variation on the yes-man style of teamwork that had spread through GM like a disease. They confused *communication* with *public relations.* The goal was to narcotize the employees so they would accept predetermined change. Granted, there was no easy way to accomplish the reorganization, no matter how they did it. But Smith and McDonald perhaps did not fully appreciate the depth of fear that the reorganization created. They might have borrowed a page from the bible of W. Edwards Deming in examining the problems GM had with communication. Deming's third commandment—*drive out fear*—might have provided a clue about what happens when the bottom-rung masses view change as the iron fist of the giant sweeping down on them. While everyone might have appreciated the rationale and need for reorganization, their concerns were basic: "I've spent years learning the ropes and establishing a career. Now I'm in a different city, reporting to someone I don't know, with no feeling of security about my future."

Ironically, it was GM itself that had long instilled pride of division in the workers. Now the company was asking them to lay it aside without so much as a glance back. "It takes time to change a culture," admitted Debbink. "We were destroying some long-lived loyalties. Here was Fisher Body just celebrating its seventy-fifth anniversary, and within a year, we come around and say, 'Fisher, you are no more.' People don't die that readily." To make matters worse, the rumored breakup of Fisher was being denied by the powers-that-be almost to the day it was announced.

From the standpoint of necessity, it was plain to see that the reorganization had to be done. But GM went at it like the sadistic dentist who yanks teeth without the benefit of novocaine. It hurt a lot.

Employees of the car companies were going through the

same gut-wrenching experience as the workers at Fisher. Most of them identified strongly with their specific makes—you were a Buick guy or an Oldsmobile guy, not a General Motors guy. But no longer.

One Buick executive told of attending a dinner for fourth-generation Buick employees—there were about one hundred—and their families in Flint, Michigan. Think of it: For these people, working for Buick was like working in the family business. Grandfather was a Buick guy. Dad was a Buick guy, his sons are Buick guys, and now the great-grandsons are Buick guys. And they were having a big dinner. But there was no more Buick—just BOC—and in a display of insensitivity that would be laughable if it weren't so sad, the Buick sign was taken down and replaced with a BOC sign, *the day of the dinner.* The executive who related this story added that after the dinner he was personally deluged with threatening letters and phone calls.

Flint was a Buick town, and it struggled to adjust to the shift in identity. A consultant recalls going to an engineering center in Flint and having a man come up to him one day. "He was wearing a Buick belt buckle, a Buick tie tack, a Buick lapel pin. And he said, 'You're with the group that are trying to help us work better together, right?' I told him I was.

"And he said, 'Well, there's something I've really never understood. My granddaddy was a Buick guy, my daddy was a Buick guy, and I was a Buick guy. So now, when I go to a party or I go on vacation and somebody asks me where I work, what do I say? They know what a Buick is, I know what a Buick is. There's a sense of identity that we've lost here.' "

At the Delta engine factory in Lansing, now a BOC factory, the name Oldsmobile remained in massive high relief, formed from bricks on a huge wall in the lobby. For many employees, it became a shrine before which they paid homage to the good old days—and a symbol of the defiant posture that their identities as Oldsmobile workers could not be so easily eradicated.

Carl Storey, a prominent Olds dealer in Lansing, told of the devastating effects the announcement had on the quality of products coming out of the plant. Lansing took another blow when compact "N" cars were moved into one of its assembly plants. Oldsmobile and "compact" were a contradiction; even worse, Oldsmobile workers now had to produce Buick and Pontiac "N" cars as well.

* * *

In its early conception, the reorganization plan looked good on paper, in spite of the outcry from the workers. But paper models rarely reflect the truth about a company's mechanics. A consultant might study the organizational chart for a particular division and get a picture of the breakdown of responsibilities and the chain of command. But he won't see the *invisible chain*, that informal network that exists in every company, large or small. And as the consultants studied the situation, they grew increasingly astonished at just how informally things were run in this company with its layer upon layer of formal management.

Explained the consultant, "Over the years, the system had become so paralytic that nothing could happen if they went through the system. What we found out is that the corporation worked by an informal network of people. They call this 'being effective outside the system.' The way they got things to work was really through this informal network. And it was very personal. It wasn't that the design engineering group did this or that. It was *Joe Sampson* did this or that."

The hard reality was that over the years General Motors had become like a corrupt government bureaucracy. The original system had been designed for conditions that no longer existed, but the bureaucrats maintained their positions in a system that didn't work by setting up their own ways to get things done.

Many people blamed McKinsey for failing to understand this. What they perceived to be blind resistance to the idea of the reorganization was largely the workers' concern that reorganization would also collapse the true operating structure.

Said one project engineer, "You knew you could call Charlie down in the model shop and you could say, 'Charlie, I need fourteen of these prototypes out by Wednesday,' and he'd say, 'You got it,' and things got done because of this trust and working relationship. But now who do you call? The person you're supposed to work with isn't downstairs anymore. You're located in Building A, and he's in Building Thirty-two, which is across town. And he doesn't know you from Adam. You can't just relate directly to him and say, 'We'll charge it to this,' like you could with Charlie. He'll say, 'No, we've got to get a purchase order. It's got to go through the system. And it's going to need fourteen signatures.' And you say, 'Oh great. See you in the year 2000.' "

To Dr. David Cole, an auto industry expert and son of the

former president, Edward Cole, one great flaw in the reorganization plan was the failure of anyone to recognize the importance of this informal network. Like others, Cole faulted McKinsey.

"I think an outside management consultant should have perceived that in an organization like General Motors there would be a very deeply entwined informal organization which is where the company really functions," Cole said. "I can see a guy like Stempel or even Smith not realizing how significant it is. But McKinsey should have seen it. I don't know of any complex organization that doesn't have a very well-defined informal network."

According to Cole, this informal structure that augments the organizational structure of a company is where the real creative juices flow. He calls it the "thought structure"—made up of managers who tend to be the "thought leaders." It is Cole's belief that ignorance of the "thought structure" created problems in the reorganization that are still felt today. "It's still a horrifying problem," he says now. "One of the most common things people said to me after the reorganization—both suppliers and people inside of GM—was, 'I don't know who to go to anymore.' Literally, the whole organization had to go fishing for that informal infrastructure. It should have been managed right along with the management of the formal structure. To me, it is unimaginable that McKinsey would not have recognized this."

Many people at GM believed that McKinsey was a fly in the ointment of the reorganization, rather than an enabler, and they were distressed that the company was placing too much faith in them.

Bob Dorn, of GM-10 fiasco fame, recalled the frustration he felt at trying to get cooperation from different divisions and having McKinsey arrive to help out. "We had people from McKinsey coming to us to tell us what we needed to do to, as they put it, 'help yourself out of this dilemma,' but their presence just added to the confusion."

McDonald takes another view of McKinsey's contribution. "Yes," he admits, "we did destroy a lot of underground communication lines and you have to rebuild those from scratch. But McKinsey really didn't have a lot to do with the fundamental changes that were made in the organization. They had a lot to do with the methodology and in advising people how to communicate." According to McDonald, McKinsey's role was as a facilitator. What they did was verify problems and offer advice on the ramifications of alternative structures. McKinsey might have been unfairly blamed for poor execution of the new structure, which was really the fault of GM.

As the two car groups began to take shape, CPC came together faster than BOC. This should have surprised no one. CPC was essentially composed of one major car company—Chevrolet—with a little one—Pontiac—attached to it, along with the marketing organization and production facilities in Canada. BOC, on the other hand, was something of a monster, with three equal and geographically separate car companies. Virtually the entire CPC organization was in Detroit; BOC was in three cities, each one about seventy miles from the other. In addition, the style of the two men heading up the companies differed greatly.

Lloyd Reuss was a true company player who took the path of least resistance. Stempel was more of a maverick, and he listened more to the staff members who were reporting to and assisting him. Once he settled on an approach, he would pursue it in spite of opposition from the Fourteenth Floor.

Tim Hunter, a former GM engineer who was at GM Canada during the reorganization, observed that "Lloyd did not like to get bad news, while Bob was more direct with people—he sat down and got on with it. Lloyd had all the right words and he could be very motivational, but I sometimes wondered how much there was behind that." Hunter has admitted that Reuss's approach contributed to his own discontent at GM. "I guess I just wasn't sure how quickly GM was going to turn."

Essentially, Reuss replicated GM's so-called matrix management structure, a series of functional departments on an organization chart, with everyone inflexibly positioned in his given vertical channel. There was no provision for cross-channel communication, except through him.

While the reorganization process was lengthier at BOC, with Stempel at the helm, many executives found the mood more invigorating. One executive recalls, "Bob used a very participatory approach. He got all the people that reported to him together and said, 'Now that we have this chance to restructure, let's go look at the competition. Let's look at what will be happening in the marketplace in the future.' "

The people at BOC reached a rather remarkable conclusion as a result of their studies. Mary Rabaut, who was on the BOC team, remembers how they reached the conclusion: If they followed McKinsey strictly, as Reuss had done, what would be gained? They would simply turn the two new divisions into two mini-GMs. There would be no GMAD or Fisher, but there would also be no structure to allow for interdepartmental communication.

"It wasn't going to get us any closer to the market," Rabaut said. "Instead of being one big nonfunctional organization, we'd be two smaller ones. We weren't going to be product-oriented. We weren't going to develop teams. We weren't going to get down to small enough entities that you could make change fast. So BOC decided to pose another structural change beyond the one they had announced."

What Stempel and his team proposed was that further changes be made inside BOC over a period of eighteen months, to create three platform groups, each with the capability of engineering a car and building it. Essentially, the inflexible organizational chart would go out the window. It was Stempel's intention to get to the bottom of what it took to build hot-selling cars and get them to market fast.

The concept was that the group would be organized around product teams that would have direct responsibility for the product—and more direct accountability, as well. "The point," explained a consultant, "was to go for parallel and concurrent and simultaneous engineering to ensure that there's at least an understanding and an empathy with what the guy ahead and the guy behind you were doing. And the product team leader would be responsible for everything."

President McDonald, Alex Cunningham, Stempel, and Reuss met to discuss the BOC proposal, with Cunningham making it clear from the outset that he entirely disapproved of Stempel's views. Recalls Mary Rabaut, "Cunningham's reaction was that this is just a cold shower, and Stempel had better turn around and go back and come up with the right answer."

In dealing with Stempel, Cunningham seemed to share the view of many who thought, "Damn it. We announced the reorganization. It's over with. Can't you just do it the way we announced it? What's the matter with the way we announced it?"

Stempel lost the first round and was sent back to the drawing board. But he and his team were even more convinced than ever that their proposal was the right way to go. His team urged Stempel to make a bold move—something almost unprecedented at GM: Go back in and fight. Take a revamped version of the plan back in to the executives and try to change their minds. The very notion was close to committing corporate hara-kiri; most fast-trackers learned not only to cease fighting for ideas that didn't fly with the brass, but to try to pretend that they had never proposed them in the first place.

Stempel was fully aware of the damage such persistence could do to his career, but he vowed to stand behind the conclusions of his team. He sat down with them and listed all the questions that Cunningham and McDonald had raised at the first meeting, and had his team construct answers. And then he went back in. McDonald and Cunningham were beginning to get annoyed. They suggested he get off this kick.

"I never saw Stempel so nervous but so committed," remembers Rabaut. "All his staff said, 'This is it, Bob. If you don't want to take it, we understand.' Everybody knew that Stempel was really sticking his neck out to go in there a third and fourth time."

But then a funny thing happened. Stempel wore them down. McDonald and Cunningham finally threw up their hands and approved the plan. Let Stempel hang himself.

"They said okay, assuming we'd fall flat on our ass," says Rabaut. "Not only did we not fall flat on our ass, we had such a good plan. All this did was force us to think through every detail—everybody was taking the helm. Everybody knew what they had to do."

Stempel's plan was such a departure from traditional GM practice that the hierarchy didn't know what to do with it. During the first six to nine months, there were people at BOC literally walking around without titles because the company couldn't figure out where they went on its master organizational chart.

But in spite of the chaos, it was just the kind of environment that allowed the apples to get shaken off the corporate tree and movement to happen. In retrospect, Debbink noted that Stempel's urging for change from the bottom up allowed the beginnings of a cultural shift that would not otherwise have happened.

"You have to be methodical about changing a culture," Debbink said. "If I had to depend on either it happening from the ground up to the top of the corporation, or from the top of the corporation on down, I don't think we could ever get there. This way, the two things came together. Of course," he added, "that's not to say that there isn't a great middle ground."

That middle ground—what Roger Smith referred to as "the frozen middle"—was the next target for change. Smith would soon begin a series of acquisitions that would shake up the company more than anything that had occurred to that point.

6

A Tale of Two Plants: NUMMI
Teamwork Versus GM Bureaucracy

One might not recognize Rick Madrid as the same man who carried, by his own admission, "a pen and a punch" as an inspector two years ago. Oh, the outward appearance hasn't changed much—tattoos and mirrored shades continue to be his trademarks. But the "Iron Maiden" T-shirt is now cleverly concealed beneath his sharply pressed shop coat provided by the company. He's a team leader now, qualified and sanctioned by his peers. He prefers to be called a team motivator, however. "I'm *part* of the team; I don't *have* a team. Let people maintain their own personality."
—*GM Today* publication

For those who believed that the Japanese industrial edge rested solely in technological prowess, the NUMMI experiment was a real revelation. The Toyota secret was, finally, no secret at all, and it was as old as history: Treat both white- and blue-collar workers with respect, encourage them to think independently, allow them to make decisions, and make them feel connected to an important effort. Combine that culture with a good car and quality parts, and the results are obvious. As a GMer who spent three years there said, "It was common sense." Going to work for NUMMI was a shock to the system of GM employees, who were accustomed to a stifling bureaucracy and an emphasis on high-tech solutions over worker initiative. At NUMMI, Toyota would demonstrate a business strategy based on trust, respect, and teamwork.

American companies tend, fundamentally, to mistrust workers, whether they are salaried employees or blue-collar workers. There is a pervading attitude that "if you give them an inch, they'll take a mile," because they don't really want to work. The idea, for example, that a worker in the plant would have the power to stop the line in order to eliminate a problem was heresy. Wouldn't such permission lead to widespread line-stoppage for every whim? Not, according to Toyota, if you instituted a system of worker responsibility and accountability. American companies might think they had a tight rein on employees, but with little responsibility resting directly in the workers' laps, there was also little accountability.

And what were the workers being held responsible for? In the first instance, *quality*. In Japanese companies, quality was part of the process, not something added on in the inspection phase. American industry focused on "quality control." Generations of business-school graduates had learned that high quality equaled high cost. GM was not different from the rest of American industry in using inspectors to find defects *after* the fact. At General Motors, the way the company demonstrated to the world its concern for quality was to add more inspectors to check for defects. The Japanese eliminated defects at all stages, from raw materials, to components, to assembly. The workers, not the inspectors, had the primary responsibility for the quality of their work, and they were given the tools to help them do a good job.

This is the tale of two plants, both in California. Fremont, the location of the NUMMI joint venture, would demonstrate that Japanese techniques can work in an unlikely environment. A few hundred miles away at the Van Nuys plant, GM was building cars the old-fashioned way, operating from very different assumptions about worker productivity, chain of command, and quality control.

TRADITION: THE GM PLANT IN VAN NUYS

Van Nuys was considered to be one of GM's more troubled plants, particularly because of its union problems. That's one of the reasons Brian Haun requested an assignment there as production supervisor. Haun was an engineer who had spent time in central staff offices, and he felt the Van Nuys experience would be valuable for his career.

Van Nuys built Pontiac Firebirds and Chevrolet Camaros. When Haun arrived, he was told that he would receive six months of training. He soon learned the nature of his training: *on the job.* And his trainers were the very people he was responsible for supervising.

On his first day, Haun was told to report to Section 25. There he introduced himself to the emergency relief operator, who was the head operator. "My name is Brian Haun and I'm your new supervisor," he told him. "I don't know anything about this." Fortunately the man taught Haun what he needed to know. "But I knew what he was thinking—what everyone was thinking. It was, 'Here comes a young college kid. Let's get him.' "

Haun was the butt of many jokes and the victim of what amounted to a plant-style fraternity hazing. He took it good-naturedly, waiting for an opportunity to show them he was on their side.

The opportunity came soon enough. Union workers were complaining about a problem with a defective welding robot. Whenever it went down, a repair operator had to pick up whatever welds the robot was missing. But the repair operator's job was limited contractually to doing repairs, not doing the welding that the robot was failing to do.

"But basically we were having the repair guy do the welding one hundred percent of the time," Haun said. "After about two weeks, he got fed up, and I thought he was right. So I went up to management and I tried to fight them on it, but they said, 'No. You make him do it, or else.' "

Haun refused, went back to his operators, and told them, "Stand your ground. Don't do it and we'll fight it out."

The union committeeman, the department superintendent, and a general supervisor who was Haun's boss argued heatedly. "They thought they could get the union to back down," Haun said. "But they couldn't, so finally, the hourly people won—and they should have. All of a sudden, I had the respect of everybody in the section. From then on, they broke their backs for me."

Despite learning his job in a confrontational environment, Haun gained a new perspective from his early days at the plant. He could see that the workers wanted to do their jobs well, wanted to be competitive, but all too often they were fighting against unbeatable odds to get their jobs done. Every problem became a confrontation; since there was a basic mistrust between labor and management, it was hard to establish a cooperative environment where problems could be solved.

Haun also found that the absence of personal responsibility and accountability could lead to costly problems.

"We had a problem with a little bracket that gets welded on the back of the car," he said, citing an example. "It holds the sunshade in place. There was a man and a woman on each side of the car who put that bracket on, but they kept missing them. The car would reach the end of the production line and have to be repaired in the 'backyard' area where defects are repaired.

"The repair man would have to take all the carpet out and all the trim out and weld that bracket in—sometimes the carpet got burned. And then it all had to be put back together and, frankly, the car was never the same. So it's a bad deal."

Haun took the two workers off the production line and asked them to go with him to the backyard. Taking workers off the line was rarely done—it was too disruptive. But Haun decided that the disruption would be worth it if it resulted in more cars surviving the gauntlet of line workers without being damaged.

"I took them out and said, 'Look, this is what happens when you miss one of those,' said Haun. 'The repair guy showed them how he had to rip out all the carpet, and they were shocked. And the woman said, 'You mean to tell me that bracket holds the sunshade?' She'd been doing this job for two years and nobody had ever told her what part she was welding."

This wasn't an isolated incident. Haun found that workers operated in a vacuum; they did the job they were told to do without relating it to the final outcome. "Basically, they didn't know who their immediate customers were. Their immediate customers were the guys who had to repair a defect they created, or the people down the line. And they didn't really know how much of an impact they personally had on the way the car was built. In the plant, you're treated like a no-mind idiot. You're supposed to come in and just put the parts on the car and shut up and do your job, and if you miss one, I'm going to yell at you, and eventually you get so used to the yelling that it doesn't do any good. If you're a supervisor, what can you do? You can't fire them—the union won't let you. I think you have to motivate them by positive means. Taking those two workers out into the backyard, for example, really worked well. The woman is fantastic. She turned out to be one of the best operators I had."

Haun said that when he returned that day from showing the two operators the problems they had been causing, "I got in trouble with my general supervisor because they were short on manpower and they didn't want to pick people off the line. He said, 'We don't have enough people for you to do that. I needed those people over at Section Thirty.' But I knew I had to do it."

What Haun encountered was an environment where workers were not partners in the task of building cars. Often they didn't know how their jobs related to the total picture. Not knowing, there was no incentive to strive for quality—what did quality even mean as it related to a bracket whose function you didn't understand? Workers were held accountable through a system of intimidation: Do your job and your supervisor won't yell at you. That was a pretty thin incentive!

It is easy to understand why such an environment would produce workers who do little without being ordered to do it. Why should they? There is no reward for putting in the extra effort. And Van Nuys wasn't unique. It was typical.

In the past, Haun had observed workers on the third (night) shift of stamping plants spending most of the night just moving around aimlessly. "Six o'clock in the morning would come around and they wouldn't have the line ready, so they would have to rush at the last minute," he said.

It was part of a vicious circle that ultimately hurt GM where it could least afford to be hurt—in the area of quality. Because of the changeover delay caused by unmotivated workers, the press time was cut. "Then," explained Haun, "we didn't have time to have the dies repaired the way they should have been. Because they weren't getting repaired in the proper way, they'd just have quick fixes on them and the quality would suffer. You'd get what they call a 'ding.' It's a small deformity in part of the die, or something gets stuck in part of the die and you get a tiny dent that you can hardly see until the car is painted. Or, worse, you lose your dimensional control. For example, when you lose dimensional control on the door, it gets twisted and then it's really hard to fit the parts together in the assembly plant."

These are the kinds of small—often minuscule—defects that turn into major problems on the showroom floor. The customer wants a perfect car. He isn't going to say, "No problem. That little dent isn't important." What Haun observed was that the traditional operating attitudes about how workers should be treated were directly responsible for the quality problems that lessened GM's competitive advantage.

The prevailing attitude encouraged an adversarial relationship between workers and management. John McNulty, GM's vice president of public relations, was concise and brutally honest in describing the us-versus-them mentality.

"We are not yet a classless society," McNulty said. "We're not in the same adversary position we used to be in with the union, but fundamentally the mission of their elected representatives is to get the most compensation for the least amount of labor. Our responsibility to our stockholders is to get the most production for the least amount of compensation. And we do it in ways that are not just taking money away from the employees—with better technology, for example."

McNulty's remark reveals the philosophy that, more than anything, has contributed to GM's loss of the competitive edge. There is no trust. No respect. Instead, it's a fight: Control the hourly workers before they can control the company, and replace them with machines whenever possible.

REVELATION: NUMMI, FREMONT, CALIFORNIA

The Fremont plant, which would be the site of the joint venture, had been closed by General Motors in 1982, and five thousand employees were laid off. When GM and Toyota first discussed Fremont, Toyota was resistant to the idea of hiring from the old work force. It was notorious as being one of GM's most unmanageable. Before the plant was closed, daily absenteeism was regularly over 20 percent; beer bottles littered the parking lot; and even the slightest dispute had to go to the bargaining table. But Toyota and GM worked together during the selection process and managed to hire workers from the original worker pool—avoiding those who were known to be troublemakers.

"I was determined that it would be the Fremont workers, and that took some hard bargaining because Toyota didn't want the Fremont workers," said Al Warren, vice president of labor relations for GM. "I'm glad they did it, because it demonstrated that a work force we thought was unmanageable could be managed. That was a tremendous process. They took almost everybody back—I don't think there was more than a handful that didn't get back eventually, but they did a masterful job of that."

In negotiating with the UAW, Toyota agreed to give the union a strong job security clause and a greater say in plant operations. In return, the union agreed to work within Toyota's system, eliminating unproductive job classifications, and setting up a team assembly system.

The secret of NUMMI's success was threefold: First, they were given a well-designed product, the Chevy Nova, to build. The Nova would be a version of the Toyota Corolla, a car Toyota was already making and selling in Japan. It would sell for about $7,500. Second, they understood that the level of technology in a plant was not the primary factor in determining the quality or cost-effectiveness of a product. Rather, the good design and the production system were the key. Third, they realized that car-making was a people business, and high productivity had to do with the way people were organized and managed. NUMMI employed management techniques that were based on the assumption that workers instinctively wanted to do a good job. They played to that instinct, driving out much of the hostility and fear. According to MIT's John Krafcik, since the troublemakers had been weeded out, NUMMI also had the advantage of a well-trained work force, eager for jobs after being laid off for a few years.

Toyota laid the groundwork for success from the outset, by taking time to set up the plant properly, and by not complicating the task of training a new work force with introducing brand-new technology. They selected suppliers and got them involved from the start in effective quality control. They developed the transportation systems to coordinate shipments from Japan and in the United States. They worked out a relationship with the UAW, carefully establishing credibility and trust with the bargaining unit.

At NUMMI, the Toyota Production System was implemented. Its operating philosophy included seven points:

1. *Kaizen,* the never-ending search for perfection (continuous improvement)

2. *Kanban,* the reduction of costs, through its "just-in-time" system

3. Development of full human potential

4. Building mutual trust

5. Developing team performance

6. Treating every employee as manager

7. Providing a stable livelihood for all employees

The striking thing about the seven points was their emphasis on human development. Nowhere did they say, for example, "the search for technological superiority." Within the framework of the seven points it was assumed that technology would or would not be included depending on its ability to enhance quality.

At the core of the human development philosophy were two premises—both new for GM. The first was that the average worker is motivated by the desire to do a job that enhances his sense of self-worth and that earns the respect of other workers. The second premise was that the worker is inspired by an employer who places value in the worker's input. Under the system developed in Japan, every worker is encouraged to think—to use brainpower and find ways of improving products and processes and eliminating waste—and is rewarded for improvements.

At NUMMI, job classifications were reduced to 4 (as opposed to as many as 183 at some GM plants) and employees were placed in teams headed by fellow hourly workers trained in Japan. If a problem was spotted, the team had permission to stop the line. The team leader functioned, not as a boss, but more as a mediator and instructor. Ultimately, each member of the team would be trained to do the leader's job when called upon. More than a year after production was under way, morale was high and quality was high. GM's surveys ranked the Nova regularly among the company's top three models in terms of quality. In fact, only three months after the first cars rolled out of NUMMI, they were already receiving 140 ratings—virtually *no* defects.

Worker productivity was also rated high. One study suggested that compared with NUMMI, it would probably take about 50 percent more hourly and salaried workers at the old Fremont plant, with comparable technology, to assemble the same car. The same study showed that increased productivity from better management-labor relations reduced the cost of building each car by about $750, compared with the traditional GM manufacturing system.

The hiring process itself was different. For one thing, the UAW and NUMMI management collaborated in personnel decisions, selectively hiring from the ranks of workers who had lost their jobs when the Fremont plant closed in 1982. The evaluation process, which included assessment by UAW and NUMMI representatives, took about thirty-five hours for each candidate. By the time a worker was hired, he knew that something special was happening at this plant. The goals of the system were spelled out in great detail, and the importance of *quality* was stressed, above all. This was quite a departure from the lack of orientation that was typical in GM plants at the time.

At NUMMI, there was great attention to detail. Space utilization, for example, was a major concern. The way space was planned reflected concern with thousands of seemingly insignificant details that, when taken together, went far to save money and maintain quality. At the old pre-NUMMI Fremont plant, 12 percent of the factory space was dedicated to reworking defective vehicles, compared with 7 percent at NUMMI, and only 1 percent at NUMMI's Takoaka sister plant in Japan.

Another system that enhanced quality and saved space was the "just-in-time" system, long used in Japanese car companies. Just-in-time means pacing deliveries from suppliers so that plants aren't storing more than a few hours' or a few days' supply of any given part. This system not only saves space and increases plant capacity, it also serves as a quality-control system, since plants don't have huge stocks available to cushion the impact of a high percentage of defects. Even though Fremont had much unutilized floor space, Toyota kept the work space tight to impress upon workers the essence of their philosophy of eliminating waste.

Work standardization amounted to a form of factory-floor choreography. Each team of workers had the responsibility for coordinating body movement, parts location, and time required to do its job. Once the team standardized its work, it found ways to constantly improve upon it. This was called *kaizen*—an ongoing attention to finding low-cost, incremental ways to improve productivity and quality. A second concept, *muda*, was the elimination of waste. At NUMMI, teams were encouraged to document any new efficiencies they discovered. Soon workers were using words like *kaizen* and *muda* as commonly as they once might have used "line speedup" and "grievance."

It was not only the hourly workers who were shocked by NUMMI; the salaried staff also found the environment very different. Stephen Bera was one of a group of sixteen GM executives assigned to NUMMI. Bera's area of expertise was production material control. He had been with GM for twenty years, working for Chevrolet, the AC Spark Plug division, and in central staff before joining NUMMI.

Bera thrived at NUMMI. "I went through a personality change out there," he admitted. "I felt better about working for Toyota. No more politics. No more doing things just for my own personal gain. The issue was, 'What's good for the company?' It was one hundred eighty degrees from everything I have ever done in my career." Until NUMMI, Bera said, his motivations were typical: "Do what is good for you as an individual . . . for promotions, for bonuses."

According to Bera, every member of the sixteen-member GM team went through a similar personal transformation. "I think everyone who went out there finally realized that it does no good for one person or one department to succeed. It's either the whole company succeeds or there's no benefit or gain."

This was not the lesson GM necessarily expected to learn from NUMMI. The technological solutions were expected to be more important than changing relationships among people. Bera recalled that he and the other group members were told, " 'Go to the joint venture and bring back this *magic* that exists in the Toyota production system.' So everyone went out there with just that in mind: 'Learn what you can. Learn your lessons well. You are going to help us alter the course of the company.'

"After the first few months, representatives from the corporation came out to California, sat with us, and basically said, 'We're looking to the future from you guys. How does it look to you right now?' Everyone said it was a fascinating experience—one that we had never encountered anywhere else in our careers. We gained so much, we learned our lessons well, and we reported back to the corporation through the personnel group."

Smith and McDonald visited too, eager to get the lowdown

on the NUMMI experience. "We had all the heads of state," Bera said. "They came to talk to us, to tell us, 'Give it your best shot, guys.' "

Of course, the team was already doing that. But the team had other concerns, as well—such as, how was the corporation geared for its repatriation? It was well and good to assign them for two years or so to learn the Japanese methodology, but then what?

"There was no answer to that question for the two years I was out there," Bera said. "No one could answer that question— no one could respond to each and every one of us and tell us just exactly how we were going to go back and give this new-found knowledge and experience to the corporation."

It wasn't that there was *no* corporate plan to incorporate the wisdom of NUMMI into the main body of the company. A liaison office was established near NUMMI whose job it was to make NUMMI techniques available to GM personnel. Videotape presentations and written materials describing NUMMI's production methods were produced, and tours of the NUMMI plant were given. But simply exposing GM personnel to NUMMI was not particularly meaningful from the standpoint of applying the NUMMI systems elsewhere in the company. For one thing, this type of exposure was too superficial to make a difference. More important, the Japanese-style business systems could hardly be implemented by random individuals throughout the company.

A 1986 report by James P. Womack, research associate with the Center for Technology, Policy and Industrial Development at MIT, made the point this way:

". . . plant tours, videotapes and manuals seem to be a poor substitute for hands-on experience. Recent interviews by the author with several manufacturing managers in the GM system who have been exposed to NUMMI instructional materials and taken on NUMMI tours reveal a very partial understanding of NUMMI's procedures, and in many cases a defensive conviction that NUMMI techniques can never work in their plant. In the words of one manager, 'All that NUMMI talk is pretty unpopular around here.' "

On the reverse side, the NUMMI employees felt that Toyota was deeply interested in the venture, and they received a lot of attention from top Toyota executives.

"The few times GM executives visited the plant, they did a

'five-minute fly-by,' " said one former NUMMI manager. "So no one believed they were really interested. GM didn't position itself to get maximum benefit from NUMMI because it lacked patience. GM wanted to learn everything in a day—that's a very American character trait. The same wasn't true for Toyota, and they seemed to get much more out of the venture."

In all likelihood, the question of how this learning experience would actually be applied was never considered. For one thing, it was expected that the answer would be technology, rather than people-oriented. It would have been so much easier if Bera and his fellow team members had returned to describe new equipment or production techniques. But, in fact, what the NUMMI team learned concerned a change in management philosophy, and company executives were no doubt reluctant to pursue this direction, for it touched the heart of what was culturally wrong with GM, and this could not be changed by one small experiment in a California town.

It is interesting to reflect about the direction GM was actually taking at the time. Consider the reorganization. It was a radical move, to be sure. But when all was said and done, the reorganization only addressed the issue of *bigness*. It did not shift the paradigm. NUMMI did. It was as though, having reached the conclusion that things didn't work (a giant step, to be sure), the company couldn't quite bring itself to go the next step—except in "experimental" projects like NUMMI or Saturn.

A former NUMMI executive expressed disappointment in how reluctant the company was to deploy the NUMMI team back into the corporation to spread their knowledge. In typical GM fashion, there was no place for them to return to. And so much animosity had developed toward NUMMI that any idea carrying its signature would never have been implemented. In fact, only one member of the team, Bob Hendry, a finance man, would move directly from NUMMI to run a production plant, and it was one of GM's most notorious plants in England. Hendry successfully changed the environment in that plant. Some left the company, others were absorbed into positions that didn't necessarily make use of what they had learned. In any case, the NUMMI "graduates" were merely tokens in the company. Given the system of rotating managers through the plant, at most only fifty managers could be NUMMI-trained by 1992. It appeared that the company wasn't prepared to learn organizational or people-oriented practices. It expected to learn mechanical or technological lessons.

It wasn't a deliberate lack of commitment. More likely, the implications had never been considered. Roger Smith billed NUMMI as an "educational experience," but his agenda may have been quite different. He may have (1) just wanted to quickly and inexpensively get a small car into production; (2) assumed that the lesson to be learned from the Japanese would be more tangible and less threatening to the General Motors culture; or (3) never really expected to learn from the Japanese as much as he hoped to shake up the company and force his own people to look at the competitive environment.

If Smith did plan to incorporate Japanese wisdom into the GM plants, his choice of method only reveals just how little understanding there was of the underlying reasons the NUMMI method worked so well. It proved how incredibly naïve American management could be when it came to understanding the foreign competition.

TEAM EXPERIMENT: VAN NUYS, CALIFORNIA

As the success of NUMMI filtered back to headquarters, GM synthesized it into its own version of "team concept," which it decided to try in some of its other plants. It did not, as might have been expected, utilize experienced NUMMI-trained executives for this task; its approach was an Americanized version that mimicked the Japanese wisdom only on the most superficial level.

More troubling still was the way GM instituted the plant experiment. Two plants would be pitted against one another— the one with the most efficiency would remain open and the losing plant would be closed. Van Nuys was up against Norwood, a suburban Cincinnati plant that also built Firebirds and Camaros.

From the start, it appeared that Norwood had a great advantage since it was more centrally located. Van Nuys was saddled with an estimated $400-per-car penalty for getting parts shipped to and cars shipped from the West Coast to markets east of the Mississippi.

But the plant manager, Ernest Schaefer, wasn't going to let

Van Nuys close down without a fight. A skilled negotiator and well-liked manager, Schaefer sat down with the union represent-atives and convinced them to join the fight. In this way, the GM version of the team concept was introduced to Van Nuys.

The first thing Schaefer did was send his people up to Fremont to observe the way NUMMI operated. Brian Haun remembers being impressed, but surprised to find an absence of high-tech tools. "I was amazed that they basically used 1950s technology, and they did a heck of a job with it. All the press lines were the same as the older types, except, of course, they were new presses. But it wasn't anything fancy."

What Haun saw was a study in plant efficiency. "The work-ers knew how to change a press line over in two hours. I watched them. I *studied* how they did it. If they wanted to rush, they could even change it in one hour."

The field trip was useful, but hardly sufficient to give the Van Nuys employees any real practical understanding of how to institute Japanese methods and philosophy in their own plant. And observing NUMMI couldn't accomplish the most important thing—to instill mutual trust and respect between workers and management. Van Nuys taught the lesson that you couldn't just shove a new philosophy down people's throats, without making it an integrated part of the corporate understanding. And you couldn't count on union support unless there was a consensus. Although a team of four NUMMI-based managers traveled to Van Nuys frequently during a period of several months to share what they had learned, there was still skepticism in the Van Nuys ranks. "We tried to act as consultants and preach the gospel of NUMMI," one of the four would say later. "But we weren't very good at it. Our approach was hard-sell, and that was the wrong way to convert these guys."

Ray Ruiz, the Van Nuys union chairman was in favor of the team concept. In his view, this was perhaps the only way the plant could survive the threat of plant closings. But there were hot debates in the union about the concept, and the primary issue was one of trust. What were GM's true motivations, union members asked suspiciously. Was this just a roundabout way of extracting concessions from the union?

Schaefer and Ruiz went to work on the workers, organizing mass meetings on each shift, asking for support from the work-ers on team concept. Union president Peter Beltran, who was opposed to the plan and called it "the most dangerous scheme ever conjured up by GM to rob workers of their union," pointed out that it wasn't team concept he was opposed to, it was GM's competition, pitting one plant against another. Argued Beltran, if GM expected a commitment from the workers, fine. Give the workers a commitment in return. "A more appropriate exchange for team concept," said Beltran, "would be a GM guarantee that the GM Van Nuys plant would remain open for at least ten years."

Ruiz had support for the plan among many workers, who saw it as a way to get more involved in the production process. Other workers stood behind Beltran. But one union member observed that "the majority are just resigned to it. They say, 'If GM says give us the team concept or we'll close the plant, why are we pretending we have a choice in the matter?' "

When the union members voted, they approved the team concept, but the vote was close and there was still dissent among the ranks. To make matters worse, Ray Ruiz was transferred to Detroit before the plan could get off the ground, and that gave Beltran new impetus because, with Ruiz leaving, a new chairman would have to be elected. Beltran's opposition to the plan hadn't meant as much when Ruiz was the chairman. The union president is relatively removed from the operation of individual plants. But with Ruiz out of the picture, Beltran decided to take a bold stand against the concept. He announced that he would run for chairman himself. He was determined to undermine the team concept at Van Nuys, no matter what it took.

According to Brian Haun, Beltran's opposition was a severe setback, but in many ways it was understandable. "He was an old-school type of guy who had been through some wildcat strikes," Haun explained. "I'm not sure he was completely wrong to say, 'I don't trust those guys'—GM management. They had not given that much reason to be trustworthy. His attitude was kind of that General Motors acts like they want what is good for people, but they don't give a shit and we need to take care of ourselves."

Until Beltran interfered, team concept was on track at Van Nuys, but the workers weren't really committed to the concept; rather, they resented the way they had been bullied into it with the threat that if they didn't go along, the plant would be closed. Beltran won the election.

"So now all the joint union-management committees that had been putting team concept together were dissolved," Haun said.

Part of the problem with implementing team concept at Van Nuys was that it wasn't ever fully understood as being beneficial to the workers or the company. It was merely billed as a way to increase efficiency—a red flag to union workers who perceived higher efficiency as leading naturally to worker layoffs. In fact, this was a legitimate concern. It was hoped that team concept would decrease head count at Van Nuys by as much as 25 percent.

Beltran was determined that this would not happen. The execution of team concept Beltran-style was a twisted version of the original intention that actually decreased efficiency. For example, before team concept, Haun supervised twenty people and had three relief people. When the concept was implemented under Beltran, teams of six were set up, with the plant hiring extra leaders. But the relief people, who were there to cover for absentees, were retained. The result was that Haun now supervised twenty-six people, not twenty-three. Overall in the body shop, at least ten people were added to the payroll.

Under Beltran, efficiency declined on the line, as well. Workers, who now had permission to halt production on the line when quality problems developed, were stopping the line so often that quality was actually decreased—and fewer cars were going out the door.

In plants where the concept was more fully explained, it wasn't perceived as a hoax on the work force. Rather, it was billed as a valuable competitive tool, a cohesive system where workers depend upon one another to be on time and do the job right. When a worker is accountable to his peers, not to a distant, oppressive supervisor, performance improves, because workers don't want to let the rest of the team down by not showing up for work or doing a shoddy job.

In spite of its poor execution of team concept, the Van Nuys plant won the contest against Norwood. In August 1987, the sixty-four-year-old Ohio facility was shut down and four thousand workers were laid off.

How could Van Nuys be the winner when its cost-per-car was $400 higher than Norwood's? President Jim McDonald would cite a number of reasons, including the age of the Norwood plant. But the real reason might have been that Norwood's workers had rejected team concept from the start. It was never implemented in the plant.

On April 21, 1988, Peter Beltran would be fired for absenteeism. GM said its investigation showed that Beltran lied in a February 23 letter when he said he missed thirty-eight days of work because of union business. Union vice president Michael Velasquez, who was also fired for signing the letter with Beltran, asserted that Beltran spent those thirty-eight days at union conferences or on paperwork.

It might be suggested that Van Nuys won the battle, but lost the war, since team concept was such a resounding failure. It wasn't all Beltran's fault. Japanese management techniques couldn't simply be overlaid haphazardly on an existing plant. NUMMI's success with team concept started with first selecting people who possessed some leadership qualities and who were open to working in teams. In most General Motors plants, a large percentage of the work force consisted of workers who had been in place for twenty or twenty-five years, and were more resistant to change. Ernie Schaeffer would eventually resolve the heated UAW debate. His successor at Van Nuys, Robert "Bob" Stramy, would bring about further improvements in cost savings and quality. But GM might have avoided many of the problems had it chosen to introduce team concept in a more legitimate way.

In setting up its team concept competition, GM once more fell victim to its habit of oversimplification. If putting workers into teams was the way to succeed, then put the workers into teams. But the team structure was only part of a much larger equation that included product, manufacturing system, plant layout, training, and company philosophy.

GM also ignored one of the most important lessons of all—the need to develop mutual trust between management and workers. Resentment was there from the start; the message that filtered down to the workers was that team concept was a sneaky maneuver to cut back on workers and, ultimately, to close plants. This was no way to establish trust! In pitting plants against one another for survival, General Motors actually may have created the reverse of its intended result—a more militant work force. The savvy union leadership in Van Nuys, for example, openly scorned the idea that in winning the competition they had really won anything at all—except time. What guarantee was there that the plant would stay open? In fact, it appears that Van Nuys will almost certainly be closed by the end of the decade, as the company deals with long-term issues of declining market share, excess capacity, and slow sales of Camaro and Firebird. Its location, with the added cost of shipping, simply doesn't make economic sense.

One of NUMMI's top executives—a veteran GMer—ranked the three most important lessons learned at NUMMI in this order:

1.   Establish good people relationships. This, not advanced technology, was the first priority.

2.   Recognize the value of a no-layoff policy. At NUMMI, this policy resulted in worker loyalty and increased productivity. The GM plants lacked such a policy, and workers were suspicious of management's motives.

3.   Pay attention to details. It was always on the details that Toyota won. GM paid more attention to the gross investment than it did to the small but all-important details, such as program timing.

Another executive, who was among the first group sent to NUMMI, summarized the lessons learned this way: "You have to create the right environment before you can accomplish anything. GM hasn't always understood the importance of establishing a nonconfrontational relationship with the UAW—it's doing better now, and I think that's because of what we learned at NUMMI. The Japanese system itself, with its constant follow-up on details, and ongoing improvements, helped create an environment where problems could get solved without confrontations. Contrary to the suspicions of many GM people, the Japanese system wasn't mysterious at all. It was simple and basic."

He noted that, in the beginning, the UAW was fearful of NUMMI. "They didn't really understand the concept, and many people thought it sounded like putting the fox in the chicken coop. But now the UAW has come around—they see how beneficial it's been for the workers. The UAW was impressed that, when sales of the Nova were weak, no one got laid off."

In October 1985, the General Motors in-house publication,

GM Today, spotlighted two workers who were rehired at the Fremont plant when NUMMI took over its operation. They were Rick Madrid and Santos Martinez. As team leader, Madrid was sent to Japan for training. "I was part of the media blitz," he said. "Management told me to talk to the press and explain what things were like. They put complete trust in me. Because of that, trust is now mutual."

Martinez echoed the sentiment. "I learned a different meaning for the word respect—one that doesn't include fear," he said. "My responsibility now is to the team, which works together like a family to solve problems and do the job. And no one places blame when something goes wrong."

Madrid and Martinez were sold on the team concept. Their transformation as workers was the direct result of the management practices employed at NUMMI. But on the Fourteenth Floor, far removed from the factories and showrooms, sat long-time GM executives who still could not trust the evidence. And so, the company continued to pay lip service to NUMMI, with plant tours and instructional videos, but it did not move aggressively to package the lessons learned at NUMMI for application in all of its plants.

It seemed that what GM was about was spinning plates in the air. There were several programs going on simultaneously, each with the mission of making the company more competitive, but there was a lack of coordination among the many efforts, and no central system for evaluating them. Was NUMMI the answer? The CPC system? BOC? Spending more on technology? Saturn? In one executive meeting, the question was raised, "Now that twenty-five studies of NUMMI have been completed and a thousand GM people have gone through NUMMI, can we say what the secret of NUMMI is and introduce it to the rest of the company?" The answer was lost in a tremendous debate that led to no conclusion, except that no one on the Executive Committee seemed to have the will to institutionalize change.

To this day, there are those within General Motors who have closed their minds and ears to NUMMI, taking a stance of "I don't want to hear it; it's a Japanese system of thought." Al Warren says this is true, "but we've done a pretty good job evangelizing about NUMMI, and there's a lot more willingness to listen than there used to be."

Resistance has also come from some old-guard managers

and unionists who view the prospect of management-labor co-operation with dread. Some union officials still complain that getting into bed with management will weaken the unions and cost jobs. In their book, *Choosing Sides: Unions and the Team Concept,* former autoworkers Mike Parker and Jane Slaughter railed against the team concept, calling it "management by stress"—a system that was built upon regimentation of workers and job insecurity.

But according to Bruce Lee, director of the United Automobile Workers' western region, that argument, and most other complaints, represent uninformed views. Lee noted in a 1988 *New York Times* article that there is no record of Parker or Slaughter ever stepping foot inside NUMMI, and that their viewpoint is based on fallacy. Wrote Lee, "NUMMI is now at the leading edge of a sea change taking place in American factory management. Decades of managerial arrogance and disregard for the consumer cost American industry hundreds of plants and millions of jobs. Today, at the eleventh hour, progressive companies pushed by progressive unions are finally beginning to put those disastrous mistakes right."

One reason it may be so difficult for some American workers to accept the Japanese labor ideology is that the concept of "continuous improvement" is anathema to their fundamental ideas of what it means to be a productive worker. In the American ideal, the payoff for developing more efficient systems is that the work becomes less demanding. In the Japanese system, the successful solving of one problem simply opens up a new, more difficult, challenge. What some NUMMI workers have termed "management by stress" is really an operating philosophy that never allows workers to stop striving for betterment.

In spite of its struggle to understand and incorporate the NUMMI learning experience, GM has gradually started to come around. Increasingly, the NUMMI-trained managers are being relocated to factories where they can transfer what they've learned. And with the wisdom of hindsight, one former NUMMI manager suggested that it may have been a good thing that the company didn't try to use the NUMMI graduates too forcefully in the beginning.

"We were like religious zealots," he laughed. "We wanted to spread our message to all of GM, but we weren't very sensitive to the concerns of the unconverted. It's no wonder that people got hostile. NUMMI graduates would go into their plants and act superior to everyone else. In some plants, they'd even form little clubs. We'd try to force the NUMMI concepts down people's throats and tell them how much they had to change. It was ineffective. It's not like that anymore, because more people are knowledgeable about it, and the company is more accepting."

The NUMMI joint venture has a legal cutoff date of 1996, but neither GM nor Toyota has made specific plans for what will happen to the work force. "I have to confess I haven't thought of it," Al Warren hedges. "Time goes by more quickly than you think it does. That's a tremendous work force and they have done a tremendous job. They are now a reservoir of a process that maybe we don't have anymore, and I think we have to look at that."

Now that Toyota has decided to build trucks at NUMMI, the possibility has arisen that Toyota will take over the entire plant when production of the current product, the Prizm, is completed.

General Motors and Ross Perot:

A Match Made in Detroit

Life's a spider web, not a corporate flow chart. You never know how these connections will relate. If money is your God, you're going to chase it all your life. I know a lot of rich guys who never have any fun. I have a lot of fun. I do everything I want.

— H. Ross Perot

H. Ross Perot had never given a thought to selling his Dallas-based firm, Electronic Data Systems. EDS was prospering—it ranked third in the fast-growing computer services industry and was well on its way to reaching a goal of $1 billion in revenues and $100 million in profit by 1987.

When John Gutfreund, the chairman of Salomon Brothers, approached him with the possibility that GM might want to acquire his company, Perot was surprised. But, he said, "When a company the size of GM approaches, you have to consider it. We were flattered they came to us. In fact, I'm surprised they ever heard of us."

Roger Smith had approached Gutfreund informally about GM's interest in making high-tech acquisitions, although exactly what constituted high tech was never spelled out. The company, he said, had to have a potential for synergy with General Motors. Although Smith was vague regarding the nature of the technology he was interested in, Salomon Brothers' investment bankers believed EDS might be a good match for the automaker.

In late 1983, Salomon Brothers made a presentation to GM treasurer Courtney Jones regarding EDS and other potential takeover candidates and told him the firm believed the business systems company could be for sale at the right price. Jones studied the report on EDS over Christmas at his Long Island home, and immediately began to visualize the possibilities. In spite of its heavy investment in new manufacturing technology, GM's utilization of data processing systems verged on the archaic. Previous attempts to computerize had led to the purchase of more than one hundred mainframes, but there was no centralized system to link the computer operations. Each group or division had its own hardware and software, so, for example, a design group could not interact with production engineers via computer; data were transmitted by paper and reentered into the noncompatible computer. It was a system whose inefficiency, according to one analyst, cost GM roughly $600 million a year. With no centralized data-processing system, it was impossible to coordinate operations from one department to another. The company desperately needed an integration of its data-processing functions.

"The whole idea of advanced business systems appealed to me," said Jones. "I had seen many, many instances where our ability to develop systems, particularly integrated systems, throughout our company was not at all up to the business challenge that we were facing. And, of course, by then we were looking at the Japanese. We were trying to think of what on earth would ever meet this competitive challenge. It was a combination of technology in its fullest form—all the way from the technology you use to process business transactions, to the technology that's inherent in your product, to the technology that's in your manufacturing processes."

Another attraction of EDS was the promise of what it could do to standardize the data-processing requirements of transactions between dealers and car divisions.

"A number of us had talked over the years about each dealer having a computer terminal on his desk instead of filling out all these crazy forms," Jones said. "When I was assistant comptroller at Pontiac, I once had to come to New York to assist a Brooklyn dealer with the paperwork that ran through his system. I became aware that he was absolutely *buried* in paper."

Roger Smith had also spoken of developing a state-of-the-art system with dealers for the Saturn project. His concept was a computer system that would link dealers to GMAC, the company's financial subsidiary. Customers could order their cars and arrange financing through showroom terminals.

GM wanted to bring its $2.3-billion health care costs under control (it was using 187 different carriers), and EDS had special expertise in processing health care claims.

Jones said that when they looked at companies that might be adept at handling GM's broad needs, "EDS had the most muscle. It wasn't what you'd call a real intellectual house, but they were very tightly run, with a tremendous appetite for work. They just never let up—and that's what we needed."

Once Roger Smith was convinced that EDS was the right company, he set out to court Perot. In Dallas to deliver a speech, he stopped in at EDS headquarters and the two men hit it off immediately.

"The early negotiations started off with a tremendous romance between Ross and Roger," corporate counsel Elmer Johnson would recall. "They really fell in love with each other. I think in Ross, Roger felt he had found his true partner in saving General Motors. And Ross felt this was going to be a new, creative stage in his life."

Courtney Jones agreed. "They appeared to be very taken with each other. Roger's a bit of a homespun chap, too, and Ross can lay that stuff on as well as anybody. There were several occasions when they walked off into the sun together and came back glowing. They both saw a great future together."

Roger Smith had a history of being attracted to people and companies that were very different from himself or the company he ran. Perhaps it was a yearning to change GM by introducing a successful example of how things could work differently. NUMMI was one such move. Now he brought in Perot and EDS and gave them unprecedented freedom in the takeover. In EDS, he found a unique organization, a reflection of the quirky entrepreneurial spirit of its founder. Ross Perot was cut from a different mold than the typical businessman. He was a creative genius and a quick-change artist who moved comfortably in and out of the many roles he played. One day an evangelist, the next an army general, he was fascinating to watch, a true charismatic leader the likes of which General Motors had not seen for a long time. He lent credence to the reputation Texans had for making grand gestures.

All his life Perot had felt restless—he was scrappy and ingenious and easily lured by the promise of adventure. He especially liked it when the stakes were high, and once he set his mind on a course of action, he never gave up. He'd started EDS in 1962 on a wing and a prayer, and the company had made him a billionaire.

In the late 1970s, Perot gained notoriety in the United States when he set up an operation to rescue two of his employees who were being held hostage in Iran. This was company loyalty carried to an extreme that only Perot would dare.

EDS's contract with the government of Iran's social security system placed two employees in the country at the time of the Khomeini takeover. The employees were arrested and held for a hefty ransom of $12.75 million. Perot would have paid the ransom if he thought it would secure the release of the employees. But it was hard to be sure of anything in the chaotic early days of the Ayatollah's regime. So Perot decided to go to Iran himself.

The Washington Post would later detail the escapade in a story by Michael Schrage and Warren Brown:

Wearing tourist garb, he [Perot] strode past the wire-tufted steel gates and the prison guards. Ramsey Clark, a fellow Texan, was there on a separate observer mission but failed to recognize Perot. He signed his name in the official prison registry—a good Presbyterian and stern moralist of the old school, he wasn't deceitful—initial "H" for Henry, initial "R" for Ross, Perot. Nobody called the Ministry of Justice, where the name would have stirred up a hornet's nest.

The small, wiry man with the broken nose of a bantam-weight boxer strode into the central compound of Iran's greatest prison like he owned the place.

"My God," said one of his long-secluded employees, "It's Ross . . .

"Can you believe this?" the man nudged his jailmate. "Perot's here."

Perot embraced his incredulous friends, gave them food, and a few words from home. "There's some long underwear in here for you," he said, thrusting a box at them. "We couldn't buy any, so this is mine and I want it back, you hear?"

Perot promised to get the men out. They promised to return his underwear.

A few weeks later, a commando team, secretly drilled at Perot's lakeside summer home near Dallas, instigated an angry mob which broke into the prison. The two employees of Perot's EDS fled through the rubble and eventually escaped to freedom with the aid of Perot's elite squad.

Not your ordinary businessman. But it was certainly not unlike Perot to stage a daring rescue when his employees' lives were in danger. He knew no distinctions between business and family loyalty. In Perot's way of thinking, you wouldn't hire people to work in your company for whom you would not also risk your life.

Perot ran EDS like a brotherhood, alternating an iron fist with a velvet glove. (In the early days of the company, employees sometimes referred to the EDS management philosophy as the Faith.) On one hand, he imposed a rigid morality in the manner of a righteous southern Protestant. Candidates for employment were rigorously screened, and would be rejected if even the smallest detail didn't line up correctly. EDS imposed a strict twelve-point code of ethics that included everything from use of drugs and drinking on the job to lighting a cigarette on the premises or discussing one's salary with a fellow employee.

On the other hand, Perot was a generous, hands-on manager, quick to reward those who did well. He estimated that he spent an average of $40,000 per employee for training (which he made people repay if they left the company before two years). An EDS staffer once made the statement that "I'd go to hell on a pair of roller skates if he asked me to, and he'd do the same for me."

EDS could sometimes feel like boot camp, with Perot playing the role of unbudgeable drill sergeant. "Can't" was a word not allowed on the premises. He pushed employees to their limits, expecting them to do the impossible. He nurtured them and prodded them and pushed them. The important thing was the goal—to get the job done, no matter what. This dedication didn't always translate into financial reward. Although the myth

at EDS was that if you work hard, you get ahead, only a handful
of EDSers made it onto the gravy train.

It is not surprising that the people attracted to this unique
work environment tended to be young, eager, and willing to
work hard for low pay. Perot gave special preference to Vietnam
veterans, knowing that proven heroes would not be reluctant to
give their utmost to the task at hand.

By the time General Motors came knocking on the door,
EDS had six thousand employees and a long list of prestigious
clients, though none in manufacturing. The timing seemed just
right for Ross Perot—he needed a new adventure.

It is hard to imagine a more bizarre match than General
Motors, the slow, bureaucratized giant, and EDS, the scrappy
gang of Perot loyalists. Perot himself, on his first visit to Detroit,
told Roger Smith that he didn't think acquisition was the solution. "Roger, you don't have to buy a dairy to get milk," Perot
said. "We'll sell you service."

Smith wanted to own EDS, but Perot was deliberately hedg-
ing. Though intrigued with the challenge of getting involved in
what he perceived to be the great industrial rescue mission of
the century—saving General Motors—he wondered if EDS and
GM could possibly find a happy meeting ground between their
two radically different cultures.

"If you cut a finger at EDS, you'd go down to the doctor's
office, get it sewed up and go home," he said, describing the
difference between the two companies. "Cut your finger at a
company like General Motors, you go in the hospital on Thurs-
day, lie around there until Tuesday afternoon, get a suntan, and
leave with a hearing aid and orthopedic shoes."

From the start, he realized that it would be disastrous for
EDS to simply be swallowed up in the GM culture. He set out
to negotiate a deal, based on the promise that EDS would maintain independence. Smith was willing to accommodate this because he maintained that he wanted the unique EDS culture as
a motivation for his own work force. He instructed Courtney
Jones, and the acquisition team who were handling the negotiations, to put together a deal that included a method of linking
rewards to EDS's performance, and a plan for maintaining its
separation from GM to protect the Dallas company's unique
culture and personnel policies.

It was from this mandate that a plan evolved which resulted in the creation of the first "alphabet" stock. EDS, it was agreed, would operate as a separate profit center, with GM contracting its data processing and other systems work on a cost-plus basis, and later moving to fixed-price contracts. To further sweeten the deal, GM would issue a separate class of stock (called Class E), the value of which would be determined in the stock market by the performance of EDS, and the dividends would be paid, equal to 25 percent of the previous year's earnings. Current EDS stockholders would be offered a choice of trading in their shares for $44 per share in cash, or accepting a package of $33.20 in cash, one fifth of a share of the Class E stock, and a contingent promissory note that guaranteed a 16-percent return for those who held their shares from five to seven years. GM would issue 13.6 million Class E shares immediately, with 22.6 million more shares to be issued by October 18, 1986. In addition, they agreed to authorize 20 million shares for an EDS employee incentive plan and 10 million for an EDS employee stock purchase plan.

The complete offer had a value of $2.55 billion, the largest acquisition GM had ever made. It was agreed to and a statement of intent was announced on June 28, 1984—coincidentally, Ross Perot's birthday. A few days later, Perot was elected a member of the board of directors of General Motors.

Until the last minute there were many, including EDS President Mort Meyerson, who thought the deal would never go through, and that ultimately EDS would simply get a contract to handle data processing for GM. There were also doubters on the GM side, including board members and individuals on the Executive Committee, who questioned the value of EDS, were leery of Perot, and failed to see how EDS could make a substantial contribution to GM's high-tech direction. But few were willing to be openly critical of Smith, so he got his way. In fact, Smith was so convinced of the deal's merits, that one associate who tried to alert him to his concerns about Perot was excised from the chairman's inner circle.

But as Roger Smith and Ross Perot were shaking hands on what they billed as a synergistic relationship, each man perceived reality in a different way. Smith believed he could bring Ross Perot into his camp as a team player—a ludicrous idea for anyone even vaguely familiar with Perot's modus operandi.

Perot, on the other hand, believed that he could infuse GM with the messianic zeal he had brought to EDS. It was an equally ludicrous idea. The rude awakening would come before the marriage was even consummated.

In the excitement of doing the deal, two rather critical details remained unsettled: the strategy for integrating EDS into the company, and the strategy for moving ten thousand GM employees into EDS. Mort Meyerson chose Kenneth Riedlinger, an executive vice president, to undertake the transition and head up the GM effort. Riedlinger would have to summon all the lessons he learned from his days as a Catholic lay missionary to travel the unfamiliar corridors of the Detroit auto giant.

The fact that Roger Smith hadn't included the GM leadership—specifically, Jim McDonald and Alex Cunningham—in discussions about an acquisition that would dramatically affect their spheres of influence made Riedlinger's job all the more difficult. "Nobody knew what the deal was," he said. "Roger Smith was totally sold on the idea of revolutionizing General Motors from a business data-processing standpoint. It was a good idea, but it was totally beyond Roger Smith's authority to see that it would be carried out. He had no backing from anyone else in General Motors.

"I drafted the announcement for Roger Smith to sign that went to the GM people. We *made up* the scope of EDS's authority and responsibility. It had never been negotiated and absolutely no plans were made. There was not a single piece of paper given to me that said, 'Here's the plan.'"

The announcement Riedlinger drafted for Roger Smith was a typical press release—heavy on self-congratulations and light on details. "People said, 'Telecommunications? What does that mean?'" Riedlinger recalled. "Mort came up with a concept that telecommunications meant everything from a satellite to the black telephone handset on the desk. That and everything in between was EDS's responsibility."

In the wake of the announcement, shock waves coursed through the GM data-processing staff, who were hearing for the first time that they would no longer be working for General Motors, but for a new company, EDS. An initial meeting with the employees, chaired by Meyerson and Riedlinger, turned into a nightmare. "They were yelling obscenities, and the whole thing got off to an absolutely ludicrous beginning," said Riedlinger.

"These were people who were key data-processing managers. They'd been told nothing. Their bosses were told nothing. I remember one guy who worked for Lloyd Reuss said, 'Obscenity, obscenity . . . just wait until Lloyd Reuss hears about this!' The whole thing was just ridiculous."

The EDS deal seemed thrown together without any semblance of a plan for how it would be executed, or any sense of the real implications for GM. And once again, lack of communication from the top led to near revolt in the GM ranks. Smith had focused his attention on making the deal, then left it to others to sort out the logistics. But how could he have been so insensitive to the tremendous implications of announcing that ten thousand workers (already shell-shocked from the rigors of reorganization) would now work for a company peopled by near-religious fanatics, and founded upon principles that would make General Patton shudder? Why did he make no effort to cushion the blow—in particular, the fact that these suddenly ex-GM employees would no longer be entitled to the generous company benefits—nor would they be entitled to their pensions. Instead they would receive Class E stock. Eventually GM wound up in litigation with its employees over these issues, and the company prevailed. But it lost hundreds of experienced data-processing people, who left to find lucrative jobs elsewhere.

Riedlinger would have appreciated a little help from the top layers of GM management, even if it was only a pep talk to the employees. But there was silence at the top while emotions spilled out at the bottom. "There were some people who had been at Fisher Body and they'd just been taken out of Fisher and put in BOC or CPC," said Riedlinger. "They were still refusing to accept the fact that they no longer worked for Fisher, but General Motors. We had guys two or three generations back who didn't even accept General Motors as their employer, let alone some outfit called EDS. It was a firestorm of emotion."

By the time the acquisition was formalized in October 1984, open hostility existed between the two companies, with Riedlinger in the middle trying to smooth ruffled feathers on both sides.

It didn't help matters that the EDS employees who accepted transfers from Dallas landed like the troops on Normandy Beach. To GMers, the EDS zealots might as well have been invaders from Mars. They had an attitude that was decidedly not GM—a smug we're-here-to-save-you demeanor. "GM just spent two point six billion dollars to buy EDS," grumbled one employee. "And they come into our area like gangbusters, like they just bought GM." In fact, among EDSers, the event was, and still is, referred to as a *merger,* which has a distinctly different connotation from an *acquisition.*

The cynicism among data processors was so deep that after EDSers had gone through one office, putting red dot stickers on the equipment they now claimed, the GM transfers began sporting the stickers on their foreheads. Totally tasteless jokes made the rounds; some were even printed and circulated throughout the company: "Why did California get AIDS and Michigan get EDS? California had first choice."

One employee observed bitterly that "if Roger Smith were to walk into our building today, he'd never get out alive. We'd nail his hide to the wall."

EDS staff were of the opinion that the GMers who had complaints were just lazy; they didn't want to work harder and lose their cushy benefits. To better educate people in "how we do things," Perot arranged for middle- and upper-level managers to attend three-day training sessions in Dallas, which included a classic call to arms.

But by November, petitions were being circulated asking for union representation for the nonunionized GM data processors. The UAW called a general meeting to discuss the petition drive—and it promised to support the workers' rights.

Said one union official, "These are people who go to work expecting a career with GM, an uninterrupted one, a chance to work with GM, the most prestigious company in the United States for the rest of their natural lives. Then all of a sudden, the carpet is pulled out from under them and they are totally abandoned by GM for a company with a totally different philosophy."

EDS took the stand that they would not tolerate unionization. "Labor unions have no place in EDS," Riedlinger wrote in a memo to GM data processors, "and we intend to do everything legally and ethically possible to prevent a single unit from being organized' . . . I want each of you to understand my firm commitment to oppose these current unionization efforts until total victory is ours: yours and mine."

He meant it. In January 1986, the UAW gave up the fight, citing the futility of trying to overcome EDS's endless string of obstacles, which included splitting up a group of workers with prounion leanings. Troublemakers were fired or laid off, and replaced with inexperienced young workers who would obediently perform jobs for less money.

EDS had taken over the data-processing operations of other companies and was accustomed to trouble-free transitions. But they had never tackled anything of the magnitude of GM. This was different. For one thing, EDS's benefits were usually better than those of the data-processing departments they were taking over—and this was definitely not the case with GM. "People were incredibly overpaid," Riedlinger said. "Because of all those automatic raises over the years, they had people who were horribly overpaid. They had people who did three hours' worth of work in eight hours on the job."

And then there was the work style. As Courtney Jones observed, the EDS staffers were high-energy, nonstop workers. "Those folks are less paternalistic than the GM people," he said. "The EDS staff told stories about people with lackadaisical work habits ingesting various substances on the job—and that horrified them. I know some of them felt very deeply that some of those GM workers were terrible folks."

In the midst of this hostile environment, Riedlinger was faced with a potentially more serious problem. The GM divisions were balking at giving EDS contracts, because they quickly figured out that data-processing costs would go up under the EDS system. They didn't understand the cost-plus price structure and were suspicious that EDS was overcharging them. GM already had a history of bad experiences with the cost-plus system, so it's amazing they allowed themselves to get trapped in this arrangement with EDS. A similar system that operated between the component groups and the car divisions had demonstrated that when prices were tied to costs, there was little or no incentive to keep the costs down. As profit centers themselves, the component groups were simply interested in making as much as they could, and would report billions in profits while the car divisions lost billions. In the case of EDS, it was even more illogical, since the value of the E stock was directly tied to earnings. Even when fixed-price contracts were eventually established, the pricing problems weren't solved. One executive complained that a four-month rental of a portable computer would cost his department $1,700. His solution was to charge it on his credit card for $180. He also found that EDS was charging for his phone, phone line, and every feature and every call at more than 30 percent above the going rate.

Riedlinger was working at a furious pace, trying to get negotiations off the ground because "these contracts take six months to a year when you've got people on both sides who *want* to do the contract, and in the case of General Motors, they didn't *want* to do the contracts."

In Dallas, Mort Meyerson was losing his patience, and he began calling Riedlinger several times a day. "He would have perceptions based on what somebody told him or what he read in the newspaper or something he invented in his own mind. I started resisting him and telling him why such and such didn't make sense. Our relationship got just unbelievable. He would call up and start screaming and yelling, but even so, I told myself these things all will pass."

In one sense, he was right. In April 1985, at a board meeting in Dallas, Roger Smith expressed dismay that the process of finalizing contracts was going so slowly. So Mort Meyerson announced that all the contracts would be negotiated and signed within ninety days.

"There was a great hurrah," Riedlinger remembers, "and everybody started dancing around. It was a carnival atmosphere. The General Motors people said, 'Good, that's settled,' and they all jumped on their plane and went back to Detroit. We had a little meeting of the EDS officers and everyone was jumping up and down, and someone said, 'Hell, we won't make a billion dollars next year—we'll make *five* billion off these guys.' People were going berserk and I just sat there. It was like the inmates were loose.

"Then Mort said, 'Well, Riedlinger, why are you sitting there so quietly?'

"I said, 'There's nothing to say. You already announced that we're going to sign all these fixed-price contracts in ninety days.'

"He looked at me. 'Well, you're going to do that, aren't you?'

" 'Mort,' I said—and I was tired, 'I'm not going to fight with you. You've already announced that we're going to do it and we're having a carnival celebration here in anticipation of the five billion dollars we're going to make next year. That's an impossible task, but I'll go back and work twenty-eight hours

a day to try to do that because that's what you said we're going to do.'

"He just went white, dismissed the meeting, and called me
into his office, and he virtually had a breakdown—screaming,
yelling, calling me names."

" 'Mort,' I said, 'I'm a grown man. I'm forty-five years old.
I've got a lot of stock. I just don't need that crap anymore. I can't
conceive, if this is what you really think of me, why you would
want me to work for you.' His answer was that of course he
wanted me to work for him. He just wanted to beat me up—he'd
done it a hundred times before, and he thought he'd do it
another hundred times. I told him I would never work for him
again. I packed my briefcase and left."

Riedlinger was replaced with EDS vice president Kennard
Hill, who inherited the thorny task of settling the contract issue.
It would not be until early 1986 that the two companies would
reach at least a temporary truce, and 1988, when 60 percent of
the business with GM was covered by contracts. The agreement
gave GM managers the right to choose from different options,
including a catalog, longer-term fixed-price contracts, or a cost-
based incentive system. The catalog concept was a way to ease
GM suspicions that EDS was overcharging for services; it outlined uniform published rates so managers could be sure EDS
was competitive.

It would take longer for GM data processors to accept the
transfer. This boxed advertisement, paid for by eight trans-
ferees, appeared in the May 21, 1986, issue of the *Detroit Free
Press:*

An Open Letter
to General Motors

We are your older, loyal, longtime data employees that were
arbitrarily transferred to your Electronic Data Systems acquisition in 1985. At that time, we lost all the promised GM benefits
and retirement after 30 years that other GM employees of all
divisions presently enjoy. We feel as older employees that we
suffer the greatest loss. It's time for Roger Smith and the board
of directors to respond to the following questions:

1. Why were your data employees selectively discriminated
against? Is GM's commitment to some employees to be hon-
ored, and not to others?
2. Why were Delco employees who are to be transitioned

to your Hughes acquisition* allowed to keep their GM benefits and we were not?

3.   If data employees were treated so fairly . . . and EDS is such a progressive place to work, why are more upset today than they were at the beginning? Why did almost a thousand employees take early retirement, or quit outright, rather than transfer to EDS, and why are many more leaving every day?

It's time for General Motors to show all employees that they are a fair and honorable corporation and stop pretending that no problems exist. We would ask if any GM executive would willingly trade his GM benefits and retirement for Class E stock worth a fraction of the value? We think not.

You can no longer ignore the grave injustice to your data employees. Other GM employees are concerned that they may receive the same "fair treatment" we received. Now is the time to resolve this problem and prove that "people really are your most important asset." Do we deserve anything less?

A GM Data Employee

By late 1986, EDS had tripled its size, with General Motors accounting for three quarters of its work and an estimated $2.4 billion in revenue. In spite of the skirmishes, EDS had successfully mounted the hill and placed its flag on GM soil. But to this day, the majority of people involved wonder if the acquisition was worth it. And Roger Smith quickly grew disenchanted with his new partner, Ross Perot, who seemed intent on acting on his personal agenda of transforming the culture of General Motors—and stirring up plenty of trouble in the process. Although Smith claimed to want Perot on board because he was an independent thinker, it seemed unlikely that he really wanted that. GM boardroom etiquette required quiet compliance with executive directives. Meetings were somber affairs, with little discussion and no criticism. Into this collegial atmosphere stepped H. Ross Perot. Perot was not about to change character. Independent he would be—both inside and outside the boardroom. Smith might have been enamored of the *idea* of Perot. But he would soon lose patience with the reality of his new straight-shooting board member.

*The Hughes acquisition was made in 1986.

High-Speed Change:
Traveling in Many Orbits

You talk to a Hughes man. He's not building a missile. He's got a whole system to shoot down an aircraft. He can detect it, find it, zero in on it, target it, destroy it, and then get it back to base. That's the way he thinks. And that's the kind of thinking we need for GM. We're not trying to build a clutch. We're trying to build an automobile that has a clutch in it.

—Roger Smith

By 1985, the Saturn project had become a giant media event, propelled by a steady stream of tantalizing announcements from Roger Smith's office. Even Lee Iacocca, a master at creating the big media splash, expressed grudging admiration. In his book, *Talking Straight,* Iacocca admitted that "I was envious. Not because I thought the car was great, but because as a huckster myself I hadn't thought of the PR scam first."

The prototypes of the car remained generalized, and no one knew what this new vehicle would look like, but to listen to the hype, one might almost expect that it would be able to fly.

With the promise of Saturn, the world was suddenly Roger Smith's oyster. When he announced that General Motors would accept bids from governors to locate the new high-tech plant in their state, the drama moved into high gear. It was a nationwide *The Price Is Right,* with states doing everything in their power to win the prize. Seven governors even appeared with Smith on the

Phil Donahue show. Smith spent fifteen minutes giving the Saturn pitch, and the governors spent the remainder of the show practicing unashamed one-upmanship as they boasted that each of their states would be the best choice for the new plant.

"Choose me!" the states were crying, mouths watering over the promise of the estimated twenty thousand new jobs and accompanying economic growth the plant would bring—not just low-paying factory jobs, but lucrative high-tech positions. The states viewed Saturn as the nucleus of a high-tech industrial base—a kind of new order, requiring highly trained individuals with skills well above those of the typical autoworker. New York even offered to establish a branch of the state university on the plant grounds. Thirty-eight states submitted proposals, often accompanied by promotion efforts and unprecedented deal-sweetening offers. Missouri erected self-promotional billboards on Detroit highways; New York accompanied its bid with a prototype Saturn license plate (hand-delivered by Governor Mario Cuomo); Ohio sent hundreds of thousands of letters to Roger Smith, mostly from schoolchildren. States flooded GM with offers of free land, tax abatements, and other incentives.

Youngstown State University's director of labor studies, John Russo, pointed out that GM's gambit (which he called "Saturnmania") was more indicative of corporate political game-playing than it was community involvement, since even while GM was dangling the carrot in front of the states, it was threatening to close plants in other locations. Said Russo of the competition to win Saturn, "It involved politicians and community leaders offering the world's largest industrial corporation tax abatements and exemptions, utility rate reductions, industrial revenue bonds, new highways and access routes, union-free atmospheres, and free land and training.

"Overall, Saturn's influence on the public consciousness is indicative of just how easily global corporations can shape the national economic debate, using sophisticated public relations techniques along with a measure of old-fashioned economic blackmail."

General Motors planned to hold out on a final announcement of the site until the Saturn labor contract was nailed down. The proposals GM was making to the UAW were substantially different from what they were accustomed to—including wages at only 80 percent of current rates; bonuses for performance, quality, and work attendance; and flexible work rules that would allow GM to shift workers from one job to another. It would have been a tough package to sell to the UAW, had not the UAW's representatives been involved in the Saturn plans since 1983. Their participation smoothed the way for an innovative contract.

The final plan was very close to what GM had originally asked for, with a tremendous amount of flexibility built into work rules and guaranteed salaries rather than hourly wages. In exchange for labor's agreement, GM promised lifetime job security to 80 percent of Saturn's workers and told them they would continue to have an important voice in the decision-making process.

The winner in the Saturn sweepstakes, announced by Smith in July 1985, was Spring Hill, Tennessee, a small town of eleven hundred people, about thirty miles south of Nashville. According to GM executives, the final selection was based on consideration of more than sixty different factors—including its attractive location as a central United States shipping point. But cynics suggested that Spring Hill might also have been chosen because of pressure from the UAW. Thirty miles from the proposed Saturn site is the nonunion Nissan plant that the UAW had been trying unsuccessfully to organize for years. With UAW influence enhanced in the area through the Saturn plant, it was thought that Nissan would ultimately be unable to resist union overtures. Saturn would be staffed with veteran GM employees, not Spring Hill natives, so it was believed that they would infuse the area with a prounion spirit. But the Saturn employees would be a different breed, since they preselected themselves to accept the new order of Saturn. So it wasn't traditional unionism they brought with them, but potentially something more palatable.

Named president of the new company was Bill Hoglund, now promoted to vice president and group executive in charge of operating staffs. As former head of Pontiac, Hoglund was widely credited with revitalizing the division. He landed the Saturn job by default; the original president, Joe Sanchez, died three weeks after he was named to the position.

Hoglund was a well-regarded, independent corporate executive, seen by many as a breath of fresh air at GM. Even his office style set him apart—his chair was a red-and-gray bucket seat from the 1984 Pontiac Fiero Indy pace car. Since he was already talked about as a potential candidate for chairman or president, his selection was designed to telegraph a message that GM took Saturn seriously.

A brand-new industrial partnership emerged as Hoglund and UAW vice president Donald Ephlin refined the plan that would have labor and management working hand in hand as equal partners. The early plans proposed a complete upending of the traditional hierarchical structure, replacing it with management-labor committees. These would include:

1.   Strategic Advisory Committee for long-term planning. This committee would involve the Saturn president and his staff, and the top UAW advisor. Hoglund and Ephlin had already set this process in motion.

2.   Manufacturing Advisory Committee for supervision of the plant. This committee would include company representatives, elected UAW members, and specialists in engineering, design, and production.

3.   Business Unit to coordinate plant-level operations. This committee would be made up of on-site managers, specialists, and UAW representatives.

4.   Work Unit Module—the divisional team structure, made up of three to six work units, led by a "work unit advisor."

5.   Work Units—Teams of six to fifteen workers, led by a UAW "counselor."

While the approach was widely applauded as utilizing the best elements of Japanese business practice, not everyone agreed that such a mating of management and labor was viable. For example, some labor officials were concerned that under the guise of gaining equality, they would really lose power and future benefits for workers. To some extent, these detractors argued, the adversarial relationship between labor and management provided a necessary check-and-balance, and guaranteed that the workers would have a protective body looking out for their needs alone. Ephlin disagreed, saying that management and labor alike had to "face up to the challenge, to recognize that we have to change the way we do business because we are suffering and losing our industrial base to very tough competitors. And if we'd like to compete, we'd better be good."

So effective was the GM public relations effort on Saturn that few people did the math that would have made them realize that the level of investment GM was predicting over six years—about $5 billion—would generate automatic fixed costs of about $2,000 on each car, assuming 500,000 cars per year—a hefty bite for a car that was billed as a cheap import-fighter. One defense of the high costs was to remind people that Saturn was, first and foremost, a catalytic agent, a new business process, as much as it was a new product. But processes can't be displayed in showrooms. You can't drive a process. The concept may have been brilliant, but when the smoke cleared, there had to be a profitable and desirable car on the other end. And that meant that the customer had to perceive the car as having value for his needs—and being reasonably priced. He would hardly be impressed by the fact that the Saturn project might impact General Motors. Over the years, Saturn had mushroomed from a skunk-works project, championed by Alex Mair and a few engineers, into an unwieldy, risky, expensive venture that would probably be unable to meet the original goal of supplying a desirable, economical car to the customer. GM insiders report that in financial terms the now scaled-down Saturn project won't go into the black for at least fifteen years. Members of GM's board have expressed concern about the logic of the project and the burden it imposes on the company.

Saturn, more than EDS or Hughes, is linked to Roger Smith. It has become the embodiment of his vision and philosophy. Like everything else done by GM, the investment scale is enormous. If Saturn proves to be a massive generator of red ink in a cost-sensitive auto world, Smith's successor will be forced to reevaluate the program. Spring Hill is a beautiful, productive facility, so no matter what happens, it will continue to build cars—possibly at the expense of another GM assembly plant. But Saturn might undergo a radical restructuring to cut losses. It would not be the first time that a program nurtured by a top executive withered after he retired. Ed Cole saw his beloved rotary engine killed within weeks of his retirement.

Had Roger Smith not been so intent on proving GM's commitment to building competitive small cars, the Saturn company might have taken a different turn altogether. Rather than being set up as a separate car-making project, it could have remained a research tool whose input was incorporated into the established operations—as are the Ford Alpha and Chrysler Liberty programs. An existing plant might have been selected to experiment with technology and worker relations.

From the start, the fundamental flaw with Saturn was GM's assumption that people who bought imports were snobs. The reasoning was that these customers would never buy a car from Chevrolet, and therefore an elite brand would have to be created to draw them away from imports. The design staff loved to tell about how they interviewed consumers in California to find out their perception of Chevrolet. The story goes that a young girl was asked about her opinion of the difference between a Chevrolet model and a Japanese import. She said, "If I had a blind date and he showed up in a Honda, I'd know we were going to a nice restaurant and then doing something fun afterward. If he showed up in a Chevy, I'd figure we were going to Jack in the Box." Stories like this demonstrated that GM insiders had an astonishingly narrow view that insulted the intelligence of the car buyer, and overlooked any changes that might take place in the market regarding the perception of domestic cars. Indeed, GM's past attempts at selling import fighters, such as the Vega, Chevette, and Cavalier, did not fail because they were Chevrolets. They failed because they were poor imitations of imports. The solution seemed apparent: Build a true import fighter. Instead, GM chose to set in motion the mystique-laden process of creating a new brand, seeming to forget that ultimately the Saturn product would be judged the same way every other car is judged—on its price, style, quality, and features. If it matches or exceeds the top imports, such as the Honda Accord, it may have a chance of being successful. If not, Saturn's razzle-dazzle will only make the effort look ridiculous. Saturn also has to survive against a time factor. The competition isn't standing still while Saturn takes years to produce its new entry. Speedy product development is critical in a highly competitive market. Already, the Honda Accord will include features not planned for Saturn.

In light of the other events occurring at GM, the start-up of Saturn appeared to be almost redundant—way off in an orbit of its own. For example, at the very time Saturn was being announced, another experiment called Buick City was started in Detroit. Buick City, championed by CPC head Lloyd Reuss, was a plan to convert thirty-four acres of factory into an advanced car-making complex, in an attempt to replicate some of the manufacturing concepts of Toyota City in Japan. Although Buick City was not designed to build small cars, in many other ways its goals were similar to those of the Saturn project. It was even called a test case, for the technological aspects of the Saturn operation (NUMMI allegedly being a test case for some of the process features of Saturn).

This was somewhat foolhardy, as the Japanese might have suggested, since technology cannot simply be separated from people. Buick City would initially be a disaster for the company, with frequent equipment breakdowns and labor problems. It would not begin to emerge from its troubles until 1988. It was a very expensive test case for Saturn.

A former employee observed, "It was to the point where there was such a rah-rah team spirit at Saturn that a lot of people just got sucked into it and didn't really want to think about what a bust it was going to be." For Roger Smith, the train was racing at 100 miles an hour. There was no way to stop it without causing irreparable harm to the company's image and his personal credibility. Now the ultimate fate of Saturn would be in the hands of the customers.

By this time, people were also wondering just how many balls Smith could set spinning at the same time without one or more of them dropping. Already, in only four years as chairman, he had announced a massive company reorganization, formed a partnership with the largest Japanese auto manufacturer, invested a sizable amount in the acquisition of EDS, and launched the Saturn project, all while the massive modernization and capital spending program were creating other kinds of turmoil. As if that weren't enough, he was to bid on another major company in 1985.

Smith had been promising to have "a lulu in the future for GM shareholders." That "lulu" would turn out to be the ultimate diversification plan that would help protect the company against the vagaries of the auto industry. The bid was for Hughes Aircraft Company, one of the United States' largest defense contractors, and the competition for the deal was fierce—Ford and Boeing were the two main contenders with GM for the prize.

The jaundiced view was that Roger Smith was so immersed

in the year 2000 that he had forgotten the business of selling cars in the 1980s. But Smith argued that his two-prong Hughes strategy would offer GM both a hedge against declines in the auto industry, by diversifying into defense, electronics, and aerospace, and an opportunity to become the kind of technologically advanced company that could thrive on into the twenty-first century. With Hughes Aircraft Company, Roger Smith finally saw a chance to create the high-tech automobiles and automated plants that had always been his dream. There was something of Buck Rogers in Roger Smith—he had once considered a career in the aerospace industry—and the potential of robotics for plant manufacturing was a theme he had repeated over and over. He had often spoken of his brother who was a scientist in a Navy missile center. "Just seeing what he was doing with electronics and things convinced me that we were going to be in for such a revolution and we had to get out on the leading edge."

Smith sent vice chairman Howard Kehrl and executive vice president Donald Atwood to lead a team that spent a week inside Hughes to evaluate its potential for GM. They returned enthusiastic.

A second team followed, and its confidential report was a more mixed review. Referring to Hughes by a code name, "The Ritz Company," the report stated: "In most respects they are complementary to GM . . . their strengths match GM's weaknesses and GM strengths are generally not present in Ritz, but in some cases should be. The exploitation of Ritz skills by GM in Detroit is likely to be of value measured by interchange of a few dozens of people. The benefit to GM of utilizing Ritz in its own current environment to participate in automotive problem solving is of much larger potential but will require creative and bold management action. To realize this greater benefit GM must be determined to make a major effort. . . ."

But at the same time, the report presented a less than awesome view of Hughes's financial benefit to GM. "It is difficult to put a monetary value on the technical synergies, but using the cost of purchased and in-house technology development as a base, we believe the long-term value of the synergy with GM may be in the area of $500,000,000."

Nevertheless, Roger Smith wanted to make a deal.

The plan GM presented to the Howard Hughes Medical

Institute, the nonprofit organization set up by the late eccentric billionaire Howard Hughes to oversee his holdings, was another example of its newly favored strategy of using letter stock to "pay" for an acquisition. The deal called for the payment of $2.7 billion in cash and the rest in fifty million newly issued Class H shares. Each H share would entitle the holder, as in the EDS deal, to a dividend equivalent to 25 percent of the prior year's earnings of a newly established unit to be called Hughes Electronics Corporation, a combination of Hughes, the Delco Electronics division, Delco Systems Operations, and the instrument and display systems business of the AC Spark Plug division.

A second facet of the deal was that three years after the completion of the acquisition, GM would be required to pay the medical institute up to $40 a share to ensure that the value of the shares the institute still held would be no less than $60 at the end of those three years. A subsequent two-for-one stock split would put the guaranteed minimum price at $30 per share, and double the shares outstanding. If the stock was trading at or above $30 per postsplit share on the anniversary of the closing, GM would pay nothing. When the bid was disclosed, GM estimated the value of H stock at $46.50 presplit.

In retrospect, it is amazing that the Hughes Medical Institute accepted the deal because it was fundamentally flawed. The institute did not receive the right to sell its shares to GM at a specified price. Instead, it received a "market value guarantee," which would expire permanently on December 31, 1989; GM was obliged to pay the institute only if the stock averaged less than $30 per share in the ninety days preceding December 31, 1989. Irving Shapiro, chairman of the medical institute's board of trustees who originally accepted the deal in 1985, became concerned later about the limited market in Hughes stock, the lack of liquidity for institute shares, and GM's ability to keep the stock price up through buying in the open market. By early 1989, Shapiro, on behalf of the institute, was suggesting that GM should buy back some or all of the stock, or change the terms of the deal. GM was backed into the corner by the possibility that Hughes might sell the stock in the open market and force the price down. In early 1989, GM would restructure the deal, repurchasing 35 million shares from the Hughes Medical Institute.

Smith wanted Hughes badly; he was talking it up as the

Mecca of high technology that would play a major role in the renaissance of General Motors. He often repeated the line that "just last week, someone told me that getting Hughes was like getting Cal Tech and MIT combined." But there were reasons to question the accuracy of this, if beating Japan in quality and costs was still the goal.

Hughes was the antithesis of the Japanese manufacturers' attention to the minute, penny-pinching details that kept their costs much lower than the United States carmakers. In the year before Roger Smith bid on Hughes the Navy, Air Force, and Army each temporarily shut off the cash pipeline to Hughes in the wake of disclosures of poor workmanship, inflated costs, and missed deadlines. The payments were eventually resumed, but Hughes continued to have problems making a success of its multibillion-dollar Maverick missile program—so much so that Congress attempted to halt the program until it could find a better supplier.

"We've poured billions and billions into Hughes for the past forty years," said a Pentagon official at the time, "and they've never built a successful missile." While that might have been more the Air Force's fault than Hughes's, it was clear that Hughes was not a company with a lot of expertise in cost control. Was General Motors to be its teacher in this arena? It seemed hard to fathom.

The winning bid was announced June 5, 1985, and the people at Hughes were thrilled it was GM. If either Boeing or Ford—both already in the aerospace business—had won, antitrust considerations might have required some operations to be sold. With GM, that wasn't a problem, and at the time, GM was thought to have the "deepest pockets" of the three companies.

The day before the winning bid was announced, Ford was set to announce that it had won the auction and had a news release prepared. Boeing believed they had won, and planned to celebrate victory at simultaneous parties hosted in Paris, New York, and Seattle.

The wastebasket-bound Ford news release announcing victory made it clear that Ford had seen no synergy between Hughes and its car business. But GM chose to downplay the diversification angle and portray the Hughes acquisition as a coup in its effort to develop the twenty-first-century vehicle corporation. Roger Smith trumpeted it as part of his strategy to develop "highly efficient new forms of manufacturing and management," aimed squarely at the Japanese.

As it was prone to do, the media swallowed Smith's vision pretty much whole. The headlines read: AUTO FIRM DIVERSIFIES FOR FUTURE, THE ACQUISITION OF HUGHES AIRCRAFT WILL PROVIDE A TECHNOLOGICAL BOOST, AUTOMAKER SEEKS EXPERTISE TO GAIN EFFICIENCY, END ITS COST GAP WITH JAPAN.

No one seemed to question whether these things were possible. And if they were, what would be the cost of development? How long would it take? Hughes knew more about defense electronics, new materials, lasers, and similar advanced technologies than anyone else, but these expensive technologies would be of limited value in the auto industry, which measured costs down to the fraction of a penny. High tech meant high costs for research and development, and very high unit costs. It was questionable whether these had a place in the car business if Japan was the standard for comparison.

But Roger Smith's sales pitch to the GM board of directors urged them to clear the acquisition for the good of the company. It was, he promised them, critical to his strategy of eliminating the Japanese automakers' cost advantage.

"GM intends to set the standards for the industry with a total systems approach to manufacturing and management," Smith told the board. "Hughes is one of the few organizations in the world that has extensive experience in systems engineering. Although this experience had traditionally been focused on military applications, the proposed GM-HAC combination would provide the opportunity to apply this expertise to automotive manufacturing systems."

A further selling point was Smith's contention that "the automobile is in the process of making a rapid transition from a mechanical product which incorporates a few electrical subsystems to one with electromechanical and electronic elements within the next decade."

And Smith also cited what was an immediate potential benefit of buying Hughes: acquiring a world leader in the design and fabrication of integrated circuits, a major item being both manufactured and outsourced by Delco Electronics.

But it was clear where Smith's real passion lay. Acquiring Hughes, he told the board, would allow top technical talent to be infused throughout General Motors and ultimately lead to its being a car company driven by advanced technology and cars filled with electronic gadgets that would allow drivers to see through fog and avoid collisions.

Within the company, support for buying Hughes was more widespread than it had been for buying EDS. Electronics was rapidly becoming an important element in car manufacturing—in engine control, anti-skid brakes, diagnostic systems, and a host of futuristic dashboard gadgets such as instrument displays.

In addition, the corporate cultures of GM and Hughes were more alike than the superficials might suggest. Hughes might have employed a more casual California management style, but it was, like GM, a company where people spent their entire working lives. And the company's prestigious reputation and generous benefits attracted and kept highly skilled people. Indeed, in their original report to the Executive Committee, Kehrl and Atwood had pegged Hughes as a place where "the integrity, character, and capability of the people we dealt with appeared to be excellent." The report further noted that "the relationship among those who were in the higher levels of management seemed one of mutual respect, admiration, and even affection due to the long tenure which most officers have had with the company."

It didn't take much to sell GM's technical people on the idea of buying the aerospace company. "Hughes is a museum piece," enthused one. "There is no company in America like Hughes." They were dazzled by the idea of working with the company that brought satellites back from space to repair and return to orbit.

Smith, perhaps to differentiate the Hughes deal from his original Saturn announcement ("truly an historic occasion"), called the acquisition "a superhistoric day for us."

One very outspoken member of the board of directors was seriously opposed to the Hughes acquisition. Furthermore, he was becoming increasingly edgy with Roger Smith's cavalier manner of dismissing criticism and relentlessly shoving his plans down the throat of General Motors.

Ross Perot was hardly accustomed to this type of treatment. In a carefully crafted and sharp-edged letter to Roger Smith, he made his feelings known in no uncertain terms—not only about the Hughes deal, but about what he considered Smith's offensive personal style. An excerpt of the letter follows:

Dear Roger:

In order to resolve my concerns about the Hughes transaction, we need to address two areas:

    —The economic and business aspects.

    —The negative impact of GM's management style on advanced technology companies, and the long-term implications to Hughes.

The business aspects of Hughes can best be resolved by having the outside—

    —lawyers

    —accountants

    —investment bankers

give me a full briefing. I will require a due diligence-type briefing, highlighting Hughes' problems as well as its strengths. Specifically, I do not want a Hughes sales presentation . . .

In addition, I would like to have GM's principal reasons for acquiring Hughes, in outline form, ranked in order of their significance to GM . . .

The next step is to openly address and solve the problems between us. Failure to do so will allow the same problems to adversely impact Hughes . . .

The only issue is the success of GM. Our compatibility is not the issue . . .

In the interest of GM, you are going to have to stop treating me as a problem, and accept me as—

    —A large stockholder

    —An active board member

    —An experienced businessman

You need to understand that I am one of the few people who can and will disagree with you.

An increasing number of GM people are asking me to tell you something that—

    —they feel you need to know;

    —are concerned that you won't want to hear;

    —they are afraid to tell you.

I will tell you anything that will build and strengthen GM, whether you want to hear it or not.

For example, Hughes is not generally considered by senior GMers to be a significant contributor in making GM quality and cost competitive. Acquiring Hughes does not resolve the fundamental management issues that place GM at a competitive disadvantage.

In our relationship—

    —I will support you when I believe you are right.

—I will tell you candidly when I think you are wrong.

—If you continue your present autocratic style, I will be your adversary on critical issues.

Let me be more specific about the problems between us . . .

For example, during the recent meeting in Detroit, you were

—Obviously bored.

—Barely tolerated what others said.

—Your attitudes and comments stifled open communication.

You need to know that

—Your style intimidates people.

—Losing your temper hurts GM.

—Your tendency to try to run over anyone who disagrees with you hurts your effectiveness within GM.

—You need to be aware that people are afraid of you. This stifles candid, upward communication in GM.

—You need to know that GMers at all levels use terms like ruthless and bully in describing you.

—There is a widespread feeling throughout GM that you don't care about people.

—You cannot correct GM's problems by focusing on single issues as they are brought to your attention. Your tendency to do this is of widespread concern within GM.

Finally, I do not believe that GM can become world class and cost competitive by throwing technology and money at its problem.

—The Japanese are not beating us with technology or money. They use old equipment, and build better, less expensive cars by better management, both in Japan and with UAW workers in the U.S.

—We are not closing the quality and price gaps in spite of huge expenditures on automating plants. The fact that we have not set a date to have competitive prices indicates the prevalent attitudes about our will to win.

I suggest that you and I visit about these issues.

Let me know when you want to meet.

Sincerely,

Ross

Neither the letter's tone nor its intention was appreciated by Roger Smith. It was to be the beginning of a steady deterioration of relationship between the two men who once thought of themselves as a perfect corporate love match. Where Hughes was concerned, Smith was unprepared to back down. As for the personal attack, he shrugged it off, although it must have hurt him. Hadn't he often said he wasn't in a popularity contest?

Determined to make his case, Perot arrived at the November board of directors meeting prepared to give a one-and-one-half-hour argument against the Hughes acquisition.

"The driving force behind the Hughes transaction is a desire to acquire additional advanced technology for General Motors," he said. "I ask my fellow board members to keep in mind that I have spent my entire business career in advanced-technology companies."

Perot's argument was simple: How could GM justify spending money on something as peripheral to the car business as Hughes, while it couldn't figure out how to get more than half the amount of profit from a small car that Chrysler did?

"Clearly, the largest and richest carmaker in the world, we are doing something wrong," Perot told the board. "We are spending tens of billions of dollars in an effort to catch up. Money and acquisitions will not solve our problems."

He quoted auto industry consultant, James Harbour: "The American auto industry usually thinks high technology is the solution." He quoted dealers, who had told him, " 'Get us a product from GM that we can be proud of.' That's what they really want. We can become so preoccupied with using capital to solve our problems that the front-end investment will be so large that it alone will make it difficult for GM to be competitive."

Perot's most specific argument against buying Hughes was its vulnerability to shifting moods in defense spending. "Less than one half of one percent of Hughes's programs produce sixty-five percent of its profits. We are paying a premium for a defense contractor at a time when defense spending is decreasing."

On the subject of cost, he noted that by the time a high-tech item was usable in a car, it was cheap and could be obtained elsewhere. One-of-a-kind million-dollar devices of the sort Hughes made seemed inconsistent with the two-dollar devices in millions of cars that GM needed.

At the end, Perot looked across the table at Roger Smith and challenged the board: "As stewards for one of the world's largest corporations, whose future success can dramatically impact the lives of several million people and the economy of the United States, I urge each of my fellow board members to think about the following ideas:

"We need to become more active in understanding what is really going on inside General Motors.

"If GM is to change, it must start at the top, and *we are the top.*

"We must change the format of board meetings from passive sessions with little two-way communication to active, participatory sessions that allow us to discuss real issues and resolve real problems.

"As board members, we must send a clear signal to the corporation that the shareholders are not simply a nuisance to be dealt with at the annual meeting, and avoided whenever possible. *They own this company.*"

It was an eloquent and fascinating presentation. Although other board members were privately in agreement, they timidly went along with the acquisition. When the votes were counted, the only dissenting voice belonged to Perot. Smith had won his deal, but the battle lines between Perot and Smith had been clearly drawn. Both were saying, in effect, "This town isn't big enough for the two of us."

As for Hughes, it turned out to be an investment for GM that would pay off in some practical ways—although not the ways some people imagined. Donald Atwood, who later headed up a group that included both EDS and Hughes, pointed out that "I think there was a misconception on the technology. People in general wondered—and I still run into this all the time—'When am I going to find a Hughes gadget in the car?'

"And the answer is *never.* Hughes doesn't make gadgets for cars. Hughes does basic technology work which they apply to their products, and it's the basic technology which we want to apply to the automobile—basic technology being the underlying technology in instrumentation. They make instruments for aircraft cockpits, but it's the *technology* that gets transferred, not the cockpit instrumentation that gets transferred."

In many respects, Hughes was just another example of the acquisition-happy mood around GM at the time. The company had money to spend, and ambitious executives on the finance staff realized they could make names for themselves by initiating high-visibility deals comparable to the Toyota joint venture or the EDS acquisition. In one case, secret meetings were held with members of the BMW supervisory board and Vorstand to explore the possibility of affiliating the two companies. Code named "Project Jupiter," the deal never came to fruition.

Likewise, a relationship with Fiat was explored during the same time Ford was also pursuing a deal with the Italian automaker. Talks with Fiat broke down over the question of which company would have the controlling share. As one GM executive said, the deal fizzled because "there were always two people trying to sit in the chairman's seat—one from Fiat and one from GM."

Dollar for dollar, the 1986 acquisition of a tiny company named Group Lotus PLC was likely to do more for automotive engineering development at GM than Hughes Aircraft.

Lotus was one of those rare little gems—a small company of talented and highly skilled geniuses who loved cars and had advanced the art of auto-making with a steady stream of innovation. Though small, it had attained one of the most prestigious names in autos, right alongside Ferrari, Maserati, and Lamborghini. Since 1982, GM had been using Lotus to work on engineering projects. But the company was struggling financially. Said Michael Kimberly, who took over the company when chairman Colin Chapman died in 1982, "Lotus, quite frankly, staggered from crisis to crisis. We were in the middle of a desperate crisis when Colin Chapman died." In 1984, Toyota bought a 22-percent stake and that helped Lotus boost its engineering consultancy business, generating the cash flow necessary to develop new car models, the true love of Lotus engineers.

But at the end of 1985, 48 percent of Lotus became available, and it seemed likely that some car company would snatch it up. Bob Eaton, head of GM's technical staffs, felt this would make a sweet little acquisition for GM. For him, it would be both a defensive and an offensive move. "We clearly had a lot of projects," Eaton said, referring to the consultancy work Lotus did for GM. "Also, we viewed it as a super, neat little company that would have ongoing synergies." GM picked up Lotus for a steal—a mere $20 million for half the company.

The acquisition of Lotus would have been relatively uneventful if it were not for Roger Smith's blunder.

Remember, Toyota, GM's "partner," owned 22 percent of

the shares. And Eiji Toyoda and Smith were personally close—
or, at least, that's what Toyoda thought. From the standpoint of
a business courtesy alone, not to mention the personal gesture,
Smith should have been on the phone to Toyoda the minute GM
made the decision to acquire the stake in Lotus. But he never
called him; it's possible that it never occurred to Smith at all.

More puzzling was that he didn't mention it personally
when he and Toyoda were in Stuttgart, West Germany, together for the Mercedes one-hundredth-anniversary celebration. Roger Smith was surrounded by members of the
European press, which were clamoring for news about the
Lotus acquisition. Toyoda knew what was going on, and he
was waiting for Smith to tell him what GM planned to do with
Lotus, given Toyota's sizable equity stake and the number of
engineering contracts it had with the company. But Smith said
nothing about it.

Toyoda was hurt by the man who had been his partner and,
he believed, his friend. The event permanently cooled the relationship between Smith and Toyoda. And although Toyota sold
its Lotus stake to GM, it canceled its plan to sell an engine and
drive train to Lotus for a small sports car, the Elan, the company
had on the drawing board. And after that, it refused to sell
components to Lotus beyond what had been previously con-
tracted. A simple phone call from Smith to Toyoda would have
avoided the whole problem. Instead, Kimberly faced long delays
and obstacles in trying to obtain parts for his dream car, and
eventually had to rely on GM's Japanese affiliate, Isuzu.

For GM's Bob Eaton, the two most appealing features of
Lotus were the productivity of its people and its technical genius. Lotus's engineers and designers were more productive
than GM's because they were hungrier and closer to the market.
They were the perfect example of how adversity could bring out
the best in an organization. Lotus had never had enough money,
but its people made the most of what they had. They were
hardworking "car nuts," and they were led by Kimberly, who,
apart from having a fanatical love of cars, was devoted to his
people and to the preservation of what was unique and great
about Lotus. Happily for him, Lotus was too small and too far
away to come under the total scrutiny of GM, and Bob Eaton,
who was promoted to chairman of GM Europe in mid-1988, has
worked to preserve Lotus's independence.

Eaton would admit that the spirit and commitment of the Lotus staff differed greatly from GM's, and he attributed it to the hunger factor. "Lotus was a company that's been on the brink of failure—bankruptcy—since it started. In 1982 or 1983, on Monday of a couple of different weeks, they didn't have any idea of how they were going to make the payroll on Friday. That mentality of just barely staying alive caused a tremendous commitment to make things work."

Kimberly and his band of geniuses were not pie-in-the-sky thinkers. Their proximity to the market forced them to balance future vision with practical technology. For Kimberly, the answer was technology. "Technology is going to be the arsenal that is necessary to win," he said. "It's not a question of standing still anymore. And it's not just a question of price and quality. It's technology. It's what you can give the customer in terms of what he perceives is value for money."

In the articulation of vision, Mike Kimberly and Roger Smith were traveling down the same road. It was only their methods of travel that differed. Kimberly never had the option of buying his way out of his troubles; effectiveness was achieved from teamwork and elbow grease. Technology was not a magic tool for future success.

The acquisition of Hughes—and, to a much smaller extent, Lotus—was one of the high-tech routes to low-cost development that Smith was so fond of, but completing the deal must have given some people inside GM—besides Ross Perot—cause for concern. It came at a time when EDS seemed to be doing just the opposite of what was intended—increasing costs and creating rebellion in the ranks—while simultaneously, high-tech failures in Buick City and Hamtramck were attracting a lot of media attention. Concurrently, GM's new cars were failing to attract buyers. The company's market share was continuing to fall while its break-even point rose, and profit margins were being squeezed.

GM posted a 24-percent increase in net income for the 1985 third quarter, but the $517 million it earned came not from selling cars but from record GMAC earnings, investment tax credits, and foreign exchange gains. The car business posted an operating loss, partly because of costly 7.7-percent car financing to clear away massive inventories that had piled up as a result of overly ambitious production. Profit was also hurt by new-model costs, programs being set up by EDS, and inadequate price hikes to cover rising variable costs. To Smith's chagrin, Ford posted record third quarter results, despite facing the same market conditions.

To further intensify concerns, a new study similar to Smith's 1981 Isuzu-GM cost comparison gave discouraging news about GM's competitive status. In comparing the cost of building the Chevrolet Beretta versus a similar Japanese car, the Japanese cost advantage was shown to be $3,611 per car. In other words, it cost GM 86 percent more to build its Beretta than it cost the unnamed Japanese company to build its car.

One BOC manager cited this latest revelation of cost disparity in a stinging internal memo entitled "The Great Domestic Turkey Shoot of 1986–1990."

He wrote:

> Despite all of GM's efforts to become cost and quality competitive during the past six years, the only thing there is to show for it is deterioration of $1,500. Worse still, there is nothing in the forward product program that even comes close to narrowing this cost gap.
>
> As long as Japanese-sourced vehicles and components enjoy a 2-to-1 cost advantage vs. GM, the North American market will be a "turkey shoot" with GM products being the turkeys.

To make matters worse, BOC, for example, was spending 57 percent of its discretionary product engineering resources on major, minor, and ornamentation appearance changes, according to this manager. "Car divisions are willing to commit hara-kiri for a 1988 Euro GT Ultra Grand Touring Brougham D'Elegance model, yet no one seems to be pressing for a solution to the problem of Japan's ability to produce value at one-half of GM's cost."

He ended on this dour note:

> Historically, almost all successful and large institutions have ceased to exist in the long run because they were unable to recognize and adapt to changing political and economic developments in the world. Hence, the Roman Empire declined and fell, there are no more czars, the great British East India Tea Company withered away, and the Cunard steamship line no longer controls the trans-Atlantic travel business. Those who are in the

best position to be aware of an emerging trend are those who are least likely to see the need for strategic change.

The historic odds are that GM will be no different in this respect than the Roman Empire. However, while I believe GM's current cost and market position is in an intolerable strategic position, there are still sufficient (but ephemeral) marketplace strengths that can be exploited to improve GM's long-term prospects. While GM may never again be the overwhelmingly dominant producer, it may be able to survive.

And while Roger Smith was engaged in his high-tech shopping spree, Bill Hoglund, president of the Saturn Corporation, was preaching a decidedly un-high-tech message. In a speech in 1985, he told of his experiences with W. Edwards Deming, whom he had brought into Pontiac in 1981 despite upper management's aversion to using a consultant who often blamed auto company executives for the industry's problems.

"We listened to him, and we learned," Hoglund said. "Deming's urgent message: There must be a transformation of the American style of management." He described what happened when Deming's concepts were applied. "Managers no longer felt secure, secluded in their offices. They could no longer crack a whip and make things happen. Instead, they found themselves explaining what they wanted done and why." This, not technology, stressed Hoglund, was the key to customer satisfaction.

Late in the year, Roger Smith was featured in *The New York Times Magazine* in a piece entitled "The Innovator." It led off with an anecdote about how fascinated he was with a robot that could pick up an egg without breaking the shell. But meanwhile, in the real world of selling cars, GM was beginning to look like Humpty-Dumpty. By the end of 1985, its share of market had skidded down to 41 percent, dropping four points in two years, as the all-new Ford Taurus and Sable created shock waves throughout the auto industry and received rave reviews from the media and motorists alike. This was an embarrassing low that would have seemed impossible in 1980, when market share was 46 percent. While GM was focusing on developing small cars to compete with the Japanese, it was losing sales in the midsize market to Ford and Chrysler. In 1985, the Hamtramck factory opened and began assembling the Cadillac Eldorado, Buick

Riviera, Oldsmobile Toronado, and Cadillac Seville. With gasoline again cheap, buyers rejected these bland, tiny, pricey versions of the cars they once loved. It has been estimated that the failure of these models cost GM about $1 billion a year in net income. In the luxury market, sales of Volvos, BMWs, Audis, Lincolns, and Mercedes-Benzes continued to chip away at the Cadillac, Buick, and Oldsmobile dominance.

Roger Smith was getting zapped from all sides as 1985 came to a close. But he ended the year with his fifth annual Christmas message to the troops, saying, "Steady as she goes—and stay the course. We have a bold strategy in place designed to ensure GM's leadership for many years to come."

But on this night before Christmas, "Sugar plums" were still dancing in Smith's head as he considered the future. He was dreaming of the day GM became a high-tech leader . . . and the day when the magic car, Saturn, would roll off the line. Perhaps it would have space age features—compliments of Hughes—that no one had ever dreamed of: navigational devices locked into satellites . . . collision-avoidance systems . . . cameras and video displays instead of rearview mirrors . . . night vision devices that could penetrate dense fog . . . who knew what was possible?

Frustration and Finger Pointing:
Vision and Reality Collide

I come from an environment where, if you see a snake, you kill it. At GM, if you see a snake, the first thing you do is organize a committee on snakes. Then you go hire a consultant who knows a lot about snakes. Then you talk about it for a year.

—H. Ross Perot

A day in the life of Ross Perot could make your head spin—especially if you were a General Motors executive sitting in your beige office staring at a mile-high stack of paperwork and waiting to go to yet another meeting.

"So, how was your day today?" Perot asked Elmer Johnson, then a vice president in charge of legal affairs. The two were talking on the phone late one afternoon.

"I'm sure I had a pretty dull day by comparison to you," Johnson laughed. "Just meetings . . . the usual. How about you? What did you do today?"

"I was with the vice premier of China—I'm still going after those POWs in North Vietnam." There was urgency in his voice. "We've got to get them out of there, Elmer."

"Uh, yeah. What else did you do today?"

"I got a call from Margaret Thatcher. She's all worried about the safety of her son. [Thatcher's son was hiding at Perot's home, waiting for the latest round of terrorist saber-rattling to die down in the Middle East.] Oh, and [then Vice President] Bush called about a million-dollar contribution.''

Roger Smith was drawn to the spirited independence of men like Ross Perot. But somehow he always got more than he bargained for. For while he imagined himself to be a paradigm-shifter like a Ross Perot, he did not possess the personal security that would allow him to run at the same fast-and-loose pace.

Smith didn't understand that Perot-like characters possessed no fear. They could watch their ideas dissolve in smoke and walk away without a backward glance. They could revel in a spate of public name-calling, loving every minute of it. They could think they had an absolutely perfect solution for a problem, then change their course on a dime when someone else's idea seemed better.

With Perot, Roger Smith was playing in the entrepreneurial big leagues. He held no winning cards whatsoever, because Ross Perot didn't need GM and he didn't need Smith.

Roger Smith might have given some thought in the beginning to why a man like Ross Perot would have been interested in this particular match in the first place. Money no longer held much thrill for the Texas billionaire, so it wasn't that. Given Perot's flamboyant history, it was more likely that he wanted to get inside GM so he could shake it up, force change. Perot was a grand-scale romantic—give him a hill, he'd charge up it. What other motivation might he have had in GM but to be the man who won the war for the American auto industry? And to do that, he had first to rescue a company that was being held hostage by the worst kind of corporate terrorists: *bureaucrats.*

The Perot-Smith honeymoon lasted about as long as it took them to sign the original agreement. Now GM's largest single stockholder, Perot didn't waste any time getting involved in the company. It was unheard of for board members to visit factories and talk to workers. But Perot did that. It was unheard of for board members to visit dealers and question them on sales problems. But Perot did that. He was like a hornet buzzing around the entire corporation, an irritant who stuck his nose in every arena. His outspokenness during the Hughes acquisition was only one example of many. He was fearless and direct—almost to the point of sounding mean—in his criticism.

According to Perot, it was criminal that the top executives of General Motors didn't seek out more one-on-one communication with the workers in the plants. He had always despised any form of elitism and, in this case, he believed it also contributed directly to the problems the company had developing a practical vision. Ironically, EDS was hardly a democracy. It was an organization where very few made the decisions—or the big bucks.

He recalled once phoning a union representative to set up a meeting with the workers. "He said, 'I can't believe the biggest stockholder in the company would talk to factory guys.' I said, 'Oh, yeah, where do you want to meet?' He said, 'We'll come to you,' and I told him, 'No, I will come to see you.'

"He got real quiet when I said that, and finally he said, 'I can't believe it. I can't believe you would come to see us.' Then he said, 'We don't really have a place,' and I said there's got to be a restaurant or something.

"There was a long pause, then he said, 'You wouldn't come to the union, would you?'

"I said, 'Sure.'

"The phone went dead, then he said it again. 'I can't believe it.'

"So I said—my exact words—'Hell, I'm not going to get AIDS over there, am I?' And he started laughing and then we cut all that stuff out. But look at the gap between us! See, I was this strange big stockholder, not just another guy dedicated to seeing the company succeed—someone who had a huge common interest with the guys who put the cars together. The only difference between me and the guys putting the cars together is that the ball bounced a different way in my life. I've made this same speech to General Motors executives and I've told them, 'You've got to remember there are guys on the factory floors as smart as we are. We got the breaks. We got to go to college. We had the parental support. We had a lot of things they didn't have, but these guys aren't dummies. They are not, quote, *those people*. They are not, quote, *labor*. They are just like us, except the ball bounced a different way.'

"So I went over to the union and it would have brought tears to your eyes—it almost did to mine, because all these old guys were playing pool and hanging around. They couldn't believe I was really coming. There was a huge crowd, just to see if I would show up. And they assumed that I'd have bodyguards and aides, and I just strolled over there and walked in.

"We had a great meeting. For two hours, they told me what was on their minds, and they never once asked for more pay or less work. The talk was all about how to make a better car. They understood to their toes that their future depended on being competitive.

"Then they wanted to know if I would go through the plant, and I said, 'Guys, the only way I can go through the plant is if I meet every single person, and I've got to be able to stand there and talk to them because I'm not going through an employee show-and-tell. I don't care how long it takes, but that's the way I've got to do it.' They said, 'That's great,' so we went to the plant.

"I went down in the pits underneath the cars, and I met a man, fifty-five years old, who had worked down there his entire career. For some reason, he liked it down there, working with his hands up. Well, this old guy, who is not a softy, literally got tears in his eyes. He said, 'Ross, you're the first big shot that's ever come down into the pits the whole time I've been working for General Motors. Why did you come down?'

"And I said, 'I wanted to meet you.'

"He said, 'Well I'll be damned,' and he wiped his hand off and we shook hands. The guy was just hungry for someone to treat him with dignity and respect and like a human being."

It was Perot's contention that the GM bureaucracy had gotten so big that the people running the company no longer understood or cared about their product. "You start out with guys who make the product, who love the product, and that is what the company is all about. Then the company gets big and successful, and you decide, we're so big, we're so rich, we've got to get guys to come in and control the money. And you put financial guys in. Then you may get bigger and richer because times are good, and then you've got all kinds of antitrust problems, and then you put the lawyers in, and the company is run by accountants and lawyers. But somehow you've got to keep finding people who love the product.

"Look at the guys at GM. They have chauffeurs. Now, how much can you learn about cars riding in the backseat? Think about it. When you're too old to drive to work, you're too old to go to work. Now, think about the symbolism of having a heated parking garage when your workers are being laid off. If I've got a guy in Flint, Michigan, marching through the snow, and I'm so damn soft that I've got to have my car warm before my heater warms it up, what am I? If I have a car that gets worked on by mechanics every day so that I never see, feel, or taste reality, and I am driven back and forth to work, what do I know about my product? I should have to buy a car from a dealer. I should have to negotiate for it. It should be picked at random and I should drive it. And when that sucker breaks down, I ought to have to take it to the dealer and get punched around. That's reality."

By May of 1986, tensions between Perot and the company had reached a strangled point of no return. When Perot wrote a letter outlining several options, one of which involved a "friendly" buyout, the company decided to pursue that direction.

Elmer Johnson flew to Dallas to discuss the possibility with Perot, but the conversation went nowhere. "He said he wasn't seriously looking for a buyout, so I forgot about it," said Johnson.

Meanwhile, Perot was trying to keep his negative opinions about GM more or less private. In public, he tried to make positive, constructive comments about the company. But an incident in mid-1986 ruffled his feathers. He was being interviewed by a television network about an unrelated topic when he was asked about GM.

"I made some very positive comments about the T-type Buick and encouraged the network people to come out and drive it on the test track," Perot recalled. "And the general reaction within General Motors was one of great resentment. They asked, 'Who authorized you to do that?' I said, 'Nobody.' And I'd told them I would come out and drive it with them. And they [GM officials] said, 'Well, you shouldn't do that. We ought to have Roger drive it.' My interest was in focusing on what I thought was a fine car. The organization's interest was in who stands where."

But once Perot let loose publicly, there was no stopping him. In October, he appeared on the cover of *Business Week*, along with his statement that "revitalizing General Motors is like teaching an elephant to tap dance. You find the sensitive spots and start poking." (Only a year earlier, Perot had used the same image in *praise* of Roger Smith, saying, "Roger knows where the sensitive spots are. In fact, he can get that elephant to dance.")

The *Business Week* story was explosive. Perot said that for GM it was World War Two in the Pacific all over again, only this time "no one gets killed, but armies of people lose their jobs."

In the November issue of *Ward's Auto World*, Perot plunged the knife into a corporate soft spot. "I'd get rid of the 14th floor," Perot told *Ward's*. "I'd get rid of the executive dining rooms. I would urge the senior executives to locate their offices where real people are doing real work—live with them, listen to them, spend time with them, find out what it would take to win, and do it."

Behind the scenes, Perot was fighting for EDS's independence within GM. Specifically, he had dug in his heels and refused to give GM auditors access to EDS data. Why? Because GM had promised at the beginning that EDS would have its independence and it wasn't working out that way at all. Also, EDS had expected that by the end of the year, GM would have signed numerous lucrative, long-term contracts, and that wasn't working out, either—now, more than a year and a half after the acquisition, the contracts had not been signed.

Publicly, Smith was saying he had no problems with Perot's fighting style, and outside GM director Marvin L. Goldberger, president of the California Institute of Technology, was quoted as saying that Perot was "making a serious contribution to the board by being smart and asking hard questions." But other board members were advising Perot to tone it down; he ignored them. It's hard to find evidence anywhere in GM's history of a person so close to GM's corporate heartbeat being so irreverent. John DeLorean is probably the only other example.

Statements Perot made in *Ward's* and other media led to a growing concern that he might be plotting some kind of takeover. There were signs that Smith was wondering if Perot might try to challenge him for the chairmanship, and at least one board member believed Perot might be looking into taking over GM through a leveraged buyout.

A GM buyout in 1986 would have cost more than $40 billion, dwarfing the biggest buyout to date, Beatrice Companies, which went for about $6.2 billion in early 1986. (In fact, Chrysler chairman Lee Iacocca said he explored the possibility of a GM

takeover in 1987, at the suggestion of megadealer Victor Potam-
kin, but dropped the idea after concluding that "it might be
easier to buy Greece.")

Perot had also conceived the idea of setting up a plan for
GM to sell all but 25 percent of its EDS shares in an effort to
restore the company to its original damn-the-torpedoes, full-
steam-ahead business approach. For a time, it appeared that
AT&T might pick up 25 percent of EDS; the remaining 50
percent would be offered to the public. But the deal fell through
and it was beginning to look like Perot's previous notion of a
"friendly" buyout might be the only course to take.

Tom Luce, Perot's lawyer and longtime friend, and Elmer
Johnson met to discuss the deteriorating relationship between
Perot and GM and reached a mutual conclusion: "Let's call it
quits."

A deal that was acceptable to the board was worked out.
Luce negotiated for Perot personally, while Johnson represented GM. Somehow, EDS's interests were sidestepped and the
deal was sufficiently ambiguous that Perot felt free to start competing with EDS and hiring away EDS employees, beginning in
June 1988. At the time, however, GM was simply concentrating
on getting Perot out. "I thought the terms were fair," Johnson
said. "The premium, if any, was very modest and more than
justified by the benefits of having what I thought was a friendly
buyout." On December 1, GM announced that it had decided to
buy back Ross Perot's shares for $742.8 million, including
amounts given to three other key EDS executives. To prevent
negative publicity, the agreement stipulated that a $7.5-million
penalty would be charged if either party cut the other up publicly.

Perot also extracted certain promises from GM on behalf of
his people at EDS: That it would keep EDS independent, give
it long-term contracts, and vest bonus stock awards to the top
two hundred EDS executives after thirteen months instead of
the normal five to ten years. From Perot, GM extracted an eigh-
teen-month no-compete agreement that stipulated he couldn't
hire away EDS staff from GM during this period. After eighteen
months, Perot would be free to compete, but only on a nonprofit
basis for another eighteen months. This clause would cause GM
problems in 1988, when EDS personnel began the newly formed
Perot Systems.

On the same day, EDS quietly fired one hundred computer specialists, all longtime employees who were in their forties or older. They were dumped without cause and replaced with recent college graduates hired at bargain rates, compared with the veterans' salaries and benefits.

GM tried to soften the impact of the announcement by producing an unusual number of press releases on December 1. A one-page release announced the appointment of Albert Whelan as chairman of Hughes Aircraft Company, a widely acclaimed move. A two-and-one-half-page release announced that Howard Kehrl was retiring as vice chairman. A one-and-one-half-page release disclosed the formation of a new unit to encompass Hughes, Delco Electronics, GM's defense operations, and EDS, under executive vice president Donald Atwood. The same release announced that Lester Alberthal, an eighteen-year EDS veteran, was named to succeed Perot as chief executive of EDS. "We have established for Mr. Perot the title of Founder of EDS," the release said. There was no mention of the buyout. This was covered in yet another three-paragraph release. The first paragraph told of the buyout, without mentioning the price. The second paragraph was Smith praising Perot. The final paragraph was a stiffly worded statement by Perot himself: "I am pleased that the process of integrating EDS with General Motors has been completed, positioning GM as a technologically stronger company, better able to compete and to capitalize on the opportunities ahead."

It didn't take the media long to find the real news buried under the pile of public relations paperwork. And once the price tag was discovered, all hell broke loose. Shareholders, employees, and industry analysts were stunned. GM had only paid $2.55 billion for EDS a year and a half earlier. Wouldn't an outright sale of EDS have been less wasteful? The buyout move enraged investors because of the amount and the premium Perot got for his shares—$33 per Class E share the same day it closed at $26.875—and the $346.8 million he got for contingent notes and tax compensation.

The public criticism GM sought to avoid with the Perot buyout simply got louder in the wake of the announcement. And the day of the announcement, Perot himself came forth to brand the buyout a waste of corporate assets. He challenged GM to rethink their decision, saying he'd put the money in escrow until

December 15 to give the company a chance to change its mind. But later the same day, the board turned down Perot's offer to reconsider. Many industry observers commenting right after the announcement said they were shocked and agreed that the terms of the buyout were outrageous. Some of them speculated that Smith was out of control. He had thrown three quarters of a billion dollars at a "problem" and what was the problem? That Perot was outspoken? That he pushed for needed change at GM?

Paul Ingrassia, *The Wall Street Journal*'s Detroit bureau chief, aired his opinion in a December 3 Op-Ed piece, saying, "Smith may resolve GM's current woes. But he's more likely to do it by using some of Perot's ideas than by simply throwing money at the problems. If money alone was the answer, GM wouldn't have problems in the first place."

Regardless of the constituency, reactions to the announcement were largely negative. Top GM executives feared the cost of the buyout would affect spending programs and bonuses. UAW leaders said it would become a stumbling block to any calls for concessions in the next contract talks. Thomas Peters, author of *In Search of Excellence,* suggested establishing an "anti-hush fund" so Perot could continue to criticize GM without fear of the $7.5-million penalty.

Automotive News ran a December 8 editorial that began, "General Motors is a loser." It accused GM of having "weak character" and "lack of moral substance." Smith was branded "a man afraid of critics—let alone a fight." And GM's "faint-hearted leaders" were called upon to retire for the sake of the company. (For its stand, the publication lost GM advertising, and the company boycotted the magazine's 1987 World Congress industry conference that summer.)

The State of Wisconsin Investment Board, a major GM institutional investor, responded quickly and negatively to the Perot deal. In a December 10 letter, it said:

> Your action in buying both Class E stock and notes from one of your directors (and other top managers of EDS) and removal of that director from your Board severely undermines the confidence we have in the Board and in the officials of General Motors. Not only is this action grossly unfair to other Class E stock holders (note holders and straight common alike) but the payment of

"hush" mail to H. Ross Perot raises serious questions about General Motors' operations and management. His presence on the Board was valuable and perceived as such by the market, as evidenced by the impact on stock prices upon notice of the buyout. In addition, the market could not ignore the waste of corporate assets which this payment—so clearly in excess of market value—represented.

But for the first time since the Smith-Perot clash began, the media started to catch wind of the fact that Perot's public criticism might not have been the only issue. Smith certainly wanted to rid himself of this thorn in the side, but he was also afraid of the way Perot was affecting GM's ability to take control of EDS and make it a more integrated, smoother-running unit. Smith might also have been concerned that Perot's high-profile campaign against GM management was beginning to look like an effort to win support for a proxy fight or buyout bid. Even rumors of such a possibility could have a crippling effect on the company's attempts to solve its business problems. Most important, though, GM needed to get Perot out of its way at EDS. He was making it very hard for GM to settle disputes about how much EDS was charging for its services, the ongoing debates over long-term contracts, and EDS's reluctance to follow directives from its new parent.

Smith would attempt to address the concerns of investors in a letter that said, "Unfortunately, we . . . concluded that Mr. Perot did not accept the fact that, having sold EDS to GM, GM was now its parent with responsibilities to all its shareholders, as well as to EDS and other GM divisions and subsidiaries. . . . In short, his pursuit of complete autonomy for EDS violated accepted standards of corporate governance." Specifically, GM cited "Perot's refusal to permit GM to audit the books of EDS. . . . EDS and GM negotiated arms-length agreements to govern the pricing of EDS's services to GM. These agreements explicitly provided for GM to audit all EDS costs wherever cost-based pricing was utilized." GM's chief internal auditor had advised Smith in September that Perot wouldn't give GM's audit staff access to EDS records.

Perot protested later that the only reason he withheld the records was to protect the job security of his own auditors. He said he wanted to guarantee that EDS auditors wouldn't end up without jobs after turning the function over to GM. This argument was less than convincing. According to a current EDS executive, "Ross never got over the fact that EDS wasn't his company anymore. His not turning over the records was a good example. He actually believed they were *his* records, and the EDS staff was still *his* staff."

Michigan State business professor Eugene Jennings saw some justification for Roger Smith's position. "If you were betting sixty billion dollars to renovate General Motors, and you saw an individual who was interfering with a most critical phase of the capital program, you would not wince at using less than a billion to get that thorn removed."

But disturbed by the depth of the antibuyout sentiment, GM officials prepared to hit the road to defend their actions. Smith himself was scheduled to meet with the Council of Institutional Investors in mid-December, but he decided to send four high-ranking executives instead: general counsel Elmer Johnson; Donald Atwood; new EDS CEO Les Alberthal, and treasurer Leon Krain.

The investors were not impressed. Where's Roger Smith? they wanted to know.

"We have a right as major holders of GM to hear an explanation from the chairman," said council cochairman Harrison J. Goldin, New York City comptroller.

When the executives explained that they had been sent in Smith's stead, an angry Goldin retorted, "If we can't hear it from *this* chairman, then perhaps some *other* chairman."

Smith got the message and hurriedly agreed to meet with the group in January. But his action was too late to prevent the rumor from seeping out—for the second time in his chairmanship—that he might be forced into retirement before 1990. The rumor would stay alive for nearly a year.

Smith embarrassed himself at least one other time during his counteroffensive in the wake of the Perot buyout. In meetings with investors, he had two stock speeches—one for holders of GM stock and another for holders of E stock. GM holders would hear how EDS was going to be kept under control and wouldn't be allowed to profit at the parent's expense. Class E holders would hear how GM was committed to signing fixed-price contracts with EDS. In at least one instance, Smith delivered the wrong speech.

"Perot is not a scoundrel and Smith is not an idiot," James T. Glassman wrote in *The New Republic.* "They're two men, more naive than anyone would guess, trying to fix the world's largest company and failing."

A few months later, Elmer Johnson would get into a cab in Chicago and start chatting with the driver about the beautiful red-and-white convertible Toyota Celica in front of them on the road.

"Those little buggers are really doing it to us, aren't they?" the driver said.

"Yeah," Johnson replied. "And once drivers go to imports, it's pretty hard to get them back to American cars."

"Well, I say General Motors deserves everything they get," huffed the cabbie. "Who was the chairman of the board of General Motors who just quit in total frustration? He was just fed up with the way his own organization was treating people and treating the customer."

Johnson frowned. "You're not talking about Ross Perot?"

"Yeah, Ross Perot. He was chairman of the board and couldn't take it any longer."

Johnson shook his head and thought, "Geez, I hope not too many people in the world are thinking this. And maybe this is part of what accounts for our sudden drop in market share."

Jim McDonald would later say that he believed the dramatic market share decline in 1986 and 1987 was due in large part to the bad publicity surrounding the Perot criticism and the buyout. "You don't get that kind of rapid decline on product alone," he said. "Our reputation suffered tremendously with the Perot buyout, and bad publicity affects market share." In reality, there is evidence that GM's market share—once considered a God-given right at 45 percent—was sliding for more reasons than just bad publicity. In a 1986 memo to F. Alan Smith and Jack Edman, GM Treasurer Leon Krain suggested that targeting a lower share of the market was critical to GM's bottom line.

Wrote Krain, "Essentially we believe that it is more prudent for the Corporation to capacitize for a 35% North American passenger car penetration level in the 1990s than to invest the capital and engineering resources necessary to achieve 45% penetration. Based on estimates . . . the financial implications of a misjudgment of GM's future North American passenger car penetration by 10 percentage points would severely depress our profitability and deplete our financial resources."

As the public drama over EDS was being played out, Don Atwood and Les Alberthal were working internally to minimize the trauma for staff. "There was a lot of concern on the part of the people that their founder, the person they had great respect for, was gone," said Atwood. "Would EDS go all to pieces? The leadership was gone. Ross Perot, Mort Meyerson, and two other leaders were gone. Who would the people in EDS rally around? Could it be made attractive for them to stay? Would the management be sound? Had GM learned how to handle them so there was not greater confusion, greater morale problems? And what about the customers? Would they feel that with Ross and Mort gone, the whole thing would blow apart? Those were very trying times. Les Alberthal and I spent many hours together trying to figure out exactly what to do."

What they did was concentrate their energies on building trust and confidence. They met with groups of EDSers and told them that the organization was going to be strong and well managed, but it was no longer going to be a one-man show. They met with many customers and potential customers, gradually building a relationship of trust with them, as well. And they instituted what is now called the Corporation Information Management (CIM) group, to provide the interface between GM and EDS.

It had been the conventional wisdom that Perot's leaving would hurt EDS, but the reverse happened. The GM "E" share price rose to the high 30s in early 1987, and EDS's non-GM revenue rose more than 20 percent each year through 1988. Once the slingshots were put away, everyone got back to the business of doing their jobs again, this time away from the limelight.

Financial analysts reached the boiling point in April 1986 when GM hosted a meeting for investors at its technical center in Warren, Michigan. After a morning of corporate hype disguised as fact, the last straw came when executive vice president of finance F. Alan Smith presented a chart showing GM's earnings growth from 1980 to 1985. His chart totally skipped the decline that took place from 1984 to 1985—the primary issue the analysts wanted to hear about. Later, during the question-

and-answer session, Bob Brizzolara, a veteran analyst with Harris Trust, stood up and pointedly reminded Alan Smith that the date marked the anniversary of the sinking of the *Titanic,* also captained by a man named Smith. (During the following days, *Titanic* jokes made the rounds of GM: "What's the difference between GM and the *Titanic?* The *Titanic* had a band.")

Only two months before this meeting, an internal GM study, addressed to F. Alan Smith, GMAC chairman, Jack Edman, and Leon J. Krain, treasurer, offered sharp criticism of GM's financial strategy:

"The Corporation's financial systems, shaped largely in the 1920s and 1930s by Alfred P. Sloan, Jr. and Donaldson Brown, were predicated upon and fit well with a set of circumstances which no longer exist.

"Through the 1970s the North American automotive markets were characterized by rapid growth, with domestic producers remaining largely unaffected by foreign competition. . . . Moreover, GM's massive scale economy advantages enabled the corporation to enjoy market leadership and a highly profitable position among U.S. producers. In an industry and organization whose profit potential was limited more by its internal resource capabilities (and eventually, antitrust considerations) than by competitive forces, this approach fit and worked exceedingly well.

". . . GM can no longer adjust pricing to achieve targeted profitability levels. Intensified foreign and domestic competition and low industry growth potential place significant limits on the Corporation's profit opportunities in the automotive sector. Accordingly, the key success elements for GM's forward financial systems have moved beyond the controlled growth and reinvestment requirements of earlier periods to an era which requires increased emphasis on the *strict rationing of capital in the automotive sector* in view of realistic limits on the profit opportunities in this industry."

Also in February, Jim McDonald wrote a letter to GM executives. He noted that the letter was not "an emotional appeal," but emotion vibrated from its pages:

     . . . after making satisfactory progress toward our product quality goals from 1982 through 1984, we lost much of the upward momentum during 1985. Many in the organization had hoped and believed that our quality progress would automatically come about as we introduced new products. Nothing could have been further from the truth. We have placed a great deal of new product into the marketplace in the last couple of years Some met our quality goals, but most have not.

Second, after making excellent progress from 1982 to 1984 in terms of productivity and the elimination of waste, we lost much of this discipline in 1985. While 1985 unit sales represented an increase, our operating profit margin per unit fell in 1985. . . . At least half the decline, in my judgment, could have been avoided by more astute management and team cooperation at all levels of the organization. . . .

Third, 1985 was a year in which we experienced further setbacks in our efforts to improve the timeliness of our product development system. The time from concept to delivery of a new vehicle appears to be stretching out rather than getting shorter. This seriously affects both our marketing effectiveness and our costs. . . .

The only question is whether we, who constitute the leadership of this great organization, will muster the dedication, discipline, and determination to make 1986 the year of execution and achievement and follow-through . . . we must take bold actions that send a clear message throughout our company which cannot be misunderstood: *Improvement must be immediate, measurable and visible.*

In June, a subdued group of eight hundred executives gathered at the Tech Center for GM's triennial conference. The difference between this meeting and the euphoric gathering at the Greenbrier three years earlier could not be ignored. Then, the company was swelled with a grand strategy for the future. Finally, it had seemed then, GM was rising victorious from the hole it had dug itself into.

Now, here they were, and it wasn't the opulence of the Greenbrier but the familiar surroundings of the Tech Center. It was cost-cutting time, and the perk of a Greenbrier retreat was no longer in the budget.

At the conference, Lloyd Reuss opened with a typical "rah, rah" speech about great cars, working hard, and getting the job done. Others were less optimistic. Executive vice president F. Alan Smith, who followed Reuss, outlined a gloomy picture.

From 1980 through 1985, he told the group, GM spent $45 billion in capital investment, yet increased its worldwide market share by only 1 percentage point, to 22 percent. Until mid-1986, the capital-spending plan called for an additional $35 billion through 1989, but that had been reduced.

"For the same amount of money," he told the GM managers, "we could buy Toyota and Nissan outright," instantly increasing the market share to 40 percent.

To illustrate the problem, Smith laid out a comparison between a Ford Taurus plant and a GM A-car plant. The Ford plant operated with thirty-two hundred hourly and salaried workers. It took them twenty-five hours to build each car. At the GM plant, there were fifty-two hundred hourly and salaried workers. It took them forty-one hours to build a car.

It was an unavoidably stark picture, and when Jim McDonald rose to his feet to speak, he looked at the gloomy executives around the room and set aside his prepared notes to address the group directly. "I hear a lot about improving the way we make cars with innovation and technology of all kinds," he said with carefully controlled anger. "I fully support the need for updating and modernizing all of our facilities. Improvements are important, but unless we interrupt the alarming rise in fixed costs (projected to be 35 percent in 1986), we could be 'improving' ourselves right out of the ball park.

"We don't need more capital expenditures," he said with an urgent feeling that he rarely expressed in a public setting. "We don't need any more mission statements." He sounded faintly disgusted.

McDonald was venting his fury for all the failures and frustrations of the past three years. He scolded the top managers like children, insisting they weren't working hard enough, weren't trying hard enough to reach for quality. "I've been going to these conferences for many years," he told them. "And inevitably somebody at the end says, 'You're a helluva group. You've done a helluva job and I'm proud of you.' Well, I can say you're a helluva group. I feel that you've worked hard, but I don't really feel that I can say I'm proud of you, because we have not accomplished what we set out to do here."

These were very tense times at General Motors—finger pointing times. The grand dreams of the early part of the decade seemed almost impossible to fulfill. So many changes. So many improvements. So much newness forced into the doddering structure. But where was the payoff. Where was the excitement? Where were the gleaming new cars that dazzled and seduced the public? Where was the revived market share, which had dipped from 46 percent to 42 percent since 1980?

It had been years now since the organization had started trying to achieve quality and efficiency. But the improvements were sporadic—a plant here, a plant there, an experiment somewhere else. It was not enough. While Roger Smith was busy laying the foundations for a twenty-first-century car company, GM's competitors were selling cars that consumers wanted to buy *today.*

With all its grand visions, General Motors just kept demonstrating that it didn't understand the people for whom it was building its cars. The redesigned Eldorado, named by *Motor Trend* magazine as the worst car of the year, was a case in point. "The problem with the Eldorado," *Motor Trend* wrote, "stems from the basic GM credo to be everything to everybody. Choose a middle ground, don't be too daring, and don't offend your established constituency. After all, vanilla is still America's favorite flavor."

What GM tried to do with the Eldorado was create a smaller, sportier Cadillac that would attract the BMW set. In the process, they alienated traditional Eldorado buyers, and BMW customers laughed at the weak attempt. It was a car built for nobody. "Longtime Cadillac owners won't like it. European sports-touring owners won't bother to look at it. Where's the market?" asked *Motor Trend.*

Chief Executive magazine had just named Roger Smith Chief Executive of the Year, writing in glowing terms of the leader who "tore up a proud, if aging, battleship and is rebuilding it into a squadron of guided missile cruisers and attack submarines." Smith beamed from the pages of the magazine, a confident corporate executive. In the interview, he spoke optimistically of the big payoff that was already beginning to be seen from the investments of the decade.

But back in the real world, rumors of massive spending cuts involving thousands of white-collar workers were in the wind, even as GM was still proclaiming to investors that all was well, and the fruits of their investments would soon be ripe for the picking.

The task of evaluating spending would become a veritable nightmare. Said one former purchasing manager, "There's a lot of flapping of arms about cutting costs a certain percentage, but what are they measuring the cuts against? They don't even know what they're spending in the first place."

Paint purchasing was a good example of the truth of this remark. GM bought about $600 million worth of paint a year. The company would invite bids from three or four major suppliers, with one supplier serving one plant. Say Supplier A bid $60 a gallon, Supplier B bid $50 a gallon, and Supplier C bid $40 a gallon. The natural response would be to give the entire paint order to Supplier C. But that's not what GM did. Instead, the company went back to Suppliers B and C and told them they would have to match the $40 bid of Supplier A. They would, of course, and all three would get the business they sought at $40 a gallon.

But this method left GM wide open to distortions that often cost more in the long run. What was the incentive to bid lower when the supplier knew it would eventually get the business anyway? Why not bid as high as possible and chance getting the business for a higher cost?

An expert was brought in to help deal with the problem, but a solution couldn't be found immediately because GM kept *no record* of how much paint it had purchased in prior years. They had to go back to the suppliers to get that information. It was a long and tedious process figuring out how much of each color was being used in each plant.

It would have shocked an outsider to see such sloppy records on purchases in the hundreds of millions of dollars, but the data simply did not exist. There was no one in the company who could tell how much it cost to paint a car this year as opposed to last year.

Once the data were created, it was possible to pursue truly competitive bids for each plant. And, lo and behold, suddenly the costs dropped.

More and more, as GM began evaluating costs it was finding evidence of sloppy record-keeping, laziness, and habitual lack of planning when ordering materials in the hundreds of millions of dollars. Many suppliers found that when they called GM, they'd either get someone who had been on the job for six weeks and didn't know what he was doing, or someone who was going to retire in six weeks and didn't give a rip. Many insiders were thinking, "Hey, this whole place is unraveling." Ironically, the reorganization had made everything worse because now suppliers had to deal with two purchasing groups and two sets of specifications for the same order.

Another target for cost evaluation was GM's internal component divisions, which were perceived to be less competitive with outside sources than they should be. W. Blair Thompson, vice president and group executive in charge of the mechanical components group, was named to head up the newly formed Automotive Components Groups, which included one group of body and engine parts producers and one group of chassis and transmission producers. Together, the groups employed 250,000 employees at 139 plants.

Jim McDonald had expressed an interest in cutting down on internally produced components and using outside companies if it meant getting a better price. He told Thompson to evaluate the groups and determine where GM was uncompetitive.

Thompson and three outside consultants developed a red-yellow-green system for evaluating the operations. Red meant the unit was not competitive, had no hope of becoming competitive, and should be shut down. Yellow meant the unit was not competitive, but could be turned around. Green meant the unit was outperforming the outside competition. Thompson hired three different consulting companies to evaluate the groups. According to Thompson, the studies showed that "roughly 54 percent of the product ended up being competitive with the best in the world. The remainder were either noncompetitive—about four percent—or in the intermediate area that they weren't at the world's best cost but not so uncompetitive that we couldn't do anything about it."

There was enormous criticism from the unions about the red-yellow-green system, especially on the point that outside consultants didn't really understand the workings of the groups. Eventually, the color ratings were scrapped altogether, and GM abandoned the idea of outsourcing components.

The 4 percent of units that received the red "no hope" rating were declared, as if by magic, competitive a year after the studies were completed. What happened? According to Bill Hoglund, "They aren't fully competitive yet, but they have plans in place to get themselves competitive in four or five years. And I think General Motors is saying, 'We're going to give them that chance rather than outsource.' "

By summer of 1986, the company was announcing its plans to cut 25 percent of the salaried work force by 1989. Production on two subcompact cars, the Chevette and Pontiac 1000, was being terminated three months ahead of schedule because of poor sales.

By the end of the second quarter of 1986, it would be clear that Ford had a tremendous edge over GM in its ability to produce cars economically. In the period 1981 through mid-1986, Ford's profit per car had risen from $839 to $1,867, while GM's had increased from $1,111 to $1,741. It was apparent that Ford was running lean. By year's end, Ford, for the first time since 1924, would exceed GM in net income—$3.3 billion to $2.9 billion.

GM posted a 19-percent drop in second quarter profit, despite a 10 percent rise in revenues. Its stock price skidded to a twelve-month low as a result. Ford's second quarter sales rose 25 percent.

Roger Smith, groping as always for a way to make bad news sound good, said GM had turned the corner and was beginning to cash in on the creation of BOC and CPC, as a way of introducing the news that GM planned to close eleven assembly and fabrication plants in the United States by 1990, laying off twenty-nine thousand workers. Observed Bill Hoglund, "Only a few years ago, we were so successful and so powerful in the marketplace that we were worried about antitrust. Now we're running for our lives."

Smith's annual Christmas messages were beginning to sound like tired reruns. In 1985, he had urged employees to "stay the course." Christmas 1986 brought a similar plea, but behind the emotion in his words was the sound of a man who had undoubtedly just endured the worst year of his corporate life. He had just spent four months being bashed, professionally and personally, in the press, among investors, and inside his own company. And he had somehow failed to communicate the vision he believed in so dearly. Now he had to listen to rumors that he was on his way out.

"For thousands and thousands of years," the message read, "families, tribes and communities, in the darkness of winter, came together to reassure themselves that no matter how dark and cold it seemed, the light and warmth would return. . . .

"I ask you to have faith."

Riding High on Automation:

A Gamble That Backfired

There exists a wide belief that "if it's automated, it must be good," but our experience shows that this is not always the case.

—Alfred P. Sloan

Donald Morris, an hourly worker at GM's Delco Remy division in Anderson, Indiana, had been with the company for thirty-two years and was looking ahead to retirement. In his career, he had seen many changes at GM, watched chairmen and presidents come and go, and rolled with the punches. But the influx of robots was the toughest challenge he had faced in all those years. Instead of streamlining operations at the plant, the robots were making his work harder. Morris found it tough to keep pace with the new machinery as it was being introduced and debugged.

At the end of his shift, Morris would drag himself home, tired and frustrated, and complain to his wife Joyce that the robots didn't work right half the time. There was always something wrong with them, they were always breaking down. Morris had been trained as well as anyone to handle the robots, but he wasn't sure what the ultimate advantage would be—except, he told his wife cynically, to eliminate more jobs.

In December 1986, Morris didn't move fast enough and a robot whacked him in the head. He was taken to the hospital for stitches, but he was lucky. His wife told him to be more careful and he was, although soon after he would duck just in time to barely miss getting whacked again. By now, Morris's nerves were on edge—he just wasn't used to viewing his job as a high-risk occupation.

Saturday, October 11, 1987, was a workday for Morris. Around noon, Joyce Morris received a call, telling her she should go to St. John's Hospital in Anderson immediately—something had happened to her husband. She rushed to the hospital and arrived to hear the news. Donald Morris was dead. He had been killed by a robot.

Details of what actually occurred were sketchy because there had been no witnesses. But when Morris was found, he was pinned underneath a robot designed to pick up heavy-duty tractor frames and drill holes in them. It appeared that he might have been trying to do some maintenance on the robot when it crushed him.

Morris's death was kept quiet—only a small item appeared in the newspaper. Concerned with liability, General Motors set about placing the blame on Morris. "They were keeping it hush-hush because they didn't want to be blamed for it," said a bitter Joyce Morris. Meanwhile, the company made it difficult for her to collect the workman's compensation. The first proposal was that they would pay her $95,000 total, reduced to $85,000 if she wanted the money in a lump sum. Joyce Morris told them that she didn't want to accept the offer before she had a lawyer check it out for her. Eventually, her lawyer advised her to take the $85,000 lump sum, but when she returned to the company, the offer was no longer available.

"Now they wouldn't give it to me in a lump sum. They said I had to take it as $195 a week for five hundred weeks. So I went to the union to see if they could help me get a lump sum, and I still haven't heard anything."

As she waited for an answer, Joyce Morris was living off her late husband's $408-per-month pension money.

Ultimately, the Indiana Office of Safety and Occupational Health would fine GM $6,000 for the incident, citing inadequate training. It amounted to a slap on the wrist in exchange for Donald Morris's life.

Like many of his coworkers, Morris had not received proper training in robotics. While management was feeling the pressure to improve quality and productivity, the union was concerned about protecting jobs and had combined some job classifications to increase flexibility. But training workers in the new technology was a slow process. In a period of three years, only about 10 percent of the work force had enough training in the technology to function even minimally. These were assembly line workers, not computer programmers. They didn't learn the complex programming skills overnight—especially when the first step in the training sometimes meant teaching the worker to read!

During the late 1970s, when General Motors was feeling the heat from foreign competition, it launched a massive long-term investment in automation, setting a course for the future that would lead the company down many blind alleys. By the late 1980s, GM would have spent many billions of dollars on technological solutions, including $40 billion for modernization and new facilities, $2.5 billion to buy EDS, $5.2 billion to buy Hughes, and billions more on Saturn.

Back at the start of the 1980s, robots and automated systems seemed to represent a dazzling new hope for the beleaguered auto industry. General Motors was vocal in its commitment to technological advancements and robotics, bragging that by the year 1990 it would have twenty-one thousand robots operating in its plants. During the first half of the decade, GM would purchase equity in five machine-vision suppliers and a company that developed artificial intelligence systems.

Ford and Chrysler, unable to afford the massive capital investment of GM, dealt with crisis by cutting back on spending programs and were forced to look for production- and management-oriented solutions, while GM was inadvertently piling up fixed costs for the future. Their timely poverty saved Ford and Chrysler from investing too heavily in a technological direction that later turned out to be a Pandora's box. Had money been available, the two companies probably would have eagerly invested in automation because, at the time, virtually all experts were lauding it as the best way to turn around the aging, sluggish American auto industry. As GM began its spending spree,

Ford and Chrysler looked on with deep concern, wondering how they would be able to compete against GM's ultramodern plants.

According to economist George Eads: "The notion of rebuilding the factories was the basic strategy that was laid out in 1980. And I think we have helped Ford by doing some of the things we have in heavy automation. We've raised some caution flags for them."

As Alfred Sloan would predict long before the high-tech era hit its stride, automation alone was inadequate to solve the problems of the company. In fact, the determination to find a "quick fix" had the reverse effect. In a 1986 *New York Times* report, Barnaby Feder told of a 1984 study conducted by Harvard's Ramchandrin Jaikumar of thirty-five flexible manufacturing systems in the United States and sixty in Japan. Ramchandrin called the United States "a desert of mediocrity" compared with Japan and noted that the technology of automation was widening, rather than narrowing the competitive gap. The Japanese system of continuous improvement on older equipment worked better than the typical American solution of investing in state-of-the-art technology that the workers were poorly trained to operate.

A management philosophy of continuous improvement allowed companies to avoid the pitfalls of overspending for the wrong reasons. Without a continuous and consistent method of evaluating its needs, GM ended up investing in million-dollar solutions for ten-cent problems—instead of finding ten-cent solutions for million-dollar problems.

All too often, GM threw money at a problem before there was a clear understanding of what the problem was. This was certainly the case in its heavy installation of automated guided vehicles (AGVs) on the plant floors. The idea behind AGVs was that they would move parts around the plant floors, eliminating the expense of hiring human workers to man forklift trucks. But nobody stopped to consider the real issue, which was, How do plants devise production and inventory systems that make the appropriate parts readily available when they're needed? The Japanese just-in-time system of production scheduling and inventory control addressed the basic problem of reducing in-plant inventory. AGVs were, too often, simply used to replace forklift-truck operators without questioning the money invested in inventory. And the AGVs proved to be temperamental, requiring trained operators and heavy maintenance.

With its drive to automate, General Motors opted for *revolution* when *evolution* would have been more appropriate. The company saw itself replacing the expensive hourly workers through automation, thereby slashing its fixed costs. But the reverse happened.

In mid-decade, the newly built Hamtramck plant was to be the "Cadillac" of GM technological prowess. The plant that had been built amid a storm of protest and hard feelings was now ready and equipped with the latest automated high-tech systems. It was here that General Motors expected to build the Cadillacs of the future, using the tools of the future. Hamtramck was to be a pilot for GM's $3.5-billion Saturn manufacturing complex, which was supposed to finally revolutionize the auto-manufacturing process.

The showcase plant opened with 260 robots for welding, assembling and painting cars; 50 automated guided vehicles to ferry parts to the assembly line; and a battery of cameras and computers that used laser beams to inspect and control the manufacturing process.

But instead of a showcase, Hamtramck became a nightmare of technology gone berserk. The stories of robot breakdowns and miscues read like a 1950s B movie that might have been titled *Robots from Hell.*

The robotic assembly line was so loaded with problems that the workers might have considered breaking out the champagne when a car made it through successfully without getting smashed, dented, assembled backward, or painted the wrong color.

The first step in the process, as the underbody started down the line, was for the equipment to read a computerized spec sheet, which noted the car's make, model, color, and equipment. Along the line, scanners read the information on the card and instructed the machines how to build the car. Display monitors told the human workers which parts needed to be built by hand.

The kinks in this seemingly simple system were so great at Hamtramck that often the workers had nothing to do but sit around drinking coffee and reading newspapers (at an estimated cost of $200 per downtime second) while yet another problem was fixed. Or they would find themselves redoing manually jobs the robots had performed poorly. For example, the robots that applied sealants to the cars' joints often missed the right locations and dripped the gooey sealant on the floor. Humans had to reapply the sealant correctly while standing in the sticky mess the robots had created. The sealing robots were so inefficient that while they were projected to eliminate ten jobs, they were only able to eliminate four.

As the assembled body reached the end of the line, it was directed into one of eight robot-manned paint booths. There, the robots painted the bodies without human supervision. Breakdowns in the paint shop were frequent, especially when the line would speed up. Often cars emerged with incomplete or uneven paint jobs, which, once again, would have to be perfected by humans. In one case, several hundred cars were shipped to an old-fashioned Cadillac plant nearby to be repainted with old-fashioned hand-held spray guns.

Tales from the dark side of high technology gained momentum as people slowly began to see that this was not the panacea the company had promised it would be. The problems existed, not only at the Hamtramck plant, but in every plant where robots had been installed to perform vital functions.

- Robots designed to spray-paint cars were painting each other instead.
- A robot designed to install windshields was found systematically smashing them.
- Factory lines were halted for hours while technicians scrambled to debug the software.
- Robots went haywire and smashed into cars, demolishing both the vehicle and the robot.
- Computer systems sent erroneous instructions, leading to body parts being installed on the wrong cars.

A common scenario, as outlined in a *Ward's Auto World* magazine report, would be a robot abruptly shutting down and no one in the plant knowing the cause of the problem. An electrician familiar with one brand of robot hurries to the scene, only to find that this is a robot manufactured by a different company, and he doesn't understand how it operates. As the entire plant slowly grinds to a halt, and the electrician begins to plow through a complicated manual, the robot's manufacturer is called for advice. A company-trained expert is flown to the scene to analyze the situation and solve the problem. He looks at the robot for a minute, then hits a reset button (the modern equivalent of checking to see if the thing is plugged in). The machine springs to life. Everyone goes back to work.

"This has happened," an official of a robotics concern told Ward's, and automakers confirmed that it happened more than once. "I'm inclined to think technology may kill us if we don't start using our heads," a process engineer at Hamtramck said.

At Hamtramck, what was intended as a high-tech solution turned into gross inefficiency. Lines were stopped so frequently for repairs that one observer described car building in the plant as being "like viewing a film in slow motion, even when the assembly line is moving—which it often isn't."

Hamtramck was supposed to produce sixty cars per hour, but after nearly a year of operation it was only producing half that number, and the software was still being debugged. By late 1988, researchers at MIT had concluded that GM's Hamtramck factory was no different from the Ford Wixom plant, which produced equally complex luxury models without all the fanfare and investment. In both instances, the plants were only half as efficient as comparable Japanese facilities.

According to former vice chairman Donald Atwood, GM learned its lesson in the costly debugging process of the Hamtramck plant. Atwood believed that if the Hughes acquisition had been made earlier, a lot of the problems might have been avoided by creating preoperation computer simulations of the factory. In other words, instead of going into full operation on a costly trial-and-error basis, the computers would demonstrate what the anticipated problems might be and fix them. But there were other problems in addition to nonfunctioning equipment. The training issue remained a serious roadblock to fully functioning high-tech plant operations. For, once the software was debugged, who would "debug" the workers?

A front-page article in *The Wall Street Journal* described the state of Hamtramck mid-1986 this way:

> So far the Hamtramck plant, instead of a showcase, looks more like a basket case. Though the plant has been open for seven months, the automated guided vehicles are sitting idle

while technicians try to debug the software that controls their movements. Hamtramck is turning out only 30 to 35 cars an hour, far less than the 60 an hour it was designed to build. "We underestimated the magnitude of the task," acknowledges GM's Jan Tannehil, who oversees Hamtramck and several other GM plants. "We are making progress but it has been very slow."

How different things were in the Japanese factory systems! It is ironic that we once feared the Japanese for their secret high-tech industrial weaponry when, in fact, they were slow to implement technology for the very reasons it was such a disaster at General Motors.

NUMMI president Tatsuro Toyoda noted that "there's no doubt that robots, lasers, and computers can improve quality and productivity while reducing costs. However, it is not the only way. A balance of technology and people can accomplish high quality and reduce costs." NUMMI, which was consistently a quality and cost leader among GM plants, used only eleven computers in the plant.

Two years after the sparkling-new Hamtramck plant opened, with its grand promise of a smooth, swift, and high-quality production line, Toyota would open a brand-new plant in Kentucky. A visitor to the plant, expecting to see the latest in technological wizardry, would be amazed to find, at the end of the 1980s, such a traditional plant. In fact, it would be explained, the factory was a complete clone of Tsutsumi, a plant in Japan. It was as though the Japanese factory had been picked up and deposited in the rolling hills of Kentucky. Since both factories would be identical, if a robotics maintenance problem occurred in Kentucky, they could receive complete and accurate instructions from Tsutsumi on correcting the problem.

When asked why there were so few robots, so little state-of-the-art equipment, the management of the new plant would explain that their intention was to minimize risk. For them, it would seem a big enough chunk to bite off that they were coming to the United States and would be starting off with a new work force. Why not keep the risks down by opening with a factory operation that they already knew how to run, rather than starting completely from scratch? New technology could be added later, once the plant was operating in a smooth, cohesive way.

Consider the compelling logic of this strategy as opposed to GM's decision to build a brand-new plant in Hamtramck, with a brand-new production system, brand-new workers, and the task of building a brand-new car. There were no constants whatsoever—not even the look of the equipment. The most experienced workers in the company could walk into the factory on the first day, look at a machine, and not know whether it was designed to make coffee or weld a car. And the Japanese devoted far more time to training its new work force, even though they had far less to learn.

Eiji Toyoda once toured the Hamtramck plant. At lunch afterward with Roger Smith and Jim McDonald, Toyoda was pressed to give his impression of the plant. He avoided answering, and later told a colleague, "It would have been embarrassing to comment on it."

Throughout the 1980s, General Motors leapfrogged past the competition in its installation of high-tech equipment. The company always selected the next generation of equipment—even when it wasn't yet fully tested. As a result, they ended up with multistage transfer presses that were not yet perfected and for which software to make them operate smoothly had not been written; they installed modular paint lines that required tremendous software capabilities to guarantee that cars were painted the right colors in the right sequence. To make matters worse, GM used several different paint systems throughout the organization, always experimenting to find something better. The company consistently bit off more than it could chew in the technological arena, in a relentless quest for higher quality and greater efficiency. Even with the NUMMI plant bearing such potent witness to the fact that technology was not, in and of itself, the solution, GM would not listen. Even when the Hamtramck plant turned into a disaster, the company took the simplistic stance that once the kinks were ironed out, everything would be great. Minimizing the problem to the extreme, Roger Smith would say, "The key is an intelligent system of robots that can say, 'Uh oh, here comes an Oldsmobile that's got to be welded differently than the Buick that just went by.' "

But is getting the technology to operate more efficiently the solution? In his book, *Attaining Manufacturing Excellence,* Robert Hall writes that experts who have observed both Japanese and American plants conclude the following:

(1) New American plants often have excellent technology that is at least equal to Japanese and usually better. That is, any technology gap still slightly favors Americans. (2) American computer systems and software are almost always superior to Japanese. They are larger, more complex, and more powerful, but this can be a weakness as well as strength if the systems mask wasteful practices that should not exist. (3) Japanese are almost always superior in their ability to improve existing plant and equipment: tooling improvement, defect elimination, layout improvement and so forth. The conclusion is that the Americans have trouble putting the pieces together and making the most of what they have.

W. Edwards Deming, remarking on Roger Smith's heavy investment in technology, quoted Smith as saying, "The future belongs to him that invests in it." Not so, said Deming. "He put forty billion dollars into equipment, buying poor quality at high cost."

Often it seemed, GM tried to find high-tech solutions without first making an attempt to identify the problem. For example, one plant manager pointed proudly to a laser-guided tail-lamp inserter, a piece of automated wizardry specifically designed to locate the holes for proper connection of the tail lamp. But the need for this machine was created by the fact that the holes were not always put in the same place. Would it not have been more sensible to make sure that the holes were consistently placed in identical locations?

A perfect example of a technological versus management-driven operation was demonstrated in the different ways BOC and CPC handled the quest for greater capacity and lower cost in their stamping plants. It was still taking GM far longer than the Japanese competition to build a car. Uptime in GM stamping plants was an embarrassing 35 percent compared with more than 75 percent in Japan.

One major stumbling block was the time it took to change dies in these plants. Reasons for the lag could be attributed to a variety of factors, including a lack of ongoing die maintenance, inefficient organization of work, and a poorly trained and motivated work force. The company began to take a hard look at what it would take to get management and labor more unified in the task of survival.

The stamping plant problems highlighted some very fundamental differences in the way BOC and CPC operated. Earlier
in 1987, Bill Hoglund had been moved from Saturn to head up
BOC, replacing Bob Stempel, who had been promoted to executive vice president. Hoglund continued Stempel's efforts to
improve efficiency and quality by concentrating on improving
the way BOC managed equipment and the people who ran it. At
CPC, Lloyd Reuss continued to take more traditional GM approaches, including the age-old route of throwing money at the
problem.

Alex Cunningham felt the basic problem was the outdated
tandem presses. He decided that the solution was to scrap the
old presses and buy up the world's new transfer-press capacity
for a year and a half. (Roger Smith, always a believer in buying
state-of-the-art equipment, regardless of cost, would brag that
GM was upgrading its stamping plants and the competition
would be forced to match them but wouldn't be able to until
GM's orders were filled.)

The problem with buying the most technologically advanced presses was that they were untested in real plant situations in the United States. Instead of becoming more efficient,
GM was actually serving as a guinea pig for the rest of the
industry in ironing out the glitches in the new systems and
debugging the software. Once the problems became apparent,
Reuss tried to cancel some of the orders, only to find that the
purchase contract carried a $100-million penalty for cancella-
tion. CPC was saddled with extra capacity, made worse by the
fact that the orders were based on a seven-plant GM-10 program, and an overall 40-percent plus market share—neither of
which came to pass.

Meanwhile, BOC stamping plants were hard at work in-
stituting improvements that made the critical difference in uptime, which is worth some $25,000 per minute on a press line.

Hoglund sent the people responsible for making die
changes at the Lordstown plant around the country to see who
did it best and what they could learn.

"They came up with all the ideas," Hoglund said. "They
can change dies in eighteen minutes with die trucks. Eighteen
minutes! They took it from twelve hours to eighteen minutes.
You get die changes down to within two hours versus twelve
hours and the uptime is going to explode. They've increased
uptime from thirty-five percent to between fifty and fifty-five

percent. On that basis, you can't justify spending two point five billion dollars on transfer presses."

At a BOC plant in Lansing, Michigan, teams were set up to make a number of incremental changes that dramatically dropped time, including a system for getting metal parts through each pressing station faster, maintaining dies better by storing them closer to the presses instead of outside, and standardizing certain die bolts so that workers wouldn't need five different tools, but only one, to make changes. With these improvements, they were able to get die-changing down to as little as ten minutes on a seventeen-year-old tandem press.

These efforts did not go unnoticed by *Automotive Industries* magazine, which announced that it would sponsor a die-changing contest, welcoming all plants that wanted to participate. Only four plants accepted the challenge: BOC Lansing, BOC Lordstown, Nissan, and Honda. (No CPC plants entered the competition.)

Two Lansing teams—North and South—competed. The North team turned in a time of 10 minutes, 36 seconds. The South team turned in a time of 13 minutes, 7 seconds.

Nissan came in behind the Lansing plants, with 13 minutes, 17 seconds.

Lordstown had unexpected problems and their score was 26 minutes.

But the winner was Honda, with a time of only 5 minutes 17 seconds.

The BOC plants might have been unable to beat Honda, but consider the vast improvement: Only a year earlier, it had taken Lordstown twelve hours to change dies; Lansing North four hours; and Lansing South ninety minutes.

GM's massive capital-spending programs substituted fixed costs for variable costs and were undertaken in a profoundly mistaken belief that the main reason for high production costs in the past were strictly a function of excessive compensation to hourly workers and overmanning of the assembly line. Ironically, even as they invested fortunes in solving the productivity problem, their man-hours per car remained higher than both Chrysler and Ford.

According to Roger Smith, "Automation came along just in time to save us." He likes to point out that Ford will "get theirs" by having to spend to automate while GM will be finished spending. But this seems to miss several points, most notably that Ford is operating efficiently before the high expenditures. Also, GM has really served as a guinea pig for all its competitors in the technology game. By the time they become more automated, the expensive bugs will already be ironed out, thanks to the generous purse of General Motors.

Finally, GM got the message that was being shouted high and low—from the profitability of his low-tech Japanese competition to his own experience with NUMMI to the massive problems of plants like Hamtramck—and that is, technology is only a tool, not an end in itself. And what good is a tool that doesn't work? Those companies that have developed a system of continuous improvement will *always* be ahead of the game, compared to those that hope that a magic new era will beam down an automatic solution.

David Cole, director of the University of Michigan's Office for the Study of Automotive Transportation, warned that technology must be applied hand in hand with sound business practice. "The real key factor here is just how good a manufacturing enterprise can be if managed properly, without the high technology," Dr. Cole said. "And this has certainly happened in spades to GM from the NUMMI experience. NUMMI is low-tech, but has roughly twice the productivity of their operations in Detroit. In terms of being competitive, or trying to develop a competitive advantage, it says that step one is really using the existing technology properly. Step two is implementation of the advanced technology. But if you begin to implement the advanced technology off of a poorly managed conventional-technology base, you won't make the right decisions."

In a 1986 survey of more than one hundred auto industry executives and managers, *Ward's Auto World* found that the prevailing opinion was that technology couldn't be relevant to American industry until other systems were set in motion first. Some of the most revealing results from the survey included the following:

- Ninety-three percent disagreed that their higher usage of high-tech devices was the main reason the Japanese were more productive.
- Seventy-one percent agreed that the productivity and quality-producing benefits of advanced manufacturing technology had

been overrated—and 71 percent cited the cause being "management's wishful thinking."

- Sixty-five percent agreed that better use of human resources would produce the biggest productivity gains in the next five years.
- Seventy-two percent disagreed that management really understood what technology such as machine vision, robots, computer-integrated manufacturing, artificial intelligence, and flexible manufacturing systems could do.
- Seventy-one percent disagreed that there would ever be a totally automated, people-free plant. (Ironically, there are already fully automated plants in Japan.)

Always outspoken about GM's misdirected technological prowess, Ross Perot suggested in *The Wall Street Journal* that perhaps a better solution to GM's problems than installing robots might be to "nuke the old GM system. It takes five years to develop a new car in this country," Perot complained. "Heck, we won World War Two in four years. We are spending billions to develop new cars. This isn't a moon shot, it's just a car."

Insiders say that there has been something of a technology backlash within the company, as employees at all levels reach a boiling point of frustration. There is a strong sentiment that Fourteenth Floor executives are so far removed from the real-life operations of the company that they continue to choose directions that have little to do with reality.

"We could probably save four times as much money if we coordinated design and production functions as we could ever hope to save through technology," suggested one plant manager.

Meanwhile, Cadillac was having a different set of problems launching Allanté, the model that was supposed to restore Cadillac's high prestige. This was the car whose body would be designed by Pininfarina to capture the European mystique of the luxury vehicle. How could it possibly go wrong?

The problems with Allanté were so numerous that it almost seemed Cadillac was engaged in a competition to see how many defects could be built into one car. Mechanically, it was a disaster—underpowered and plagued by mysterious rattles and squeaks. It was outrageously overpriced at $55,000—even if the car had worked perfectly. This went against conventional wisdom that an image car should start priced below the competition; the price can be jacked up when demand is established. And the goals for volume were way out of line for $55,000. With classic marketing bravado, Cadillac's general manager, John Grettenberger, projected that seven thousand cars would be sold the first year.

Originally, GM's internal staff projected sales of three thousand cars, with a $45,000 price tag. But at that volume and price, the project failed to generate a 15-percent ROI, so the division's answer was to raise both estimates to make the project work on paper.

The storm of complaints from the first owners was so severe that hundreds of the cars had to be "corralled"—GM's term for an informal recall of cars riddled with defects. The list of defects was long; these are some of the problems that existed in a car that sold for the price of a small house:

- The car leaked in the rain because of defects in the weather stripping.
- The digital instrument panel was hard to read and unnecessarily confusing.
- The interior looked cheap. Customers complained that there was too much plastic for such an expensive car.
- Squeaks and rattles abounded. They were built into the car, as they are in the hand-built Italian cars, but hardly conformed to the quality image of a Cadillac.
- Windshield glass had ripples in it, apparently caused by complex curvature.
- Seat adjusters had a tendency to break, causing the seat to rock back and forth.
- The door was hard to open and the automatic door locks tended to break. (One owner got trapped inside and had to climb through a window in his tuxedo. Another had to have a friend call the 800 number to get herself freed.)
- Taking the convertible top down and putting it back was so complicated that a video was produced to show customers how. This didn't help those who were simply not tall or strong enough to manage the operation.

To add insult to injury, owners complained that a toll-free, twenty-four-hour phone line established to handle Allanté problems often went unanswered.

One customer wrote sarcastically about the prestigious gold car keys. "I think you are having a problem obtaining the image you are looking for on the Gold Key Delivery System, as long as the gold flakes off the keys."

The most remarkable aspect of the entire Allanté fiasco was that the problems customers were finding with their new cars weren't news to Cadillac. They had all been duly noted at the Milford proving ground long before the car hit the market. For example, drivers of prototype and pilot cars complained of getting soaked whenever it rained because of a weather stripping problem that Pininfarina once tried lamely to fix by stuffing brown paper behind the weather stripping!

How on earth could the cars be allowed to go to market having so many defects?

A key engineer on Allanté shrugged when asked the question, commenting that often first-year cars had defects that weren't fixed until later. He said, "It takes time to get the bugs out."

But how could General Motors blithely charge customers $55,000 for a car riddled with defects? Customers responded by not buying the car. With only three thousand cars sold, GM was forced to offer a $9,000 rebate to dealers in 1988. Resale values collapsed, and classified ads today often list Allantés with less than 10,000 miles selling for as little as $25,000.

The Allanté fiasco is perhaps the most searing example of the cynical attitude General Motors has traditionally had toward its customers. Let it go to market, they figured. We'll fix the problems later—if the customers even notice them.

It also underlines the dangerous internal approval system, still firmly in place in spite of all the changes in organization and philosophy. Everyone was scrambling to present the best picture to the top brass and no one was considering the customer.

"No single individual is to blame," said one former Cadillac executive wearily. "It's all of the committees and telephone calls you get, and the approval steps that you have to go through . . . and you just wear down. You get so many calls from people saying, 'I don't think this is going to sell. My boss isn't going to support it if you have this.' And you start trying to figure out ways to get around that maze." In the case of Allanté, transcripts of meetings among team members were often altered or purged of bad news, even though most people associated with the car admit that it wasn't ready for market.

But there was one positive outcome. The experience with Allanté woke the company up to the realization that brand identity was a critical element of success for Cadillac. Searching for a way to strengthen Cadillac's image and productivity, BOC head Bill Hoglund organized a team to pursue new directions.

"The one that surfaced and seemed to make the most sense," said John Grettenberger, "was to let Cadillac reestablish itself in terms of being a car division." The move would give Cadillac, for most of its products, complete responsibility for product planning, design, engineering, manufacturing, and marketing.

Grettenberger remembers the day it was announced that there would be a Cadillac Car Company again. There were as many as fifteen hundred employees crammed into the room at the Merritt Street warehouse, and when the word came down, they let out an enormous cheer. There were tears in the eyes of many veteran Cadillac workers who had suffered a blow when their beloved insignia was replaced with the BOC logo. After the meeting, a group of employees went out in front of the plant and hauled down the BOC flag. Up went the proud yellow Cadillac flag with its wreath and crest—the symbol of a stature that Cadillac was struggling to regain.

By the end of 1986, publicity about Saturn had reached a saturation point, even though the volumes of information reported in the press about revolutionary management systems, new dealer contracts, technological advancement, and so on still failed to shed light on one not so insignificant factor: the car itself. During the next two years, as the bustle of activity involved in setting up the Tennessee plant reached a fever pitch, the theretofore patient media would become testy. "Remind us, please: What was the point of this exercise?" asked one *Fortune* magazine article, and the question had merit. Although Roger Smith could wax eloquent about Saturn at the drop of a hat, he was beginning to sound like the doting father who could not see the obnoxious side of his offspring.

There were good reasons to wonder why General Motors was continuing to pile big bucks into Saturn. For, what might have seemed a brilliant move in late 1983 almost seemed redundant four or five years later. Consider these facts:

- When Saturn was announced, the idea of reorganizing General Motors was just a gleam in the eye of president McDonald. The company had changed dramatically since those days, and presumably was capable of bringing high-quality cars to the market faster than in the past.
- When Saturn was announced, the GM-Toyota joint venture was not up and running. Since then, NUMMI had proven to be a quality-production success story, using the labor-management techniques GM was unveiling at Saturn. Why not take the lessons from NUMMI and begin to funnel them more directly into the company? By the time Saturn was up and running, it would be too late to start.
- And how many experiments would GM implement before they instituted the *real thing*? NUMMI, Buick City, Hamtramck, and now Saturn. Might it be that GM thought it could satisfy its need for change with spot solutions?
- Finally, wasn't the idea of a space age Saturn car simply an indulgence for the GM chairman, who dreamed of exotic accoutrements that were not within the reach of current technology? (A Hughes executive laughed at the visionary talk of the day cars would have fancy gadgets like night vision systems. "Sure, I could give you a night vision system," he said. "It would be twenty-thousand-dollar glasses that you fit over your head and they'd weigh about ten pounds. Or I could put a television set in your car, with cameras attached to the fenders. It's anybody's guess what that might cost.")

It was apparent from the numbers that a Saturn car coming off the line in 1990 or 1991 could not possibly be profitable for GM, given the massive expenditure. So, if its value was to be the *process,* not the *product,* as some GMers have suggested, how and when would this process be incorporated into the larger body?

At least one important lesson seemed to be learned from the failure at Hamtramck and other robotized factories: Technology alone was not the answer. For Saturn, GM was placing the emphasis on people management, NUMMI-style, and scaling back on original plans to make Saturn a fully automated plant.

But as time went on, GM also seemed to be retreating point by point from its originally declared intention. When the program was first announced, it was stated that the company would produce 500,000 cars in its first year. Later, that number was reduced to 250,000 cars. Also, Saturn was supposed to be a "paperless" corporation. Together with EDS, all of Saturn's administrative tasks, and communications to dealers and suppliers, were to have been done electronically. Much of this has been pulled back on or entirely abandoned.

There was also a retreat from the great employment boon that had governors from thirty-eight states drooling. The original announcement was that six thousand people would be hired. That number was later halved to three thousand—with only fifteen hundred being hired during the first year.

Most notable, the company seemed to be pulling a rather dramatic retreat from its intention to build an import fighter. The car was expected to be larger in size than was originally planned—and was expected to be priced in the $9,000 to $12,000 price range.

And what of the product? Finally, it came down to the product and, frankly, GM's credibility as a producer of import fighters had been stretched pretty thin. This wasn't the first time the company had announced a new product designed to stop the Japanese in their tracks. Remember the Vega? The X-cars? The J-cars? What about the S-cars that were never completed because Smith believed the company was unable to build a competitive subcompact of its own? Some GMers were concerned that inflated expectations might lead the media to butcher Saturn, even if the car *is* an innovatively designed and produced vehicle for the 1990s. "It's not going to be atomic-powered or go zero to one hundred in two seconds," said one executive wearily.

At the core of GM's dilemma as it prepared to begin plant operations for the new product was the growing sentiment that customers didn't know what General Motors stood for anymore. And for those purchasers of foreign imports, GM certainly didn't stand for the leading edge of reliable, innovative small cars that they'd ever consider buying. In a 1986 article published in *The Economist,* the problem was stated directly: "Put rudely, GM's cars are seen by too many as boring and second-rate. In every segment of the market some other company produces a better car."

And now, after listening to the grand talk of Saturn for several years, people were suggesting, "It's all talk and no action . . . how about showing us a car?"

Unable to focus on the car itself, the company went to great extremes to focus on the process, continuing the game show atmosphere that had surrounded Saturn since the beginning.

The next rabbit to be pulled out of the Saturn hat was the dealership grab. At a cost of between $3 and $4 million apiece, GM announced that it would franchise one hundred Saturn dealerships. It hired a team of architects and designers to plan them. The team was called the Red Team ("Red" stands for "retail environmental design") and the architects spoke eloquently about the need for newly designed car dealerships that were "consumer friendly" rather than the traditional, glass-enclosed design, which, they sniffed, was intimidating. (While the point is well-taken, one might also make the argument that what car dealerships need to be "consumer friendly" is cars the customers want to buy.)

Applications from dealer hopefuls began pouring in. Most of them were from current GM dealers who wanted to get in on the ground floor of the hot Saturn project, but many were merely curious about the program and thought this was a good way to find out details. The attrition rate of interested dealers was high due to GM's insistence that they provide three years' worth of personal income tax returns, and that they build showrooms according to GM's specifications. Dealers also wondered if two models were enough to provide an acceptable return on investment; several dealers, who ultimately took Saturn franchises, privately believed it would eventually become a part of Oldsmobile or another car division.

Applications were also pouring in from employee hopefuls. It was expected that more than forty thousand applications would be received for the three thousand jobs at the Spring Hill facility. The hiring process would be the most carefully approached aspect of the program, since the company was banking on its enthusiastic, team-spirited employees to make things really work. The company showed extreme care in the selection and hiring of employees, as was demonstrated by this clip from the *Chicago Tribune:*

Vickie Jones handed the five engineers two sheets of paper. The first listed the problem, the second a number of potential causes.

"You've got 15 minutes," said Jones, a human resources staffer for Saturn Corp.

All the tires on the cars coming off Saturn Corp.'s assembly line were out of balance. The task of the five engineers was to determine the order of importance of 12 possible causes for the problem.

Other than the time limit, there were two other hardships—the five had to work as a team to decide how to rank the 12 causes, and the five weren't engineers; they were reporters.

Vickie Jones was putting reporters through an exercise similar to what prospective Saturn Corp. job candidates face—the team approach to problem-solving.

To be sure, the integration of the team system, along with the revolutionary pact with labor, was the most exciting aspect of the plan. It was, at the very least, a hopeful sign that the company was moving away from bureaucratic rigidity. At the most, it could make the difference in whether Saturn was the car of the future or just a Chevy with a new paint job.

Meanwhile, GM had Madison Avenue spinning with the lure of the Saturn Corporation account for a deserving ad agency. The account, whose estimated billings were projected to exceed $100 million a year, would be a big prize to land, and the agencies came courting. To further hype the selection process, GM appointed to its advertising agency selection team both a UAW representative and a dealer. And the entire selection process generated plenty of snickers throughout the industry. *The Wall Street Journal* called it "one of the more curious mating rituals in the ad business . . . more like a corporate version of 'The Dating Game.' " Explained the *Journal:*

The candidates—Saturn calls them prospective "communications partners"—never proposed any ads. Instead, they were judged on strategic thinking, enthusiasm and compatibility with Saturn. GM officials gauged "personal chemistry" over elegant dinners at which shop talk was discouraged. The eight-person selection team includes not only advertising and marketing executives but also a GM dealer and a union representative. . . . All this has elicited more than a few chuckles in the ad world, especially among those who doubt the need for such intimacy. "I think it's terribly important that we feel comfortable with our ad agency," says Jack Collins, executive vice president of marketing for Hyundai Motor America, recalling his company's three month search in 1985. "But I wasn't marrying them or sleeping with them, and it didn't mean I wanted to have dinner with them."

(The eventual winner was Hal Riney and Partners; the most shocking part of the announcement was that the agency would forgo the sacred cow 15-percent agency commission in favor of a nontraditional cost plus performance arrangement.)

The hoopla surrounding Saturn received mixed reviews—from wildly enthusiastic to cautiously hopeful to extremely critical. Some of the criticism came from expected sources. Lee Iacocca, for instance, wrote of Saturn in his book, *Talking Straight:*

> The press danced a jig over it. The details were blazed from coast to coast: Saturn will be a $5 billion program; Saturn will produce a revolutionary new car; Saturn will have the President of the United States ride in its first prototype. . . .
> Sure enough, little by little, the Saturn project is coming unglued . . . Saturn, unfortunately, is just one of GM's headaches—and they're all Excedrin ones.

And in a letter to *The Wall Street Journal,* which, ironically, identified the problem at Hamtramck, Glenn T. Wilson, an associate professor of operations management at the Southern Illinois University School of Business at Edwardsville, articulated a concern shared by many:

"There is a common-sense management maxim that it is unwise to ask an organization to do too many things at the same time," Wilson wrote.

> GM's Saturn project aims at producing a new car at a new location with new methods and new workers. It might work, but it will require superhuman efforts to avoid producing a bumper crop of lemons.
> What would be preferable? If you want to build a new "green-field" auto factory (a dubious idea anyway, when there's so much surplus capacity), it should produce a standard model of car. If you want to test high-tech robots, do it at an existing factory where the workers already know what they're doing. If you want to produce a small cheap car, do it at an existing plant

where the machinery is already fully depreciated. And if you want a cheap car design, why not produce a two-seater designed for local travel by normal-size people, instead of a sedan for a family of four midgets?

Richard "Skip" LeFauve became Saturn's third president when Bill Hoglund was moved to BOC to replace Bob Stempel in 1987. LeFauve was an enthusiastic spokesman and defender of the Saturn strategy. Interviewed frequently, LeFauve demonstrated great facility for answering some of the toughest questions about Saturn. Asked, for example, whether people who see the Saturn car for the first time will have the sensation of seeing something entirely new and out of the ordinary, LeFauve replied, "I think we've got a good design. That's exactly what happens when people see Saturn for the first time. They just look at the car and then they say, 'I really like that. I really like the car.' But at first you don't say, 'Wow! Bam! Look at that!' It's as though it takes a moment of silence to register all the information. It's a good thing to get that kind of a reaction. But it's not going to be some super-duper image car that you can't make at a low cost."

LeFauve promoted the view that one of Saturn's selling points might be that it won't be seen as a General Motors car. "We're not quite center line General Motors, so maybe they're going to give us a shot. They will come into the Saturn showroom and take a look and listen to people who bought a Saturn to see what they think about it. Today, they don't even want to talk about Cavalier. They won't even ask you if you're driving it how you like it. They wouldn't be caught dead in a Cavalier. They're very intelligent, good shoppers."

In spite of the skepticism that surrounds this launch, it's hard not to be moved to consider the utter significance of a company like GM embarking on such a radical culture-shifting experiment. "Something happens at Saturn," mused LeFauve, "because we're bringing cultures, not only from all over General Motors, but from all over American industry. We're bringing people from outside GM and it's a melding of cultures. A little bit like America was built on, I guess. It sounds kind of corny, but it's the melding of cultures that if people are willing to listen about change, to think about doing things a little bit differently, our strengths start to come out."

But no matter how important the philosophy or how grand the vision, it is plain to see that Saturn will not have more than one chance to get it right. The car that comes off the line in 1990—or whenever—better be perfect from the outset. GM's credibility is at stake.

If the car fails to deliver against very strong competitors, then everything else Saturn stands for may be discredited. If it works, then Saturn's operating principles might find their way throughout GM more easily.

The Road to Recovery:

Eating Humble Pie

People have a human dignity, people want to do the right thing, people want to be treated like people. It's been amazing when you realize that for many years our own people were almost like the enemy. It was a we-they kind of thing. You find out that when you treat people as you would like to be treated, the organization just matures and grows up.
—Robert Stempel

Bob Stempel and Lloyd Reuss were like the two boys, in everyone's childhood experience, who were always competing to be at the head of the class. And in 1987, they would have a real prize to strive for. Jim McDonald was retiring as president of GM and the two men were considered to be the top contenders for the job.

The competition was watched closely, both internally and by outsiders. This was a critical make-or-break time for GM. What kind of president was needed?

Jim McDonald had brought a reorganization about at GM, but many believed that he and Smith were badly paired. Neither was a very effective spokesman for the company—Smith tended toward bravado and appeared to be the company's only spokesman, while McDonald spoke mostly to less visible engineering groups. A forceful, believable voice might enhance GM's image as it moved toward the end of the decade. That description fit

Stempel well. Now the executive vice president of Truck and Bus and overseas operations, Stempel was comfortable in public settings, a natural speaker whose booming voice carried warmth and credibility. Someone once said that Stempel even "wrote loud"—his notes to staff were easily recognizable by their all-cap lettering.

Reuss, now executive vice president of North American car operations, was an articulate speaker, but he lacked Stempel's warmth and easygoing style. His small, tense body was always on the alert. He rarely unbuttoned his three-piece-suit jacket, and his smooth, hard voice carried the tone of an unrelenting salesman.

Another factor to be considered was the working relationship between chairman and president. Smith and McDonald were never a team. The 1980s were Smith's show, and McDonald deferred to and even seemed somewhat intimidated by the chairman for most of that period. But McDonald's style was to let his anger simmer for a long time before it reached a full boil, and by 1986, he was so frustrated and beside himself with the problems in the company that the relationship between the two men became notably tense. There had been rumors for more than a year that Smith was trying to force an early McDonald retirement. And, although McDonald never spoke out openly against Smith, he got his digs in by roundabout means.

On one occasion, the day after Smith had made a public statement that "we now have the basic building blocks in hand necessary to reach our goal of providing competitive transportation and services for the twenty-first century and beyond," McDonald spoke at a commencement ceremony at Michigan Tech University. He said, "Don't listen too closely to anyone who says he can tell you what the future is going to be like. What we're looking at is a whirlwind of change, speeding up in ever-tightening cycles. We have no illusions about how much of an edge advanced technology will give us. It could be only a year or two before it becomes outdated by yet another generation of innovation."

It was often noted in the press that GM needed a charismatic public figure, a "great communicator," who could reshape the company's image in the media. And it was further noted that the struggling chairman might be the beneficiary of a strong second who could take some of the heat. But the choice had to be someone who could relate to Smith as the domineering man he was. It would not be good for the company to have public sparring between the president and chairman at this point in history.

There was little chance of that with either Reuss or Stempel. Reuss was the classic company man, with sharp political instincts. Stempel had a history of being more nontraditional, but he too was a company man, and he possessed the rare talent of being able to raise objections without sounding critical. Stempel had the additional edge of being popular inside the company; those who worked for him enjoyed a participatory atmosphere and a greater degree of responsibility. He was known as a boss who really listened to his people.

McDonald's pending retirement was timely for another reason. He seemed to be at the end of his rope. The old GM workhorse could not fathom why success was so elusive after all that had been accomplished through the reorganization. One staffer recalled a meeting in McDonald's office during which the president appeared to come close to breaking down in tears of frustration over his inability to get the quality message across. Voice cracking with emotion, McDonald cried, "What can I do? What more can I possibly do to turn this thing around?"

McDonald subscribed to a simple, old-fashioned view that quality attainment was easy—you just look in a mirror and say, like a mantra, "It's up to me." He shunned what he thought were "fancy" techniques; gurus like Deming angered him—they just seemed to cloud the issue. Once McDonald even passed out little blue plastic mirrors to managers at a quality conference and told everyone to look in the mirror and "just zap out that poor quality."

But there was a crack in the mirror that was far deeper and more fundamental than McDonald realized. Quality wasn't a tangible thing that could simply be there by wanting it to be. As one observer remarked, "You can't take a magic quality pill." And it didn't happen by looking in a pocket mirror. The mirror had to encompass the entire organization, from the top down. And the commitment to quality had to be shared on every level.

Furthermore, quality wasn't the necessary outcome of change. Reorganization was necessary, but it only served to clear out the cobwebs; the task of creating a new mythology was a lengthier process.

W. Edwards Deming would say of McDonald, "I think Jim McDonald is a great man. He had only his employees at heart. But he had no guidance. He tried to put quality in the hands of the plant managers. The plant managers had no idea what quality was. Quality to them meant meeting the specifications, grading on conformance. It was like building a highway down the tubes."

In the spring of 1987, the horse race was over, and it was announced that Bob Stempel would be the new president, effective, September 1, 1987. Keith Crain, publisher of *Automotive News,* made the comment, "He's walking into a buzz saw." Indeed, at the end of 1987, GM's market share had slipped 3 percentage points from the previous year, to an all-time low of 36.8 percent.

There was a crackle in the air at General Motors as the new year approached. This was fish-or-cut-bait time and everyone felt it. Roger Smith was still talking about the payoff being just around the corner; by 1990, he would say, GM's market share would be back up to 40 percent, *and* the company would be more profitable. But how? Empty promises were becoming the norm and Smith's boasts were beginning to sound a lot like the little boy who cried wolf. Furthermore, most analysts agreed that in the short-term, GM could not have both increased market share and increased profit. It was widely believed that the company would forgo profit and concentrate on building its market share, after a disastrous year of pursuing a reverse strategy. In 1986, only 17 percent of GM's cars were six years or older, compared with 50 percent of Ford's cars. Yet Ford's "old" cars were beating GM's new ones. While GM continued to throw money (and cars) at its problem, Ford had identified the market and cultivated its customers. GM was trapped in an old concept that the more cars a company built, the higher its market share would be. But in 1987, GM's passenger car sales had fallen by one million—the equivalent of losing Chrysler's entire United States passenger car operation!

General Motors seemed to be getting weaker and weaker, while its competition was getting healthier. Ford's share of market had grown from 18.2 percent to 20 percent in 1987, and though its revenues were only two thirds what GM earned, its profits were higher for the second year in a row. Ford, whose letters had once been used as an unflattering acronym for "fix or repair daily," or "found on road dead," was now considered to be the hot domestic car company—as evidenced by its widely praised and popular Taurus and Sable models. Analysts who once hailed Smith as a visionary leader, were now criticizing him for doing too much too soon and being negligent about the present. GM, they said, had been so busy with the business of change that the company had forgotten the business of building cars.

In fact, the company's reaction to a market study conducted by an outside research company for the public affairs department seemed to confirm that perhaps they *had* lost sight of the product. The Wirthlin Group surveyed thousands of Americans, including GM's own employees, and handed General Motors this fact: In assessing American opinion about General Motors, the research group found that, hands down, "the *product* was more important than any other factor." An advertising spokesman for the company, seeming surprised by the response, said, "In the study, the product turned out to be about twice as important as we had thought." But what could he possibly mean? Was not the product the *only* factor, ultimately? On what other basis could consumers possibly judge GM? Goodwill? This, more than anything, illustrated that the company had once again lost touch with its ultimate mission: to build high-quality, competitive cars and trucks. While Ford was touting its philosophy, "Best car wins," GM was counting on a customer loyalty that had long since eroded.

As 1988 dawned, there were some signs that the company was beginning to get its act together. But GM would have to work overtime to convince the public, which had been bruised one time too many by cars that underperformed or fell apart during the first year of use. It would have to depend on that anticipated public goodwill to bring consumers back to try again.

As Roger Smith looked ahead to 1988, he had to know that this would be his last chance to show the business community, shareholders, the board of directors, and dealers that his long-term strategy was working. Smith was hoping that a program of severe cutbacks (a projected $13 billion by 1992), combined with a lift in sales, would help him meet his objectives in 1988. He might also have used the excuse of the stock market crash in late 1987 to cancel or postpone some of GM's more expensive

ventures—such as the ever more questionable Saturn project—
but he did not do this.

Mindful of the importance of achieving big results in 1988,
Smith started off the year with a bang, hosting what he called the
Teamwork and Technology Show, a $20-million extravaganza
that opened at the Waldorf-Astoria in New York. The show was
widely applauded as a sign that GM was back on the track; its
lineup of concept cars was praised for being distinctive, moving
at long last away from the look-alike syndrome that had plagued
its products for so many years. Particularly impressive, observers agreed, was the new Cadillac Voyage, a beautiful, innovative
design that seemed to carry the old-fashioned Cadillac style and
luxury, without trying to mimic foreign models.

However, at a press conference where *Motor Trend* magazine announced that the Pontiac Grand Prix had been selected
its Car of the Year, Smith slipped into an exchange with a reporter that would prove embarrassing.

"How come Chrysler can put a six-passenger car on the
road for seven thousand dollars and you can't?" Smith was
asked.

The chairman hedged a bit, and finally declared, "I think
that our best competition in General Motors against that car
right now happens to be a two-year-old Buick that you can get
down at your dealer. And you will get better value for that than
you will for the new Chrysler at that price."

The reporter blanched. "A *used* car, sir?"

"Yes," insisted Smith, perhaps unaware of the implications
of his remark. "There is great value in it and I think if you look
and see who is buying what, you will find that out."

Stempel's role in a recovery surge was hard to gauge. Although he had worn many hats during his tenure at the company, like most fast-trackers, he had not worn any of them long
enough to demonstrate a capacity for start-to-finish endurance.
Like most executives who made it to the high seats of power,
people knew very little about how Stempel might operate in the
hot seat.

Much would hinge on the success of the GM-10 models,
which were finally coming to market after five years in production. GM-10 was the ambitious midsize revitalization strategy
that ran into major snafus in the days before the reorganization.
Later, it was assigned to the jurisdiction of CPC with the task of

replacing older lines in all divisions except Cadillac. The success of GM-10 was absolutely critical to GM's hope of reestablishing its rightful position as the midsize leader. This was the traditional bread-and-butter of the company's business. The stakes on GM-10 midsize cars were raised by a domestic and foreign competition that was pulling all the stops. Not only would GM be competing with Ford's Taurus and Sable, but also with its sporty Thunderbird. There was also Chrysler's Lebaron, Toyota's Cressida and Camry, Honda's Accord LX, and Volkswagen of America's Audi 5000. The vehicle rollout would begin in 1988 with the Oldsmobile Cutlass Supreme coupe, the Pontiac Grand Prix coupe, and the Buick Regal coupe.

The success or failure of the GM-10 program would also present a verdict on many of the improvements GM had tried to put in place during the 1980s. It would be the first major postreorganization effort and would demonstrate not only if the system worked, but also if the company could maintain the identity of the car lines that inspired customer loyalty—in other words, would the Buick Regal be a *Buick?*

It would also reflect on GM's efforts to improve the quality of its supplier network and the efficiency of plant operations. In its new Fairfax, Kansas, plant, the company could assemble a 1988 Grand Prix in 28.3 hours, compared with 45.5 hours in the old plant, at an hourly labor cost saving of $450 per car. (Of course, while this would make GM more efficient, it wouldn't necessarily make it more competitive—the competition was cutting costs, too.)

According to Paul Schmidt, product manager of the GM-10 program, the Buick Regal looked like a winner going into 1988. "At the 1988 dealer show in Toronto, we had fifty-eight cars that we let the dealers drive," he said. "And the reaction was spectacular—to the Buick, in particular. They were saying, 'God, I'll take as many as you can give me tomorrow.' Their only concern was, 'Don't do something crazy when you price it.' "

Schmidt noted that GM really had the competitive edge when it came to midsize cars—the others were just pretenders to the throne. "If you have to sit in the backseat of a Thunderbird versus sitting in the backseat of a Buick Regal or Cutlass Supreme, I think you would really appreciate the difference between a true midsize car versus being perceived as a midsize car and really being a compact," he said. "Because that's where you lose it—in the backseat. You can look at the outside of the car and say, 'Oh, that's a midsize car'—which is fine if you only drive it and never have anyone in the backseat."

At the end of 1988, saddled with more than a hundred days' supply of GM-10 cars, the company would announce temporary plant closings to reduce the surplus dealer inventories.

Part of the problem was due to the lack of four-door models. Although approximately 70 percent of all cars sold in the United States have four doors, GM opted to introduce the two-door GM-10s first; four-door models were not scheduled to be available until the second half of 1989. This may be the first time in the history of an auto company that the two- and four-door models of the same car line would be launched so far apart. The reason for the delay is traceable to capital-spending cutbacks of $395 million taken out of GM-10 in calendar year '87 to calendar year '88 in a move to reduce capital investment. GM argues that the cars simply weren't ready on time, which, of course, they couldn't be because of the delay in funding.

With the race for the presidency over, speculation in 1988 centered on the people in line for Smith's job. A new chairman would be announced in 1990. One name that came up frequently in the press was Elmer Johnson. Johnson, the outsider whom Roger Smith had wooed and won, had achieved, in only four years, what would once have been unheard of—an executive vice presidency and a seat on the GM board of directors.

Johnson was a GMer the press could love. A tall, good-looking man with a charming, almost owlish pose, he could charge up a room with humor, honesty, and a well-articulated clarity about the challenges facing the industry. His willingness to throw an occasional jab at GM was considered refreshing.

But if Johnson's direct, nontraditional style appealed to outsiders, it never made him very popular with those on the inside who still grumbled that Johnson had not paid his dues to the company. It didn't help that he was at the forefront of efforts to shake the tree—such as trying to convince Roger Smith to abolish the executive dining room. And he openly despised the nonproductive aspects of the corporate game—endless meetings, committees, and the like. Furthermore, he criticized the bonus system that gave large payouts to top executives, even in years when blue-collar workers did not receive profit-sharing payments.

The salaried workers began to resent Johnson too, once he

implemented a pay-for-performance scheme. In 1987, he publicly proclaimed that GM had grown "fat, dumb, and happy," then proceeded to officiate over the slimming down process of cutting nearly forty thousand white-collar employees from the payroll. He instituted a long-overdue system of employee evaluation that actually included the category "unsatisfactory"—a first at GM. And to the ire of many old-timers, he promoted a forty-nine-year-old plant manager who had been with GM only ten years to the position of vice president in charge of personnel administration and development, bypassing others with more seniority.

Johnson had been impressed with the skill Roy Roberts had shown as manager of an aging assembly plant in Tarrytown, New York. Roberts had effectively forged a coalition of management, labor, and government that was responsible for saving the endangered plant.

Only the second black man to receive a vice presidency in GM's history, Roberts was known as a strong leader and a tough negotiator, but he was also described by his colleagues as having "warm, human values." Johnson might have hoped the appointment would quiet the perception that the white-collar cutbacks would be a "hatchet job."

Roberts shared Johnson's point of view about the need to trim the fat on the organization—as he once said, "If Elmer was standing next to me, you couldn't get air between the two of us in terms of goals and objectives." Roberts understood that the policy of rewarding staff for being "good soldiers" was ultimately damaging to the objectives of the company. Hard choices had to be made, but it was Roberts's goal to make those choices with a respect for the dignity of the workers.

"We walk a tightrope between being competitive and doing the right thing for our people, and being honest with our people, being *truly* honest with our people, *blatantly* honest with our people about what's in front of us and what we have to do to get it done," Roberts would say.

So, how does a company go about cutting forty thousand people from the payroll? On what basis do the choices get made?

"If I owned a business or a store," said Roberts, "and I had ten people working and I only needed eight, I would keep the eight best performers. That's who I would keep." The system of evaluation, he stressed, had to be based on performance, not a false sense of entitlement. "It's like having people on welfare entitlement programs. You do it long enough, you can kill people. You kill their initiative, you kill their creativity, and everything else. We don't need to do that to people at General Motors. We have extremely bright and brilliant people who are willing to pull their way. But over the years we've led them to believe that they're entitled to certain benefits with no thought about reciprocity. And now we've got to turn that around to make sure that if you work for us, you have some kind of contract and you understand on a daily basis that you have to compete and you have to make a contribution. And that's how you get compensated and rewarded."

The toughest part of Roberts's task was the process of separating the wheat from the chaff in the corporation. For there were two types of people who would be affected by the cutbacks. The first were those who simply were not performing. Those were to be ferreted out and severed from the rolls first. Once that was accomplished, however, there would still be the issue of having to cut more people. Then it was a task of determining who would be asked to retire early, or accept a buyout.

Roger Smith was enamored of the way Johnson could remain cool under fire and smoothly handle controversy—from directing the "downsizing" (Roberts called it "rightsizing") of the staff to handling a Department of Justice suit related to safety aspects of the X-car, to dealing with the incorrigible Ross Perot.

Of course, Elmer Johnson wanted to be chairman—and it could happen. Since the sitting chairman usually handpicked his successor, Johnson's apparent closeness to Roger Smith seemed to put him very high up in the running, and when Johnson was named to the Board of Directors in 1987, it threw the other contenders into a panic, which might have been exactly what Smith intended. It is unlikely that Smith, who was so loyal to the GM family, could have ever named an outsider to be its leader. But here is where Johnson threw tradition another curve. Conventional wisdom if you were a candidate for the top job was, "Don't rock the boat." This wisdom would be well taken when dealing with Roger Smith, who was known to dislike criticism, even when it was delivered under the guise of being "constructive." In Smith's eyes, a critic was nothing more than a person

who didn't have the vision to understand the course he was
taking.

It's hard to pinpoint exactly when the relationship between
Roger Smith and Elmer Johnson began to sour, since neither
one is talking. It probably began with Johnson's outspoken opposition to Saturn, voiced in late 1987 when the Board had to
formally fund the effort. Coupled with Johnson's high profile in
the press (a no-no in Roger Smith's regime), this destroyed his
chances. Then, in what proved to be a suicidal act, Johnson
wrote a memo to GM's Executive Committee, a twenty-five-page
document entitled "Strengthening GM's Organizational Capability." The memo, dated January 21, heightened the tension.
Johnson had approached Smith prior to writing the memo about
ideas he had related to a change in the committee process. Smith
told him, "You come up with any ideas you want and I'll consider them."

Johnson was simply doing what came naturally. It was a
thoughtful, even brilliant memo that tied together the themes of
the 1980s and suggested where the company had fallen short of
its vision. In particular, he attacked the culture and its systems
that encouraged lack of accountability, fattened up the central
staff to no practical gain, gave too much power to the finance
staff, and hindered the company from moving efficiently. In the
memo, he proposed a brand-new committee and decision-making structure and suggested, in recognition of the way things were
done at GM, that a task force be created to study the matter.

A further controversial aspect of the memo was Johnson's
suggestion that BOC's model was a better one than CPC's. In
a follow-up memo to Roger Smith on March 30, he outlined in
great detail how he would change CPC—and even offered to
take on the job himself. He never mentioned Lloyd Reuss
by name, but there was no ambiguity about where the blame
should fall.

In the wake of these two memos, the only sound to be heard
was the sound of feathers being ruffled. There was no direct
discussion with Johnson about his comments. Suddenly Smith
was not as accessible as he once had been. There were no meetings called, no task forces set up. Just silence.

So this was the way it was going to be. The circle was
tightening. And Johnson, who for a brief time really believed he

could help make the big difference at General Motors, was once again the outsider. On June 27, 1988, it was announced that he had resigned to return to his law practice with Kirkland and Ellis. In public statements, Roger Smith said that Johnson resigned "to go back to his first love of being a lawyer," and not because he felt frustrated by his inability to make changes in the GM bureaucracy. Johnson refused to be interviewed by the press, but items quoted anonymous insiders as saying that Johnson had been growing increasingly frustrated. The memos had probably been designed to give GM one last chance to show that it really meant all the big talk about change. Not long after Johnson left, Roy Roberts also resigned. It did no good for one's career to be known as "Johnson's man." Roberts would later explain why he left GM to become vice president and general manager of truck operations at Navistar International Transportation Corporation. He said, "All I would have had to have done was breathe, and I would have become a millionaire if I'd stayed at GM. There's no question about it. But I believe in working and building, not just pushing paper."

Johnson's experience illustrated the baffling contradiction within the change dynamic at General Motors. For even while a new openness seemed to be cracking through the hard shell of company tradition, the leadership was only willing to carry it just so far. And, as Johnson discovered, the line of demarcation was not always clear.

Johnson might have had an eye-opener had he stayed around to witness the leadership conference in October. The Traverse City, Michigan, conference was an effort to slay the sacred cow of layered management. The three-day meeting witnessed occurrences that might have caused old-timers to blink their eyes and ask, "Am I dreaming?"

- There was Roger Smith, laying aside his stock speech on the power of technology and admitting that it had been a hard transition for him to make, but he was now convinced that teamwork was the only way the company could grow and prosper.
- There were nine hundred-plus GM managers, sitting in small groups with their shirt sleeves rolled up, to hammer out new directions of the company without anyone pulling rank.

- There was a company whose bureaucratic chaos was legendary, utilizing the most sophisticated techniques for problem solving to forge a consensus about the company's direction.
- There were the men and women who had spent the past three years in automakers' hell as they watched profits and share-of-market take a nose dive, looking excited, animated, hopeful . . . and like they were having fun!

Traditionally, management conferences were exercises in tedium or terror, depending on the company's outlook. Managers would be seated in straight rows to listen while the GM leadership gave speech after speech. In other words, the leadership was on the stage, the workers in the pit. But at Traverse City, the formula was dramatically shifted. Here the sessions were not one-way speeches, but team efforts—the leadership was everyone in the room. The methodology was a workshop format that divided all the managers into "Breakthru Teams."

It had taken the company a lifetime to reach this point, but the seeds had been planted two years earlier with GM's decision to do something about its deficiencies in the management training arena. It had been McKinsey's concern at the time of the reorganization that the lack of executive training was a problem for the company. According to the consultants, too much of the change at GM was taking root at the bottom, and too little was being done to foster change at the executive levels. Without trust and cooperation at the top, teamwork at the bottom could not be effective.

It was McKinsey's contention that while a company's structure could be changed in one year, the "culture"—that is, the style and process—of a company could not be changed in less than five years, and then only if it was facilitated by an educational component.

In 1986, Alex Cunningham headed up a training practices committee that hired Forum, a Boston consulting firm, to conduct a series of training courses for three thousand of its managers. The program, called Leadership Now, was specifically designed by Forum to meet GM's needs. By 1988, nearly two thousand executives had participated in Forum training sessions, organized by Mark Sarkady, the trainer assigned to work closely with the corporation.

Executives who attended the sessions experienced initial

culture shock as they were asked to drop their inhibitions and relate to one another with complete trust. One exercise had two executives stretch a rubber band between them, each trusting the other not to let go and snap the band at his partner. Another aspect of the training was to distribute questionnaires to the employees who reported to the executives, asking for anonymous evaluations, which were then discussed openly in the sessions. Words like "open" and "honest" were used frequently. It was a very different experience for the people at General Motors—part sensitivity training, part personal "empowerment." The tone of the sessions threw people off guard—they were the epitome of everything GM had never been.

Forum's goal was to shift the fundamental context of the executives and teach them "a new way of being." Its role was to move people along, to loosen them up and make them open to the evolution of a new cultural mode in the company. Executives who took the training seemed to have undergone—for the short term, anyway—something of a religious conversion. One executive compared the emotional power to an Alcoholics Anonymous meeting. Graduates were eager to spread their new sensitivity, but many within the company were skeptical. One emotion-packed week does not a corporate revolution make. How would it translate into the kind of practical change that would make the critical difference? For one thing, the reasons behind low worker morale went a lot deeper than "attitude." At the center of the organization was what Roger Smith liked to call GM's "frozen middle." But why was it frozen? While the hourly workers had the support of the union, and the bonus-eligible employees had incredibly lucrative incentives, those salaried workers who were not bonus eligible were stuck with the status quo. In the early part of the decade, there was still the sense that a young and talented person could get ahead at GM. But with the cost pressures that burdened the company in the mid-to-late 1980s, very few employees were now granted bonus eligibility. A thirty-year analysis of bonus-eligible employees would offer slight encouragement to a young business-school graduate In 1960, there were thirty-two bonus-eligible employees age thirty or younger; in 1965, there were seventeen; and only seven or eight since 1972. Also, raises were harder to get and benefits had been cut. A system of merit awards had an annual cap that couldn't compare with a cost of living increase, and the awards applied only in the year they were given—it wasn't the same as getting a raise. For GM's "frozen middle," Forum's goal of teaching "a new way of being" might have offered little in the way of motivation. In a letter to the editor of *Ward's Auto World* in early 1989, Andrew J. Zaglaniczny, a retired Fisher Body employee, articulated the frustration. "I have to take exception to Mr. [Roger] Smith's not comprehending that there is a very serious morale problem at General Motors. . . . It is more severe in the salaried than the hourly ranks, due to takeaways and ever-changing personnel policy. Also still smoldering are the effects of a well-conceived but horrendously implemented corporate reorganization. There is so much infighting and self-serving individualism going on, but it's being covered over by middle management because of the old 'shoot-the-messenger' syndrome."

But from the people-management standpoint, several efforts were merging by mid-1988 that strengthened the company's drive to compete. In 1987, a radical UAW contract addendum titled "Attachment C," first instituted by Ford and later picked up by General Motors, called for the establishment of management-labor committees. Among other tasks, these committees would concentrate on improved efficiency by sharing data and working together, instead of operating as adversaries. Part of the deal was the establishment of Job Security and Operational Effectiveness Committees, which would explore ways to fully utilize the work force. Even before Attachment C, GM had been involved in pursuing management-labor cooperative efforts—most notably in its Saturn plant, and in other plants as well. Attachment C formalized the commitment within GM to make labor-management relations work for the betterment of the company. It would become the basis for the profound improvement that has occurred in GM component operations that were once thought to be living on borrowed time. The Quality Network was the name given to the joint people-involvement program created by GM management and the UAW. The program borrows from the Japanese practice of teamwork training and continuous improvement to ensure the highest quality and competitive cost. Quality Network was substituted for the GM Production System, which focused on the physical processes of engineering and assembling vehicles. But Quality Network, unlike other initiatives, makes no distinction between hourly and salary workers. It sees all employees as partners in the process of serving the customer and it is potentially the most powerful weapon that General Motors has created in its effort to regain its stature.

Both the Quality Network and Leadership Now programs inspired powerful attitudinal changes, but they lacked the framework of a strategic plan. A born-again leader still needs a battle plan.

It was this understanding that led to the establishment of the Group of Eighteen, consisting of the top executives who would begin meeting together to begin building a strategic plan the company could live with in the coming decade.

According to Marina Whitman, vice president and group executive in charge of the public affairs staffs, the process began informally. "In one sense," Whitman said, "I was a ringleader. We were sitting around at lunch one day and I asked, 'Wouldn't it be interesting if we all [other group executives] took a look at each other's business plans and tried to see how they might fit together and interact?' "

Whitman recalled that Jack Edman, one of her colleagues at the table, responded by joking, "Gosh, Marina, you may just be new enough and dumb enough around here to know that you can't do that." But it was an idea that took root—to create one plan instead of many, in effect making the whole greater than the sum of its parts.

Mike Naylor had been preaching the gospel of strategic planning since the early 1970s; maybe after witnessing the chaotic process of change in the 1980s, the company was finally ready to listen. The timing was right for other reasons. As growing numbers of executives came out of Leadership Now, the question of "overall vision" was suddenly on everyone's lips.

The group executives began meeting, with Naylor as facilitator. What were the company's priorities? What was its long-range practical vision? How could the different divisions interact to bring about a cohesive change?

Eventually, the group went to Bob Stempel and executive vice president F. Alan Smith. "We're working on these issues," they said, "and we think we could make more progress with Executive Committee involvement. Would you take the leadership and chair the meetings?" They agreed.

In early 1988, Mark Sarkady facilitated a two-day meeting

of group executives to focus on the topic of Product Simplifi-
cation.

"There was a sense of pulling together that came from that
meeting," said Whitman. "We decided that the Group of Eighteen would start meeting regularly and start planning the overall
direction of the corporation."

Out of these meetings grew the realization that the planning process had to reach out and encompass a broader group,
and the Traverse City Leadership Conference was born.

The small groups—called Breakthru Teams—would work
on six topics selected by the Group of Eighteen as being the
areas where GM most needed to overcome obstacles and provide added urgency. These were:

1. The people philosophy

2. Strategic business management

3. The global corporation

4. "Great cars and trucks"

5. Technological strategy

6. Vehicle and component partnership

At the end of the workshops, group leaders gave reports on
the consensus of their groups, to the enthusiastic cheering of
nearly one thousand managers who had never before had a
voice in decision making. Roger Smith, who many would say
seemed to have grown overnight into his position as a corporate
leader, sat and beamed as he watched his management discuss
principles that had seldom been vocalized at General Motors.
These included:

- A people philosophy founded on the beliefs and values of trust
  in our people, teamwork, continual improvement and customer
  satisfaction
- Linking rewards to performance
- Effective strategic planning that includes the development of
  contingency plans
- A global awareness and an understanding that all of GM's busi-
  ness is international
- A need to be the best, not just the biggest
- A need to listen to the voice of the customer

- An integration of Quality Network concepts in the technological strategy
- A need to have people who love the customer and who love the product

Said Marina Whitman of the leadership conference, "We are all very conscious of the fact that we raised expectations at Traverse City. There was an immediate afterglow and there will be an immediate letdown, because the world is not going to change overnight. But even the letdown will leave us at a higher level than we were before. Once you've raised the consciousness, you can't just retreat."

At the end of the conference, Roger Smith, the man who had been caretaker of both collapse and renewal during the 1980s, stood on the stage and looked out on the gleaming faces that represented the next generation of leadership at General Motors. And he found the right words in a visionary voice from the past.

"Alfred Sloan once said, 'Each generation must make a change—the work of creating goes on.' A corporation, like any living thing, must change if it is to survive. You see, we—that's you and I—have the vision to point the way for change. And we—that's you and I—have the courage to change. So I say Mr. Sloan would be proud of us. He'd be proud indeed that, at his and our General Motors, the work of creating goes on."

At the end of 1988, an elated Roger Smith reported that the company had closed the year with record profits—proof that GM was on the road to recovery. While many of the company's new products—such as a highly successful pickup truck and a restyled Cadillac—received favorable reviews, there was more to the 1988 profit picture than met the eye. A close look at the numbers shows that GM's record year was due more to accounting changes than to sale of cars. In fact, using comparable standards, 1988 earnings would have been only 60 percent of those reported for 1984, the previous record year, even though costs were down and quality had improved. But the company rewarded bonus-eligible employees and shareholders nevertheless.

GM's profits were the result of substantially higher earnings in Europe, where real improvements in products and costs were paying off. GM's international operations contributed more than $2 billion to the bottom line in 1988. Without a lot of fanfare, Ferdinand Beichler, retired head of GM Europe, set out to revamp GM assembly plants, launch an array of new models, and strengthen the dealer organizations throughout Europe. The plants are now operating more efficiently, every new car has been a success, and GM's market share has risen. Jack Smith has to be credited for creating GM Europe and getting its multinational work force to function harmoniously. He accomplished this by inspiring the employees to think of themselves not as British or German companies but as one European enterprise.

The second factor in GM's 1988 profit picture was the elimination of 42,000 jobs. The year closed with the company in better control of its destiny, although by no means having solved all of its problems. However, the record profits allowed Smith to reward hourly workers and shareholders. Shareholders received their reward in the form of a 20 percent dividend, the first since 1984. And, for the first time since 1985, profit-sharing payments were made, although the 450,000 hourly workers received only $254 each, a paltry sum by any reckoning. Ford paid at least ten times that amount, in spite of the fact that GM and Ford's net income was nearly identical and the formula by which profit sharing is calculated is the same. One can only wonder how much GM would have to earn for the average worker to receive the Ford award of some $2,800. (Ford credits the visible and meaningful payments to its employees as a sign of true sharing in the company's good fortune and partnership with management.) Nevertheless, it would be a welcome sign of health were it not for the disproportionately huge sums the bonus-eligible employees received.

In the face of what appears to be the beginning of a very real turnaround at GM, the jubilation over the profit numbers could have a dangerous side effect. Adversity has a way of sharpening managers to work more effectively. It would be a pity if they took the self-congratulations as an indication that they could go back to the comfortable old ways.

Racing Toward the Twenty-first Century: Can GM Win?

Alfred P. Sloan is reported to have said at a meeting of one of his top committees: "Gentlemen, I take it we are all in complete agreement on the decision here." Everyone around the table nodded assent. "Then," continued Mr. Sloan, "I propose we postpone further discussion of this matter until our next meeting to give ourselves time to develop disagreement and perhaps gain some understanding of what the decision is all about."
—Peter F. Drucker, *The Effective Executive*

In the first chapter I outlined several aspects of the cultural malaise that has afflicted General Motors. And I raised the question of whether or not the movement that has occurred during Roger Smith's chairmanship in the 1980s has constituted a revolution, or whether the changes have only redrawn the superficial profile of the company.

On the face of it, it is obvious that General Motors has changed a great deal. The 1980s, under the leadership of Roger Smith, have been full of surprises and high drama—from the decision to build cars hand in hand with the Japanese, to undertaking the most massive reorganization ever attempted in corporate America, to the creation of a new model for labor-management relations, to the aggressive pursuit of technological solutions for industrial dilemmas. No one can accuse Roger Smith of sitting still!

General Motors is undeniably a different company as it

approaches the end of the decade. It is impossible for a company to be slammed against the wall of change with such velocity and not become different in fundamental ways. But a car crash can break your nose, and still leave your head intact, and the dramatic gestures of the 1980s may not have necessarily shifted the cultural reality for the better. And even if General Motors has been cured of its complacency and is on the road to recovery, can it happen fast enough to get the company on track for the 1990s?

Let's evaluate the major events of the 1980s as a way of answering the question.

1. The GM-Toyota Joint Venture.   More than any other decision made during the 1980s, the choice of partnership with Toyota had the most potential for reshaping the cultural mode. Had Roger Smith actually been dedicated to his professed objective of learning what was behind the success of Japanese car-making, NUMMI might have made a dramatic difference for the entire company. This is not to suggest that NUMMI's impact has been minor; GM grasped enough of the Japanese methodology that it has been able to duplicate the team concept in a variety of experimental settings, and, more important, to understand the essence of Japanese product development and manufacturing systems. But the leadership had a hard time bringing itself to hear the real message of NUMMI—that management must change right along with everyone else. It wasn't enough to simply put workers in teams and expect automatic results. In some ways, the company only paid lip service to the experience, perhaps being embarrassed to learn its lessons at the knee of the Japanese competition. Full implementation of Japanese methodology necessitated a behavior change by everyone in the company, not just the people on the factory floor.

Only recently, with the development of the Quality Network, have the concepts of teamwork and continuous improvement made it into the everyday language of General Motors. But teamwork does not just mean working in teams; rather, it implies that all groups of people are working to achieve a common goal.

2. Reorganization.   What has reorganization accomplished at General Motors? First, it has torn down some of the old dynasties that were so resistant to change. The present organization is more suitable to the business of making cars. The design, manufacturing, and production functions are each becoming part of a single coordinated effort. No one can deny that GM cars are better quality today than they were in 1980.

The second benefit of the reorganization is that for the first time ever, people actually sat down and evaluated employees on the basis of the quality of their contribution to the organization.

The third benefit is simply that, having gone through the reorganization, General Motors is a more pliable organization than it was before. The idea of change is no longer such a shock to the system: Witness the smooth restructuring of the component operations that took place in 1988 and 1989.

But company executives must guard against the danger of BOC and CPC simply becoming smaller versions of the old company. If they are not attentive to this, the two divisions might easily become new dynasties, weighed down with the same problems that faced the old organization.

The reorganization appeared to have the effect of reducing the powers of the president, and GM had to change to eliminate at least one layer of executives. But in what appears to be the essence of redundancy, the heads of the car and truck groups now report to Lloyd Reuss, who reports to the president. The end result: one more layer was added.

Finally, it must be understood that the reorganization heralded physical and structural changes, but it did not address the deeper cultural malaise. It did little to control the power of central office staffs over operating divisions, or the finance staff over the entire company. Those who might have believed that reorganizing alone would cure all GM's ills were sadly mistaken.

3. EDS and Hughes Acquisitions. Clearly, General Motors got off on the wrong foot with the acquisition of EDS. In the beginning, Roger Smith really didn't know what he was getting with EDS. He didn't understand that data-processing systems served mundane operational functions. He expected EDS to play a role in writing software for his complex plant automation systems. Nor did Smith or his negotiators truly understand the turmoil that would result from their poorly planned consolidation of GM's internal data processing with EDS—not to mention the consequences of allowing EDS to negotiate fixed price contracts when they were the only possible source for the service.

To further exacerbate the problem, Smith turned the transition details over to EDS, rather than organizing a transition team that would more sensitively handle the concerns of GM data processors. Instead, the transition had all the sensitivity of the bombing of a city. The long-term repercussions are hard to gauge, but there remains, at this writing, a strongly felt suspicion at GM that EDS is overcharging for its services. For their part, EDSers live in fear that "the elephant might roll over" on them.

Ross Perot contributed enormously to the chaos, with his habit of tossing a hand grenade into the room, then fleeing while others were left to plow through the rubble. Perot may have been a dynamic leader in his own rarefied company environment, but he knew nothing about the "sandbox politics" of such a bureaucratic company.

Having said this, Perot must be credited with one positive result: He woke up the GM board of directors and forced them to take responsibility for their charge—to represent the shareholders, rather than just believe what they are told without question. Today's board of directors is far more active than it was during Perot's time. They don't want to repeat the embarrassment they experienced when they were confronted with their lack of information after the Perot buy-out.

Hughes may end up being a savvy decision in the long run. Once General Motors got past the idea that Hughes was going to build road-running versions of spacecrafts, the potential contribution of Hughes as a partner in sophisticated software development became apparent. The nature of the Hughes acquisition avoided all the transition politics that marred the EDS deal. But even with Hughes, it's hard to evaluate the worth of the deal, much less see tangible benefits worth $5 million. In any case, whether Hughes and EDS are good or bad acquisitions is tangential to the real issue of building good cars. Acquiring EDS and Hughes was like a four-hundred-pound woman coloring her hair and doing her nails. It wasn't tackling the real problem.

4. Saturn Corporation.   Saturn is a tangible General Motors pilot company, which states that its mission is to: "Market vehicles developed and manufactured in the United States that are world leaders in quality, cost and customer satisfaction through the integration of people, technology and business systems and to transfer knowledge, technology and experience throughout General Motors." But Saturn already shows signs of being a boulder around the neck of the company. When it was first conceptualized, there had been no reorganization, no Quality Network, and no experience yet gained from NUMMI. In light of these developments, Saturn has seemed increasingly redundant—and an expensive redundancy at that.

The big problem, of course, is the car. Sometimes it seems that the importance of producing a good car is lost amid the flashy promotion of the Saturn concept. The question remains: Will Saturn produce an import fighter—a car that measures up to market leaders like the Honda Accord? If not, it will be doomed to failure, as many previous efforts before it. The irony is that even if it lives up to the inflated expectations, it will not generate profit for the company, given the level of investment. This fact leaves the value of the project in doubt during a time when cost cutting is a major imperative. It is also ironic that GM is spending billions on a plant in Tennessee while simultaneously closing plants elsewhere.

GM's standard answer to questions about the car is that Saturn is more a process than a car. Even when one ignores the question of what good is a process without a car, it is valid to wonder what practical value the model project will serve for the entire company. Are there specific plans to incorporate the lessons of Saturn into all GM plants? Will these be different lessons from those GM has already learned and is putting into practice? If so, won't they come too late to make a difference?

Roger Smith has made Saturn the cornerstone of his chairmanship, promising to drive the first car before he retires at the end of 1990. The momentum of his early dream has grown to such an extent that he can't back down. It will be up to his successors to deal with Saturn and attempt to minimize the losses. Meanwhile, the costs pile up. In early 1989, Saturn president Skip LeFauve announced that one thousand people would be added to the work force and approximately $1 billion would be spent on tools and equipment during that year.

5. Quality Network. Forward thinkers like UAW's Don Ephlin brought into being what amounted to a revolution in the traditional relationship between labor and management with the 1987 contract and the creation of Quality Network.

But for those who might be basking in the new experience of warm feelings between the former adversaries, it should be recognized that there is a long row to hoe in bringing true labor-management cooperation into being. The Quality Network implies more than being "warm and fuzzy" with labor. It implies a corporate commitment to see beyond class distinctions and view both blue- and white-collar employees as equal partners. Its success will require a major shift in GM mentality, and it is certainly not a universally supported idea within labor. Some opponents fear that GM might use the new spirit of cooperation to take more away from the workers. They point out that the company still holds the best cards, and indeed, this is true. For example, although the new contract prohibits plant closings, it allows for "suspension of operations for an undetermined period of time." For workers, the end result is the same: no jobs. From a bottom-line perspective, it is hard to see how GM can avoid such suspensions in the future.

Ephlin has argued that cooperation still nets the unions more, since GM is now more accountable for such decisions. But only time will tell whether the new cooperation will take root. One influential factor will be what happens in the wake of Ephlin's retirement in June 1989. Ephlin has been a controversial figure in union circles—he is often accused of climbing into bed with management. His departure will almost certainly bring to a head the clash between the traditional and progressive wings of the UAW. And while the survival of the Quality Network will ultimately depend on how well it works for the rank and file, Ephlin's leaving will deprive the process of its most passionate proponent. And there are many at GM who are uncomfortable with the new order of things and would just as soon go back to the "good old days" of management-labor confrontation.

6. Leadership Now.   The transformation of GM's leadership is a work in progress. The Traverse City Leadership Conference was a remarkable occasion—one that could not have been imagined ten years ago. Today, General Motors is more closely aligned with current thinking with regard to effective management attitudes and procedures. A focus on training is long overdue, although it remains to be seen whether Forum's "sensitizing" process is the best method. It seems that GM could use a little more of the Deming flavor in its training.

It must also be remembered, as Marina Whitman noted, that core changes do not happen overnight. And they do not happen automatically. Corporate change cannot be achieved by holding a revival meeting and converting people to a new way of thinking. Rather, it must be woven painstakingly into the very fabric of daily operations. It must have an ethical foundation that rejects the temptation to compromise or slip back into more comfortable ways. And it must place at the top those leaders whose vision is consistent with the consensus of the total body— not those who have the greatest longevity or the strongest power base.

As we consider the importance of strong leadership to the ultimate success of General Motors in the coming years, it is clear that the company's immediate destiny is linked with the vision of the next chairman. What are the characteristics that the new chairman must have in order to effectively lead GM into the twenty-first century? I offer the following ten points for consideration:

1. *He must articulate the company's vision.*   As the spokesman for the company, he must communicate the positive messages of change, quality, and strength. In order to do that, he must believe himself in the direction GM is headed. He must have a vision that is simple, consistent, and understandable. And that vision must have an independent focus. That is, it must be more than saying, "We're going to beat the competition." A better articulation might be, "We're going to build the cars that address the wants and needs of the consumers, and, by doing so, we'll come out ahead."

He must avoid the public perception that he is on the defensive or mouthing platitudes. He must be ever sensitive to the human implications of making hard choices—particularly when plants are closed and workers are laid off.

2. *He must get out of his office and into the world.*   One is always struck by the limited perspective GM executives have about the world around them. To cite an example, a reporter from a prestigious business journal tells the story of a dinner he and several of his colleagues shared with a couple of top GM executives. "We were talking, as we would at any gathering of business people, about what was happening in the world, the economy— things like that. But the GM people didn't seem to be interested. All they wanted to talk about was *cars.* You got the feeling that

they didn't know or care what was going on in the world. It was embarrassing."

The chairman for the 1990s must have an interest in and understanding of the world that exists outside his doors—whether that means being able to judge the implications of economic policies or being an observer of consumer trends. He should visit the dealerships across the country. Talk to the customers. Stop the guy he sees driving a Honda and ask him what he likes about the car; what he doesn't like; why he bought it. Host frequent focus groups and really listen to what people are saying. Possess a *curiosity* about the customer. Hold the customer in deep regard. The capsulelike existence of top GM executives limits their contacts with the outside world. A chauffeur, private elevator, private office, private dining room, and private jet make it hard to get a feel for the "real" world.

3. *He must challenge and be challenged.*   The hierarchical structure of American business has been an experiment that has drowned in its own arrogance. The corporate leader of today must see himself as the conductor of an orchestra, not as a one-man band. He must appreciate that if even one instrument is off-key, the quality of the work will be gravely diminished. The old leadership style that encouraged a management team of yes-men can no longer be tolerated. The company is too big for its direction to reside in only one individual. With all the other changes he set in motion, Roger Smith struggled mightily with the nature of leadership. It has only been recently that he has appeared to grow into the role. As one high-ranking executive noted, "In the last year, I've seen Roger Smith change from an accountant into a leader." But the chairmanship should not be a training ground for leadership.

Another facet of this characteristic is that the new leader must open himself up to the input of experts, whether they come from within the company or from outside the company. He must probe into the companies he sees that are operating effectively and ask questions and learn from them.

4. *He must embrace the global culture.*   The chairman of a company the size and scope of General Motors cannot afford to be just the chairman of a midwestern car company—or even an *American* car company. It is no longer possible to view foreign competition as a temporary business problem. Indeed, the world is in partnership with American business as never before.

This fact produces a mandate for today's American business leader that he not only consider the global business community and respect the foreign competition, but also that he strive to understand the *ontology* of non-Western cultures. And he must be willing to be open to learning from the successes of his competitors.

5. *He must establish a broad leadership base.*   To this day, the primary leadership at GM rises up through the finance divisions of the company. It is essential that the new GM leader break this trend. For one thing, finance operations must be incorporated into the consensus body of the corporation, working hand in hand with the design, manufacturing, and production staff. As long as they remain separated from the heartbeat of the corporation, they cannot be truly effective. And as long as the unwritten rule stands that the best way to achieve success at GM is to be a good finance man, the bad habit of juggling numbers in order to present the picture people *want* to see cannot be broken. This is one of the most deeply ingrained cultural problems at General Motors. The new chairman must reduce the lock on power that the finance staff has and open the company up to the insight of those who have served on the front lines of engineering and production. Furthermore, he must accept the fact that true change in a corporate culture happens from the top down, not the bottom up. Ford demonstrated this when it required its leadership to make drastic changes. The results are apparent in Ford's current strength.

6. *He must understand the limitations and attributes of technology.*   General Motors has learned the hard way that automation isn't a magic wand. But neither is it dispensable. To take the lead in technological advancement means that the new chairman will have to know how to integrate man with machine. He will need to know when to move and when to wait to incorporate advancements into the plants.

This seems to be a lesson that GM has a hard time learning. As recently as January 1989, Roger Smith was telling *The Detroit News* that "technology management" was an essential part of a leader's job description. One would hope that the new chairman understands that *people-management* skills will have far more value.

No doubt, Smith still envisions a car of the future built in an automated factory, a car fully equipped with the latest in space age gimmickry. But the real car of the future is more likely to be one that focuses on more safety, more comfort, a better arrangement of components—the kind of elements people can't *see*, but will *feel* and respond to.

Unfortunately, the new chairman will also have the unwelcome task of sorting through the automated jungle that GM has become. Once the investment has been made, it is not possible to *un*invest in technology. He must decide how to make the most of billions of dollars of equipment that is currently inoperative.

GM's high-tech plants were failures that have triggered a technology backlash in the company. It is estimated that as much as 20 percent of the capital investments made in plant modernization has been wasted and substantial amounts of machinery have been scrapped. GM ends the decade with its plants unable to build cars as productively as Ford, which has yet to modernize most of its facilities. Furthermore, the investment program was based on the assumption that GM's market share would blossom, necessitating the use of all facilities at full capacity. With a shrinking share, it was pointless to spend some of the billions on new assembly plants and stamping plants since the decreased penetration didn't warrant it. For too long the company has hidden behind a manipulation of the numbers rather than facing its problems head on. The new chairman must not forget that the company's purpose is not to *appear* to sell cars; it's to sell them.

7. *He must motivate, inspire, and excite the workers.* He must stay "in the fray" and find ways to let everyone in the company know that he is working side by side with them, not secluded in a faraway office. His commitment to the employees must be more than superficial. (Don Ephlin once joked, "Three years ago you had to be a car guy. Now they want you to be a people person.") He should be the one who finally takes a stand and closes the executive dining room, which has become a powerful symbol of the line of separation between workers and central office staff. In conjunction with that, he should encourage the staff to spend less time on the Fourteenth Floor and more time where the action is. He should insist that every manager, every designer, every engineer, spend one day a month on the line— and he should start with himself—so they understand the implications of their directives and become more effective. And he should insist that every single manager at General Motors be

required to drive a GM car to and from work and begin to "live" the business.

Perhaps the Fourteenth Floor should be abandoned altogether. In this age of high-tech communications, there is no reason why executives could not be in immediate contact with one another, should the need arise. Would not the organization be better served if the top executives were dispersed?

The chairman must communicate to his management that it is responsible for the jobs of the company's employees. That means being sensitive to the consequences of its decisions. An incorrect decision might mean smaller bonuses for some—but it means *no jobs* for the workers building unpopular cars. No longer can GM afford to blame external circumstances for its failures. The leadership itself must take responsibility.

8. *He must delegate responsibility and hold people accountable.*   The new chairman must be willing to pursue without fear the direction of the team concept, and all it implies regarding delegating responsibility and holding people accountable for their decisions. Promotions and raises should be based solely on the merits of the workers' contributions. Furthermore, those who are considered on a fast track should no longer be moved from assignment to assignment so frequently. Rather, they should be assigned to see projects through from start to completion, and should be held accountable for the outcome.

9. *He must take the lead in environmental and social concerns.* The chairman of General Motors cannot ignore critical issues that affect society—such as environmental safety, employment opportunities, worker equality, and education. He is, by virtue of being the head of the largest company in America, a national figure, and it is his responsibility to represent the best of business. Remember that business is a human dynamic—it cannot be divorced from the community it serves.

The new chairman can make a tremendous impact by taking the lead in safety issues and pollution control. The car industry has had a pattern of fighting virtually every major safety and clean-air policy ever created. It has never gone down without a fight. But what would happen if this was reversed? What would be the advantage of the chairman taking the initiative in working with government regulatory agencies to bring about safety and pollution-control policy? First, it would send a positive message to the public that GM is taking responsibility for public welfare.

There is no question that this would translate into sales, as GM would have grabbed the pro-consumer imprint. Second, it would put GM in a position to help shape the debate and shape the nature and time frame of change. Its competitors would be left to play catch-up.

10. *He must set a personal example.*   When GM management awarded itself millions in bonuses, even as it was telling workers that profit sharing would not be paid because of declining sales, this was the action of a chairman who didn't understand the power of symbols. During one of those years, 1987, Roger Smith earned a bonus of $2.2 million. In 1988, when employee profit sharing paid individuals $254 apiece, Smith earned a bonus of $3.7 million. It is only valid to ask employees to accept hard times if the leadership is also willing to make sacrifices. The new chairman must be personally committed to the process of change, even when it reaches into his own pocket. It is about time, at General Motors, that the leadership aligned itself with the workers. The new chairman can make that a reality.

General Motors still faces monumental challenges that will demand great skill and sensitivity from its leaders. Although Roger Smith was responsible for many changes, some of them positive, the root problems have not disappeared. Smith had many of the right ideas, but he seemed unable to implement them in a cohesive way. He was like a cook who gathered all the ingredients for making a cake, then just tossed them in the oven randomly, thinking they would come together on their own. I would point to six key areas of concern:

First, although it has improved somewhat, GM's relationship with its hourly workers is still fragile. The company suffers from substantial excess capacity given its market share, 36 percent in 1988 (including GM imports), and 35.5 percent in the first quarter of 1989. Upwards of three to four assembly plants will have to be closed during the next four years if the company is even to improve its break-even point to match Ford's. With Don Ephlin's departure from the United Automobile Workers in June 1989, General Motors must learn to work with his successors, who may not be as willing as Ephlin to withstand criticism from union dissidents regarding cooperation with management.

How GM mitigates the impact on jobs from the projected

plant closings will have a long-lasting effect on its relationship with hourly workers, whose continued cooperation is essential.

Second, GM appears to be backing down from its often stated goal of achieving a 40-percent market share. Recently, Bob O'Connell, vice president and group executive in charge of the finance groups, stated that the company could be profitable with a 36-percent share. This indicates a belief that a higher penetration is no longer attainable. If GM's presence in the American vehicle market has permanently eroded to 36 percent or less, another wave of white-collar layoffs will be needed.

A third problem faces GM in the form of yet another challenge from the Japanese. Japanese carmakers have demonstrated an adroitness in responding to altered circumstances that has prepared them for a new, high-stakes battle in North America during the 1990s. The new threat from the Japanese auto industry is not increased volume and market share, but rather an intrusion into those segments of the vehicle market that have traditionally provided Detroit with the bulk of its earnings—large cars and, ultimately, lightweight trucks. However, for all its problems, at least GM and the rest of the American auto industry is still fighting the foreign competition. Other industries, such as consumer electronics, textile, and steel have not done as well. But the strong yen has forced the Japanese to move upscale into high-priced cars, and they are making the transition to full line manufacturing with confidence and conviction. If General Motors does not take this challenge seriously, it will once again be caught unprepared by the foreign competition.

Fourth, GM has to take seriously the strength of its domestic competition. Ford has made a remarkable comeback from economic hardship, and it seems to have learned lessons that still elude GM. Ford is building innovative cars like the Taurus that translate into record profits and higher owner loyalty, while GM has been distracted with projects like Saturn instead of revitalizing all of its product lines.

Fifth, the look-alike problem still persists in new car models, despite Roger Smith's repeated promise that distinctive models would be created for each of its divisions. A clear sign that this is not happening is the upcoming APV van that was to have been shared only by Chevrolet and Pontiac in a ratio of 65 percent to Chevrolet and 35 percent to Pontiac. Now it has been announced that 10 percent of the van production will go to Oldsmobile, in a weak move to give that division a piece of the lightweight truck market. But it amounts to nothing more than badge engineering. Having made such definitive statements about solving the look-alike problem, and waxing poetic about building unique division images, the company has shredded its credibility by doing the same thing it has always done—in effect, putting leather seats in a Chevrolet and calling it an Oldsmobile.

The sixth challenge lies in a fundamental change that is taking place in the ranks of GM's leadership. A new generation of leaders is growing up at GM—men and women who began their careers at a time when imports were already threatening the company. These are not people like Roger Smith and his peers, who spent their formative years in GM's glory days and learned to view the company as invincible. Although they may not have been able to communicate their fears and concerns, it is obvious that it left an impression. Their voices will be the ones heard during the 1990s, and a new chairman must be prepared to be challenged in ways that would have been unthinkable during Thomas Murphy's or Roger Smith's era.

Roger Smith once said in an interview that he admired Fred Donner, who might be called "the father of GM's financial structure." He described Donner as having "stuffed the mattress." Unfortunately, the 1980s were a period of financial decline for the company. Only numerous accounting changes created the illusion of massive profits. In reality, General Motors earns less today on a U.S.-made automobile than it did a decade ago.

It is ironic that while the 1980s began with the worst recession since the 1930s, it also included the largest postwar expansion. Not only has the United States experienced seven good sales years, but also a weak dollar has slowed the Japanese in their quest for ever-increasing sales.

This climate, which has made Ford more profitable than GM despite its being only two-thirds the size, only highlights the company's problems. The 1990s will not be any easier for General Motors. They will include new challenges.

Clearly, whoever assumes the chairmanship for the 1990s will have a full plate of problems—many of them caused by the reckless investments of the past decade. Given the urgency of the times, the choice of chairman is particularly critical. How will the next chairman be selected, and who might it be?

Thomas Murphy described the process of selecting a chairman as a massive talent hunt, with as many as two hundred executives being considered potential candidates. According to Murphy, Roger Smith rose to the top of the talent bank and that's why he was selected. But it was common knowledge that Smith was the heir apparent *years* before it was announced. And while it is not so clear today who will succeed him, it will almost certainly be one of six men, and more likely one of two.

GM president Bob Stempel, fifty-seven, had long been considered the front-runner in the chairmanship race. He was favored by the operations people who wanted a "car guy" to get the company back to the basics of building good cars. Stempel, it was hoped, would be a high-visibility president, perceived by dealers and outsiders as a take-charge leader. But within GM, many now express disappointment that Stempel hasn't had the hoped-for impact—although that might have more to do with the nature of the presidency than with Stempel himself.

Nevertheless, the selection of Stempel would send a very clear message that GM is moving back to product emphasis and away from control by the finance staffs. Such a message may be needed. Whatever voodoo the finance people have been able to work on the company's balance sheets, the simple fact remains that General Motors has not been building great cars. Indeed, to judge from the press the company has received during the 1980s, it has focused on everything *but* building great cars. Selecting a strong chairman with an operations orientation might be both a symbolic and a practical move in that direction.

A second scenario places F. Alan Smith, fifty-nine, executive vice president and director for the operating and public affairs staff group, in the chairmanship, with Stempel continuing as president. For a long time, Smith seemed to be out of the running—particularly after his embarrassing 1986 performance in front of financial analysts. But Smith seems to have undergone a phenomenal metamorphosis. During the past year and a half, his star has been rising, in large part because of his speeches. His memorable presentation at the Traverse City conference dazzled everyone, and a speech to the University Club in Chicago in December 1988, titled "The People Factor in Competitiveness," stressed human factors above all else, positioning Smith beyond the narrow finance role. "The company," he said, "must set the climate for people to succeed. This means we must demonstrate through deeds as well as words that we truly believe people are our most important asset. That means *living* by a philosophy of the importance of people, rather than merely printing one and putting it on a bulletin board." Even operating people who were terrified of another finance-groomed Smith at the helm are giving him high marks and saying they could work for him.

In transcending the narrow attitudes that are characteristic of the GM finance staff, Smith has endeared himself to the operations people. In late 1988, in what looks like an effort to appear less aloof, he began occasionally to drop the "F" from the front of his name.

From the current vantage point, a Smith-Stempel team seems a strong possibility. A Stempel-Smith team is less likely, since a finance man has never been selected to be president.

But there are other candidates who bear watching. Lloyd Reuss, fifty-four, seemed halted in his move toward the top when he lost the presidency to Bob Stempel. And it would be practically unthinkable for Reuss and Stempel to become a chairman-president team, since both come from the product side of the business. Reuss possesses a strong power base within the company, and this puts him in a position of great influence, but the combination still seems remote.

Three more distant contenders for the chairmanship are executive vice president, components, Bill Hoglund, fifty-six; chief financial officer Bob O'Connell, fifty-two; and executive vice president, GM International, Jack Smith, fifty-two.

Bill Hoglund bears the distinction of having started his career in finance and later making a transition to operations. He is popular inside the company and with the dealers, although many insiders believe he's too outspoken and controversial. It's possible that he could be a contender for either the presidency or the chairmanship in the next round. (Since retirement is mandatory at age sixty-five, the next round might not be that far away; Alan Smith, for example, would only serve about six years before he reached retirement age.)

The primary factor that puts Bob O'Connell on the list is his close association with Roger Smith. Indeed, under the traditional mentoring system, O'Connell might be the accepted heir apparent—just as Roger Smith was. But there are serious road-blocks to O'Connell achieving the chairmanship this time around. He is singlemindedly a finance man, and is not particularly knowledgeable about the operations side of the business. In fact, those in operations who are familiar with him fear O'Connell because of his obsession with numbers. They believe that the choice of a chairman who is so out of touch with both people and products could spell disaster for the company.

Jack Smith is a strong leader and savvy businessman who has presided over a period of unprecedented growth in GM's European operation. In 1988, while BOC and CPC combined lost about $2 billion (excluding the transfer pricing effects of the component divisions), the overseas operations contributed in excess of $2 billion in earnings. In Europe, the secret of success has been simple: great cars and wise investments. In fact, GM has won Car of the Year awards in Europe twice during the past five years. Smith's easygoing style and facility with people are credited for the harmonious structure of GM Europe.

But in spite of his success overseas, Jack Smith is handicapped by the fact that international operations is not a traditional stepping stone to the top. However, Smith is young enough to be a strong contender in the next round. In the meantime, he might be considered for a prominent position at home when all the cards are shuffled next year.

The final outcome of the race for leadership of General Motors will not be known until early 1990. In that time, the fortunes of the top six contenders could rise and fall by means yet unknown. But when it comes, the announcement should serve as a good indicator of the kind of company General Motors will be during the next decade and on into the twenty-first century.

Then again, one never knows. We said the same thing about Roger Smith.

BIBLIOGRAPHY

Bender, Marylin. *At the Top.* New York: Doubleday & Company, Inc., 1975.

Bennis, Warren, and Burt Nanus. *Leaders: The Strategies for Taking Charge.* New York: Harper & Row, 1985.

Blache, Klaus M., ed. *Success Factors for Implementing Change: A Manufacturing Viewpoint.* Dearborn, Mich.: The Society of Manufacturing Engineers, Publications Development Department, 1988.

Bohon, C.D. "What's Wrong with Detroit?" *Auto Age,* May 1987.

Brody, Michael. "Can GM Manage It All?" *Fortune,* July 8, 1985.

Brown, Warren. "GM Steps on the Gas." *The Washington Post,* March 27, 1988.

————. "In Multibillion-Dollar Numbers Game, What's Good for GM Is Good for U.S." *The Washington Post,* January 15, 1989.

Cole, Dr. David E. "NUMMI: The GM-Toyota Joint Venture in Learning." *The JAMA Forum,* February 1986.

Colello, Ralph G., Nancy Gardella, Phillip G. Gott, Donald A. Hurter, Michael J. Kay, Harry W. Mathews, Jr., and Ellen I. Metcalf. "The World Automotive Industry in Transition." Cambridge: Arthur D. Little Decision Resources, November 1985.

Crandall, Robert W., Howard K. Gruenspecht, Theodore E. Keela, and Lester B. Love. "Regulating the Automobile." Washington D.C.: The Brookings Institution, 1986.

Cray, Ed. *Chrome Colossus—General Motors and Its Times.* New York: McGraw-Hill, 1980.

Deming, W. Edwards. *Out of the Crisis.* Cambridge: Massachusetts Institute of Technology, 1982.

DeVoe, Raymond F., Jr. "Roger Smith's Variation on John Le Carre's Observation." *The Devoe Report,* June 17, 1988.

Drucker, Peter F. *The Effective Executive.* New York: Harper & Row, 1966, 1967.

————. *Management—Tasks, Responsibilities, Practices.* New York: Harper & Row, 1973.

——. *The Practice of Management.* New York: Harper & Row, 1954.

Dunham, Tony B., and Lawrence R. Gustin. "The Buick: A Complete History." *Automobile Quarterly,* 1987.

Feder, Barnaby J. "The Drive to Speed Automation." *The New York Times,* June 15, 1988.

Fisher, Anne B. "Behind the Hype at GM's Saturn." *Fortune,* November 11, 1985.

——. "GM Is Tougher Than You Think." *Fortune,* November 10, 1986.

Fleming, Al, and David C. Smith. "GM's J Cars: The Full Story." *Ward's Auto World,* January 1981.

Flint, Jerry. "The Ghost of Alfred Sloan." *Forbes,* May 25, 1981.

——. "GM—Yes, It's for Real." *Forbes,* November 28, 1988.

Fulmer, William B. "Case Study: Electronic Data Systems." Colgate Darden Graduate School of Business Administration, University of Virginia, 1986.

Goldschmidt, Neil. Secretary of Transportation. "Report to the President on the State of the Automobile Industry." Washington, D.C.: Department of Transportation, 1980.

Gooding, Kenneth. "Mr. Smith Answers His Critics." *Financial Times,* September 30, 1985.

Gordon, Maynard M. "Saturn: Putting It All Together." *Auto Age,* October 1988.

Gustin, Lawrence R. *Billy Durant, Creator of General Motors,* 2nd ed. Flushing, N.Y.: Craneshaw Publishers, 1984.

Hampton, William J. "Reality Has Hit General Motors—Hard." *Business Week,* November 24, 1986.

Harvard Business School. "The 'New' General Motors." Boston: July 1987.

Holusha, John. "Advice for Detroit's Humbled Giant." *The New York Times,* December 17, 1986.

Iacocca, Lee, with William Novak. *Iacocca—An Autobiography.* New York: Bantam Books, 1984.

——, with Sonny Kleinfield. *Talking Straight.* New York: Bantam Books, 1988.

Kleinfield, N. R. "The Irritant They Call Perot." *The New York Times,* April 27, 1986.

Krafcik, John F. "Triumph of the Lean Production System." Cambridge: MIT International Motor Vehicle Program, *Sloan Management Review,* Fall 1988.

Kanter, Rosabeth Moss. *The Change Masters—Innovation and Entrepreneurship in the American Corporation.* New York: Simon and Schuster, 1983.

Krebs, Michelle. "Hughes Emerging as More than Diversification for GM." *Automotive News,* April 7, 1986.

———. "Stempel Brings Cool Hand to GM." *Automotive News,* August 29, 1988.

———. "The GM-10 Design Strategy." *Automotive News,* September 28, 1987.

Lawrence, Paul R., and Davis Dyer. *Renewing American Industry.* New York: The Free Press, 1983.

Lee, Bruce. "Worker Harmony Makes NUMMI Work." *The New York Times,* December 25, 1988.

Levin, Doron P. *Irreconcilable Differences: Ross Perot Versus General Motors.* New York: Little, Brown and Company, 1989.

———, and Dale D. Buss. "Titanic Battle: GM Plans Offer to Pay $700 Million to Buy Out Its Critic H. Ross Perot." *The Wall Street Journal,* December 1, 1986.

Lowell, John. "Perot's Rx for GM." *Ward's Auto World,* November 1986.

McElroy, John. "For Whom Are We Building Cars?" *Automotive Industries,* June 1987.

———. "Outsourcing: The Double-Edged Sword." *Automotive Industries,* March 1988.

Mann, Eric. *Taking On General Motors—A Case Study of the UAW Campaign to Keep Van Nuys Open.* Center for Labor Research and Education, Institute of Industrial Relations, University of California, Los Angeles, 1987.

Mitchell, William. "Move Over, Here Comes Elmer." *Detroit Free Press,* September 1987.

Mitsukini, Yoshida, Tanaka Iko, and Sesoko Tsune, eds. *The Compact Culture—The Ethos of Japanese Life.* Tokyo: Cosmo Public Relations Corporation, 1982.

Moore, Thomas. "Make-or-Break Time for General Motors." *Fortune,* February 15, 1988.

Moritz, Michael, and Barrett Seaman. *Going for Broke—The Chrysler Story.* New York: Doubleday, 1981.

Moskal, Brian S. "Is GM Getting a Bum Rap?" *Industry Week,* January 12, 1987.

Musselman, James P. *Cadillac—The Heartbreak of America.* Washington, D.C.: Essential Information, Inc., 1988.

Nader, Ralph, and William Gaylor. *The Big Boys: Power and Position in American Business.* New York: Pantheon Books, 1986.

Nora, John J., C. Raymond Rogers, and Robert J. Stramy. *Transforming the Workplace.* Princeton: Princeton Research Press, 1986.

Nussbaum, Bruce. *The World After Oil.* New York: Simon & Schuster, 1983.

O'Reilly, Brian. "EDS After Perot: How Tough Is It?" *Fortune,* October 24, 1988.

Perot, Ross. "How I Would Turn Around GM." *Fortune,* February 15, 1988.

Peters, Thomas J., and Robert J. Waterman. *In Search of Excellence.* New York: Harper & Row, 1983.

Peters, Tom. *Thriving on Chaos—Handbook for a Management Revolution.* New York: Alfred A. Knopf, Inc., 1987.

Reich, Cary. "The Innovator—The Creative Mind of G.M. Chairman Roger Smith." *The New York Times Magazine,* April 21, 1985.

Rescigno, Richard. "Race to the Future: Can Billions and Mr. Smith Make GM a Winner?" *Barron's,* June 30, 1986.

Sloan, Alfred P., Jr. *My Years with General Motors.* New York: Macfadden Books, 1963.

Smith, David C. "1986 State of the Industry—Roger Smith, GM: As Far As We've Come, We've Still Longer to Go." *Ward's Auto World,* December 1985.

Spinella, Art, Tom Black, and Ralph Gray. "Saturn: The View from Earth." *Ward's Auto Dealer,* March 1988.

Taylor, Alex, III. "Back to the Future at Saturn." *Fortune,* August 1, 1988.

Tichy, Noel M., and Mary Anne Devanna. *The Transformational Leader.* New York: John Wiley and Sons, 1986.

Treece, James B. "It's Time for a Tune-up at GM." *Business Week,* September 7, 1987.

———, Mark Maremont, and Larry Armstrong. "Will the Auto Glut Choke Detroit?" *Business Week,* March 7, 1988.

Vorderman, Don. "General Motors Fights Back." *Town and Country,* April 1988.

Weiss, Stephen E. "Creating the GM-Toyota Venture—A Case in Complex Negotiation." *Columbia Journal of World Business,* Summer 1987.

Weitz, John. "Automotives." *The New York Times Magazine,* March 27, 1988.

White, Joseph B. "EDS Scrambles to Grow as Its Parent, GM, Cuts Costs." *The Wall Street Journal,* December 2, 1987.

———. "The Ride Gets Rough at Hughes Aircraft." *The Wall Street Journal,* May 16, 1988.

Williams, Douglas. "GM's Project Charlie." *Automotive Industries,* September 1988.

Winter, Drew. "High Tech's Midlife Crisis." *Ward's Auto World,* June 6, 1986.

Wright, Patrick J. *On a Clear Day You Can See General Motors—John Z. DeLorean's Look Inside the Automotive Giant.* Grosse Pointe, Mich.: Wright Enterprises, 1979.

Yates, Brock. *The Decline and Fall of the American Automobile Industry.* New York: Empire Books, 1983.

INDEX